Teacher's Manual with Tests

Encuentros
CURSO DE INTRODUCCIÓN

HOLT, RINEHART AND WINSTON
Harcourt Brace & Company
Austin • New York • Orlando • Atlanta • San Francisco • Boston • Dallas • Toronto • London

Credits

Editorial

Project Director: Fannie Safier
Editorial Staff: Belén Ayestarán, Laura Baci, Sonya Canetti-Mirabal, Daniela Guggenheim, Bobbi Hernandez, Jennifer E. Osborne, Cintia M. Santana
Editorial Support: Isabell Coffey, Barbara Sharp Turner

Production, Design, and Photo Research

Athena Blackorby, Betty Mintz

Cover Photography
Michael Scott / Tony Stone Images

Cover Photo Research
Angi Cartwright

Cover Design
Bob Prestwood and Katie Kwun

Contributors

María I. Cruzado
Translator and Teacher
New York, NY

José Del Valle
Translator and Editor
New York, NY

Carroll Moulton
Formerly of Duke University
Durham, NC

David Ochoa
Teacher
Columbia University
New York, NY

Yolanda Purseglove
Facilitator
Long Beach Unified School District
Long Beach, CA

Samuel A. Southworth
Writer and Editor
New York, NY

Lawanna Trainor
Long Beach Unified School District
Long Beach, CA

Copyright © 1997 by Holt, Rinehart and Winston, Inc.

All rights reserved. No part of this publication may be reproduced or transmitted in any form or by any means, electronic or mechanical, including photocopy, recording, or any information storage and retrieval system, without permission in writing from the publisher.

Permission is hereby granted to reproduce Tests in this publication in complete pages for instructional use and not for resale by any teacher using ENCUENTROS.

Acknowledgments appear on page viii, which is an extension of the copyright page.

Printed in the United States of America
ISBN 0-03-095165-8

Table of Contents

	Scope and Sequence of the Program in *Encuentros*	ix

Collection 1

Desafíos

	Collection Overview	1
	Introducing the Collection	2
Esmeralda Santiago	***de* Cuando era puertorriqueña**	2
	Literatura y ciencia	
	Los huracanes	3
	Lengua y literatura	
	En busca de palabras precisas	5
Rose Del Castillo Guilbault	**Trabajo de campo**	6
	Elementos de literatura	
	Autobiografías, biografías, ensayos y artículos	9
Onelio Jorge Cardoso	***de* Negrita**	9
	Estrategias para leer	
	Cómo utilizar pistas del contexto	11
	Escena cultural	
	Comunicación animal	11
Isaac Bashevis Singer	**La cabra Zlateh**	12
	Taller del escritor	
	La narración/Episodio autobiográfico	13
	Taller de oraciones	
	Mil maneras de combinar oraciones	15

Collection 2

Si tú supieras...

	Collection Overview	16
	Introducing the Collection	16
Gregorio López y Fuentes	**Una carta a Dios**	17
	Elementos de literatura	
	Cuentos I: Argumento y ambiente	19
Antonio Robles	**El adivinador de máscaras**	20
	Literatura y tradiciones populares	
	El Carnaval	20

	Estrategias para leer	
	La relación de causa y efecto	22
Pablo Neruda	**La casa de las tres viudas**	22
	Lengua y literatura	
	La sensación que producen las palabras	25
Nicolás Guillén	**Adivinanzas**	26
	Taller del escritor	
	La descripción/Ensayo de observación	26
	Taller de oraciones	
	Dime con quién andas y te diré quién eres	28

Collection 3

Enfrentarse a los riesgos

	Collection Overview	29
	Introducing the Collection	29
Santo Neiva	**El pescador y la Madre del Agua**	30
	Lengua y literatura	
	Las palabras que pesca el pescador	32
Gary Soto	**La bamba**	33
	Elementos de literatura	
	Cuentos II: Caracterización, punto de vista y tema	36
Sandra Cisneros	**Chanclas**	36
	Estrategias para leer	
	Los resúmenes nos ayudan a recordar	38
Huynh Quang Nhuong	*de* **La tierra que perdí**	38
	Taller del escritor	
	La narración/Cuento	39
	Taller de oraciones	
	Palabras de enlace	41

Collection 4

Un más allá

	Collection Overview	43
	Introducing the Collection	44
Horacio Quiroga	**El cuendú**	44
	Literatura y ciencia	
	El cuendú	45

	Escena cultural	
	El origen de las palabras del español	47
Ray Bradbury	**Todo el verano en un día**	48
	Literatura y ciencia	
	¿Lluvia en Venus?	49
	Estrategias para leer	
	Distinguir hechos de opiniones	50
Rubén Darío	**El trópico**	50
	Elementos de literatura	
	Poesía I: Recursos de sonido e imágenes	52
Norbert Wu	**La isla Sangalakki**	52
	Literatura y ciencia	
	Tortugas marinas	53
Nicolás Guillén	**La Osa Mayor**	55
	Taller del escritor	
	La exposición/Artículo informativo	55
	Taller de oraciones	
	La aposición: Un segundo nombre	57

Collection 5

La convivencia

	Collection Overview	58
	Introducing the Collection	59
Don Juan Manuel	**Los dos labradores**	59
	Lengua y literatura	
	Cómo se construyen las palabras	62
	Elementos de literatura	
	Drama	63
Lope de Vega	**Los ratones**	64
	Escena cultural	
	Deportes latinos	66
	Estrategias para leer	
	Hacer predicciones	67
Emma Pérez	**Se cayó la luna**	67
	Taller del escritor	
	La persuasión/Ensayo sobre problemas y soluciones	68
	Taller de oraciones	
	Una norma para poder leer	70

Collection 6

El paisaje de la amistad

	Collection Overview	71
	Introducing the Collection	71
Ana María Fagundo	**La canción del árbol**	72
Gabriela Mistral	**El ruego del libro**	74
	Elementos de literatura	
	Poesía II: Figuras retóricas y de estilo	75
Maya Angelou	***de* Yo sé por qué canta el pájaro enjaulado**	76
	Estrategias para leer	
	Los detalles te ayudarán a hacer deducciones	78
Cristina Lacasa	**Las manos de la abuela**	78
	Taller del escritor	
	La descripción/Semblanza	79
	Taller de oraciones	
	Oraciones sin principio ni fin	81

Collection 7

Todos somos iguales

	Collection Overview	82
	Introducing the Collection	82
José Martí	**Los dos ruiseñores**	83
	Lengua y literatura	
	Semejanzas y diferencias de significado	87
	Elementos de literatura	
	Cuentos populares, fábulas y leyendas	87
José Martí	**Los dos príncipes**	88
	Estrategias para leer	
	Uso de métodos de comparación y contraste	90
Jorge Luis Borges	**Los dos reyes y los dos laberintos**	90
	Taller del escritor	
	La persuasión/Evaluación	92
	Taller de oraciones	
	El arte de dar información	94

Collection 8
Huellas de grandes espíritus

	Collection Overview	95
	Introducing the Collection	96
Ana María Matute	**El árbol de oro**	96
	Lengua y literatura 　Las palabras tienen más de un significado	99
Maricarmen Ohara	**La leyenda del maíz**	99
	Literatura y cultura 　El símbolo del maíz	100
	Escena cultural 　El jaguar en el mito y el folclor	101
Susana Mendoza	**Cuentos de junio**	102
	Estrategias para leer 　Evaluación de un libro	104
	Elementos de literatura 　La novela	105
Juan Ramón Jiménez	**El pájaro libre**	105
	Taller del escritor 　La exposición/Especulación sobre causas o efectos	105
	Taller de oraciones 　La oración es flexible	107
	For Further Reading	109
	Transparencies	117
	Tests	119
	Answer Key to Tests	163
	Index of Authors and Titles	172

Acknowledgments

For permission to reprint copyrighted material, grateful acknowledgment is made to the following sources:

Agencia Literaria Carmen Balcells: From "La casa de las tres viudas" from *Confieso que he vivido: Memorias* by Pablo Neruda. Copyright © 1974 by Pablo Neruda and Fundación Pablo Neruda.

Susan Bergholz Literary Services, New York: From "Chanclas" from *La casa en Mango Street* by Sandra Cisneros. Copyright © 1984 by Sandra Cisneros: translation copyright © 1994 by Elena Poniatowska. Published by Vintage Books, a division of Random House, Inc., New York.

Ediciones 29: From "Las manos de la abuela" by Cristina Lacasa from *Mis primeras lecturas poéticas* by Angelina Gatell. Copyright by Angelina Gatell.

Editorial Lumen, S. A.: From *Yo sé por qué canta el pájaro enjaulado* (Spanish translation of *I Know Why the Caged Bird Sings*) by Maya Angelou; translated by Carlos Manzano. Copyright © 1969 by Maya Angelou. Translation copyright © 1966 by Editorial Lumen, S. A.

Provincia Franciscana de la Santísima Trinidad: From "El ruego del libro" by Gabriela Mistral.

SCOPE AND SEQUENCE OF THE PROGRAM IN *ENCUENTROS*

Colección 1: DESAFÍOS

Selección	Estrategias para leer	Elementos de literatura	Lengua y literatura	Escritura	Hablar y escuchar	Otras actividades
de *Cuando era puertorriqueña* Esmeralda Santiago (pp. 3–7)		Autobiografía (p. 2)	En busca de palabras precisas (p. 11) Palabras que inspiran miedo (p. 11)	Compilación de ideas para un episodio autobiográfico (p. 10)	Planea de antemano (p. 10)	Investigación: Averígualo todo (p. 10)
Literatura y ciencia: Los huracanes (p. 8)						
Trabajo de campo Rose Del Castillo Guilbault (pp. 13–17)	Pistas del contexto (p. 12)	Tema (p. 12)		Compilación de ideas para un episodio autobiográfico (p. 19) Redacción creativa: El placer del trabajo en el campo (p. 19)	¿Trabajo o placer? (p. 19)	Investigación/ Dibujo: Producto de California (p. 19)
Elementos de literatura (pp. 20–21)		Autobiografía, biografía, semblanza, diarios, memorias, cartas, artículo de noticias, artículo de opinión, ensayo, hecho y opinión, conflicto, caracterización, argumento, clímax, imágenes sensoriales, figuras retóricas (pp. 20–21)				
de *Negrita* Onelio Jorge Cardoso (pp. 22–25)		Ambiente (p. 22)		Compilación de ideas para un episodio autobiográfico (p. 27) Escribe el guión: Negrita: la película (p. 27) Redacción creativa: ¿Y después qué? (p. 27)	Negrita y Zlateh (p. 27)	

Colección 1: DESAFÍOS (continuación)

Selección	Estrategias para leer	Elementos de literatura	Lengua y literatura	Escritura	Hablar y escuchar	Otras actividades
Estrategias para leer (pp. 28–29)	Cómo utilizar pistas del contexto: Definiciones y paráfrasis, ejemplos, comparaciones, contraste, causa y efecto (pp. 28–29)					
Escena cultural: Comunicación animal (pp. 30–33)						Actividades para empezar (p. 30) Actividades de cierre (p. 33)
A leer por tu cuenta *La cabra Zlateh* Isaac Bashevis Singer (pp. 34–41)						
Taller del escritor: La narración (pp. 42–46)				Episodio autobiográfico (pp. 42–46)		
Taller de oraciones (p. 47)			Mil maneras de combinar oraciones (p. 47)			

Colección 2: SI TÚ SUPIERAS...

Selección	Estrategias para leer	Elementos de literatura	Lengua y literatura	Escritura	Hablar y escuchar	Otras actividades
Una carta a Dios Gregorio López y Fuentes (pp. 51–55)	La relación de causa y efecto (p. 50)	Ironía (p. 50)		Compilación de ideas para un ensayo de observación (p. 57) Redacción creativa: Lo que quiero (p. 57) Redacción creativa/ Teatro: Hablemos claro (p. 57)		
Elementos de literatura (pp. 58–59)		Cuentos I: Argumento, trama, exposición, conflicto, suspenso, clímax, desenlace, finales inesperados, ironía, flashback, anticipación, ambiente (pp. 58–59)				
El adivinador de máscaras Antonio Robles (pp. 61–65)				Compilación de ideas para un ensayo de observación (p. 68)		Investigación/ Redacción: Conviértete en crítico de arte (p. 68) Redacción creativa/ Música: Música de Carnaval (p. 68) Artesanía y trabajos manuales: El arte de hacer máscaras (p. 68)
Literatura y tradiciones populares: El Carnaval (p. 66)						
Estrategias para leer (p. 69)	La relación de causa y efecto (p. 69)					

Colección 2 : SI TÚ SUPIERAS... (continuación)

Selección	Estrategias para leer	Elementos de literatura	Lengua y literatura	Escritura	Hablar y escuchar	Otras actividades
La casa de las tres viudas de *Memorias* Pablo Neruda (pp. 71–77)		Figuras retóricas: símil, metáfora, personificación (p. 70)	La sensación que producen las palabras (p. 81) El cuento casi sin fin (p. 81)	Compilación de ideas para un ensayo de observación (p. 80)	Un archivo de personalidades (p. 80) Recuerdos que perduran (p. 80)	Dibujo: El viaje de Neruda (p. 80)
A leer por tu cuenta *Adivinanzas* Nicolás Guillén (p. 82)						
Taller del escritor: La descripción (pp. 84–88)				Ensayo de observación (pp. 84–88)		
Taller de oraciones (p. 89)			Dime con quién andas y te diré quién eres (p. 89)			

Colección 3: ENFRENTARSE A LOS RIESGOS

Selección	Estrategias para leer	Elementos de literatura	Lengua y literatura	Escribir	Hablar y escuchar	Otras actividades
El pescador y la Madre del Agua Santo Neiva (pp. 93–98)	Resumir (p. 92)		Las palabras que pesca el pescador (p. 101)	Compilación de ideas para un cuento (p. 100)	Lectura fragmentada (p. 100)	Arte: Un mural (p. 100)
La bamba Gary Soto (pp. 103–107)		La anticipación (p. 102)		Compilación de ideas para un cuento (p. 109)	Una entrevista con la estrella (p. 109)	Teatro/Arte: Un taller de talentos (p. 109)
Elementos de literatura (pp. 110–111)		Cuentos II: Caracterización, punto de vista, tema (pp. 110–111)				
Chanclas Sandra Cisneros (pp. 113–115)				Compilación de ideas para un cuento (p. 117) Redacción creativa: Ritmo narrativo (p. 117)	Un poema improvisado (p. 117)	
Estrategias para leer (pp. 118–119)	Los resúmenes nos ayudan a recordar: Resumir, parafrasear, palabras de enlace, generalizar (pp. 118–119)					
A leer por tu cuenta de *La tierra que perdí* Huynh Quang Nhuong (pp. 120–125)						
Taller del escritor: La narración: (pp. 126–130)				Cuento (pp. 126–130)		
Taller de oraciones (p. 131)			Palabras de enlace (p. 131)			

Colección 4: UN MÁS ALLÁ

Selección	Estrategias para leer	Elementos de literatura	Lengua y literatura	Escribir	Hablar y escuchar	Otras actividades
El cuendú Horacio Quiroga (pp. 135–138)	Distinguir hechos de opiniones (p. 134)			Compilación de ideas para un artículo informativo (p. 141) Redacción creativa: Libre al fin (p. 141)		Investigación: Protección natural (p. 141)
Literatura y ciencia: El cuendú (p. 139)						
Escena cultural: El origen de las palabras del español (pp. 142–143)						Actividades para empezar (p. 142) Actividades de cierre (p. 143)
Todo el verano en un día Ray Bradbury (pp. 145–151)		Personaje (p. 144)		Compilación de ideas para un artículo informativo (p. 154)		Arte: Propiedades fabulosas (p. 154) Dramatización: El monólogo de William (p. 154)
Literatura y ciencia: ¿Lluvia en Venus? (p. 152)						
Estrategias para leer (p. 155)	Distinguir hechos de opiniones (p. 155)					
El trópico Rubén Darío (p. 157)		Aliteración (p. 156)		Compilación de ideas para un artículo informativo (p. 160)		Arte: Pintar el trópico (p. 160)
Elementos de literatura (pp. 161–162)		Poesía I: Recursos de sonido e imágenes: Rima, ritmo, verso libre, repetición, paralelismo, onomatopeya, aliteración, imágenes (pp. 161–162)				

xiv SCOPE AND SEQUENCE

Colección 4 : UN MÁS ALLÁ (continuación)

Selección	Estrategias para leer	Elementos de literatura	Lengua y literatura	Escribir	Hablar y escuchar	Otras actividades
La isla Sangalakki Norbert Wu (pp. 164–171)		Las imágenes (p. 163)		Compilación de ideas para un artículo informativo (p. 174) Redacción: Desde el punto de vista de la tortuga (p. 174)		Dibujo: Un diagrama del océano (p. 174)
Literatura y ciencia: Tortugas marinas (p. 172)						
A leer por tu cuenta *La Osa Mayor* Nicolás Guillén (p. 175)						
Taller del escritor: La exposición (pp. 176–180)				Artículo informativo (pp. 176–180)		
Taller de oraciones (p. 181)			La aposición: Un segundo nombre (p. 181)			

Colección 5: LA CONVIVENCIA

Selección	Estrategias para leer	Elementos de literatura	Lengua y literatura	Escribir	Hablar y escuchar	Otras actividades
Los dos labradores Don Juan Manuel (pp. 185–187)	Hacer predicciones (p. 184)	Drama (p. 184)	Cómo se construyen las palabras (p. 191) Un lenguaje antiguo (p. 191)	Compilación de ideas para un ensayo sobre problemas y soluciones (p. 190) Redacción: ¿Qué me aconsejas? (p. 190)		Dramatización: ¡En vivo! (p. 190)
Elementos de literatura (pp. 192–193)	Cómo leer una obra teatral (p. 193)	Drama: Representación, argumento, exposición, conflicto, clímax, desenlace, diálogo, acotaciones escénicas, director, utilería (pp. 192–193)				
Los ratones Lope de Vega (p. 195)		Rima (p. 194)		Compilación de ideas (p. 197) Solución de problemas: Tu propio invento (p. 197)	Detengan al gato (p. 197)	
Escena cultural: Deportes latinos (pp. 198–201)						Actividades para empezar (p. 198) Actividades de cierre (pp. 200–201)
Estrategias para leer (p. 202)	Hacer predicciones (p. 202)					
A leer por tu cuenta *Se cayó la luna* Emma Pérez (p. 203)						
Taller del escritor: La persuasión (pp. 204–208)				Ensayo sobre problemas y soluciones (pp. 204–208)		
Taller de oraciones (p. 209)			Una norma para poder leer (p. 209)			

Colección 6: EL PAISAJE DE LA AMISTAD

Selección	Estrategias para leer	Elementos de literatura	Lengua y literatura	Escribir	Hablar y escuchar	Otras actividades
La canción del árbol Ana María Fagundo (pp. 213–214)				Compilación de ideas para una semblanza (p. 216) Redacción: Haz que el ruiseñor regrese (p. 216)		Arte: Conserva tus recuerdos (p. 216)
El ruego del libro Gabriela Mistral (pp. 218–219)		Tono (p. 217)		Compilación de ideas para una semblanza (p. 221) Redacción: Diálogo con el libro (p. 221)		Arte: Juzgar un libro por su portada (p. 221)
Elementos de literatura (pp. 222–223)		Poesia II: Figuras retóricas y de estilo: Símil, metáfora, personificación, símbolo, hipérbole (pp. 222–223)		Escribe un «poema disparate» (p. 223)		
de *Yo sé por qué canta el pájaro enjaulado* Maya Angelou (pp. 224–227)	Hacer deducciones (p. 224)			Compilación de ideas para una semblanza (p. 229) Redacción: Bailey habla (p. 229)	El origen del título (p. 229)	
Estrategias para leer (p. 230)	Los detalles te ayudarán a hacer deducciones (p. 230)					
A leer por tu cuenta *Las manos de la abuela* Cristina Lacasa (p. 231)						
Taller del escritor: La descripción (pp. 232–236)				Semblanza (pp. 232–236)		
Taller de oraciones (p. 237)			Oraciones sin principio ni fin (p. 237)			

Colección 7: TODOS SOMOS IGUALES

Selección	Estrategias para leer	Elementos de literatura	Lengua y literatura	Escribir	Hablar y escuchar	Otras actividades
Los dos ruiseñores José Martí (pp. 241–250)	Comparar y contrastar (p. 240)	Sátira (p. 240)	Semejanzas y diferencias de significado (p. 253) Símbolos chinos (p. 253)	Compilación de ideas para una evaluación (p. 252) Redacción creativa/ Ciencia: Las máquinas inteligentes (p. 252)	Investigación: ¿Máquinas frente a humanos? (p. 252)	
Elementos de literatura (p. 254)		Cuentos populares, fábulas y leyendas, cuentos de hadas, tradición oral (p. 254)				
Los dos príncipes José Martí (pp. 255–256)		Paralelismo (p. 255)		Compilación de ideas para una evaluación (p. 258) Redacción creativa: Amigos por correspondencia (p. 258)		
Estrategias para leer (p. 259)	Uso de métodos de comparación y contraste (p. 259)					
Los dos reyes y los dos laberintos Jorge Luis Borges (pp. 261–262)		Alegoría (p. 260)		Compilación de ideas para una evaluación (p. 265)		Dramatización: Los dos reyes en escena (p. 265)
Taller del escritor: La persuasión (pp. 266–270)				Evaluación (pp. 266–270)		
Taller de oraciones (p. 271)			El arte de dar información (p. 271)			

Colección 8: HUELLAS DE GRANDES ESPÍRITUS

Selección	Estrategias para leer	Elementos de literatura	Lengua y literatura	Escribir	Hablar y escuchar	Otras actividades
El árbol de oro Ana María Matute (pp. 275–278)		Punto de vista: primera persona, punto de vista omnisciente de tercera persona, punto de vista limitado de tercera persona (p. 274)	Las palabras tienen más de un significado (p. 281) ¡Albricias es alegría en árabe! (p. 281)	Compilación de ideas para una especulación sobre causas o efectos (p. 280) Redacción: Ivo en la torre (p. 280)		Dramatización: El teatro del lector (p. 280)
La leyenda del maíz Maricarmen Ohara (pp. 283–284)	Evaluación (p. 282)			Compilación de ideas para una especulación sobre causas o efectos (p. 287)	El nombre de los árboles (p. 287)	Investigación/ Arte: Las leyendas del maíz (p. 287)
Literatura y cultura: El símbolo del maíz (p. 285)						
Escena cultural: El jaguar en el mito y el folclor (pp. 288–293)						Actividades para empezar (p. 289) Actividades de cierre (p. 293)
Cuentos de junio Susana Mendoza (pp. 295–302)		La literatura fantástica (p. 294)		Compilación de ideas para una especulación sobre causas o efectos (p. 304) Redacción: Elogio del sol (p. 304) Investigación: Solamente los hechos (p. 304)		Dramatización: Leyendas del sol (p. 304) Arte: Un poema sobre el sol (p. 304)
Estrategias para leer (p. 305)	Evaluación de un libro (p. 305)					
Elementos de literatura (pp. 306–307)		La novela: Ficción, argumento, personajes, ambiente, punto de vista, tema, ciencia ficción, novela histórica, novela policiaca, novela de misterio (pp. 306–307)				El placer de leer (p. 307)

SCOPE AND SEQUENCE xix

Colección 8: HUELLAS DE GRANDES ESPÍRITUS

Selección	Estrategias para leer	Elementos de literatura	Lengua y literatura	Escribir	Hablar y escuchar	Otras actividades
A leer por tu cuenta *El pájaro libre* Juan Ramón Jiménez (pp. 308–309)						
Taller del escritor: La exposición (pp. 310–314)				Especulación sobre causas o efectos (pp. 310–314)		
Taller de oraciones (p. 315)			La oración es flexible (p. 315)			

Selections that have been recorded on audiocassette are identified by this symbol:

xx SCOPE AND SEQUENCE

Collection 1: DESAFÍOS

Collection Overview

The selections in the opening collection focus on the ability to meet challenges, especially those encountered in nature. Most sixth-graders will enjoy the excitement and suspense generated by these true-life and fictional tales that revolve around the theme *Desafíos* (Challenges).

The collection begins with an excerpt from Esmeralda Santiago's *Cuando era puertorriqueña* (*When I Was Puerto Rican*). Santiago was born in Puerto Rico and eventually moved to New York. Her autobiography, which she translated into Spanish herself, gives insight into the bicultural experience. Santiago relates her family history in simple, clear prose, describing what it means to be Puerto Rican both on the island and on the mainland. This excerpt is set in Puerto Rico, where a hurricane forces the family into a storm shelter. As the eye of the hurricane passes overhead, the men emerge to explore the wreckage of the yard. Santiago's narrative emphasizes the strength in family unity.

The second selection is a newspaper article in which Rose Del Castillo Guilbault recalls a childhood experience of picking garlic during California's harvest season. Told with graceful humor, "Trabajo de campo" ("Field Work") demonstrates the author's fortitude in the face of a daunting task. This selection and the Santiago piece furnish excellent examples of the personal narrative for students to refer to when they write their autobiographical incidents in TALLER DEL ESCRITOR (see page 42).

In the next selection, a chapter from the novel *Negrita* by Onelio Jorge Cardoso, a farmer and his two sons encounter a man about to drown a small dog. They save the puppy and adopt her into their family. The suspenseful and heartwarming scene is rendered with rich visual details and will appeal to most students.

The final reading in most collections in this anthology is called A LEER POR TU CUENTA. Intended for enrichment, these culminating selections are not accompanied by apparatus. In Isaac Bashevis Singer's story "La cabra Zlateh" ("Zlateh the Goat"), a boy and a beloved family goat survive a winter storm through their mutual protection and love, and they return home in time to celebrate Hanukkah. The translation preserves the flavor of the original and clearly conveys Singer's gifts as a storyteller.

Throughout the collection, questions, exercises, and activities give students a wide range of opportunities to respond to the literature in both analytical and creative modes. The instructional material also encourages students to relate the literature to their own experiences.

In the feature titled ELEMENTOS DE LITERATURA: AUTOBIOGRAFÍAS, BIOGRAFÍAS, ENSAYOS Y ARTÍCULOS (page 20), students are introduced to nonfiction. The discussion highlights the central role of plot, characterization, and vivid imagery in all narratives, whether they are fictional or nonfictional. Students will be able to derive many practical hints for writing their own autobiographical incidents.

This integration of materials also extends to the opening assignments in OPCIONES: PREPARA TU PORTAFOLIO, which are designed to prepare students progressively for the major writing assignment. Further activities in OPCIONES challenge students to explore themes and ideas in a variety of modes, such as research, art, and film. ESTRATEGIAS PARA LEER builds students' proficiency in reading through the use of context clues. LENGUA Y LITERATURA focuses on the importance of precise words in writing. VOCABULARIO gives students the opportunity to work with words encountered in selections or related to the collection theme. An essay on animal communication, included in the feature ESCENA CULTURAL, offers stimulating links with *Negrita* and "La cabra Zlateh." The assignment to write an autobiographical incident, presented in TALLER DEL ESCRITOR, synthesizes many of the skills that students have been developing throughout the collection. At the very end of the collection, students are provided with a further opportunity to hone their writing skills in TALLER DE ORACIONES, which introduces ways to combine sentences.

Introducing the Collection

Encourage students to explore the unifying theme of this collection by presenting them with a choice of opening activities. Possibilities include the following:

1. Have students draw a line down a page. On the left-hand side, have them write a list of five challenges that they have faced in the past six months. On the right-hand side, have them write a list of five challenges they would enjoy meeting in the next year or two. Call on volunteers to share some of their past and future challenges with the class as a whole.

2. Write the word *desafíos* on the chalkboard. Then have students form word associations and call them out so you can write these words and phrases on the board in a cluster diagram. Call on volunteers to suggest where lines can be drawn to connect the terms so that similarities and relationships are graphically represented.

3. Tell students that most good stories contain at least one conflict or struggle. This conflict often involves a challenge: a test that the main character must face. Invite students to verify this aspect of storytelling by sharing some of the challenges confronted by characters in their favorite movies, television shows, or stories.

4. Ask students to explore the collection theme by composing a cinquain, a simple five-line poem, on the theme of challenges or tests. The format for the cinquain can be as follows:

    Line 1: One noun (such as *desafíos*)
    Line 2: Two descriptive adjectives
    Line 3: Three verbs
    Line 4: Four words to express feelings
    Line 5: One word referring to the first noun

When students have finished writing, call on volunteers to share their poems by reading them aloud.

de Cuando era puertorriqueña
(*from* When I Was Puerto Rican)

Esmeralda Santiago   **page 3**

Into the Selection

Summary

As Hurricane Santa Clara approaches Puerto Rico, the author and her family prepare for the worst. Papi and Mami stow the family's possessions, while Esmeralda rounds up her siblings, including month-old baby Raymond. The family trudges next door to Doña Ana's one-room cement house, where the windows are boarded and every crack and chink has been plugged with rags to keep the wind out. Doña Ana's dwelling is small but sturdy, and as thirty people prepare to ride out the storm there, the author finds comfort in the room's warmth, the aromas of good cooking, and the hushed play of the children. The men play dominoes as the women prepare food and brew coffee.

As the children try to sleep, the eye of the hurricane passes over the house. The men open the door and emerge cautiously to examine the debris in the yard. A sliver of sun breaks through the clouds, forming a rainbow on the ground. The children who are big enough to stand cluster at the door in awe of the spectacle.

Antes de leer
(Before You Read)   (page 2)

Punto de partida (Focus)

Desafíos y recompensas
(Challenges and Rewards)
You may wish to encourage students to work in pairs for this activity. You might also model the activity by mentioning some of your own

experiences. Guide students to understand that meeting a challenge may result in more satisfaction than is gained through achieving one's goal without effort or struggle.

Toma nota (Quickwrite)

Suggest that students freewrite for five minutes or so without stopping. Assure them that they need not worry about spelling, grammar, or mechanics. The important goal is to get their ideas down on paper. Suggest that visual learners draw a rough sketch to illustrate the situation or challenge they describe.

Diálogo con el texto (Dialogue with the Text)

An ongoing dialogue with the text is a key element of this program. Suggestions for handling the activity are provided below, under DIARIO DEL LECTOR.

Elementos de literatura (Elements of Literature)

Autobiografía (Autobiography)

Supplement the discussion in the text by telling students that a brief narrative presenting one incident from a person's life is often called an autobiographical incident. An autobiographical incident is usually told in chronological or time order, and the author includes his or her feelings about the events.

Through the Selection

Diario del lector
(Reader's Log) (pages 4–5)

The sample marginal annotations exemplify several reading strategies, including questioning, making inferences, challenging the text, and reflecting on its meaning. If you think some of your students will benefit, you can extend this activity, modeling similar annotations for the next page of the text or for the entire selection. Alternatively, you can pause at the end of each section, allowing enough time to monitor and discuss students' notes on an individual basis.

Adueñate de estas palabras
(Words to Own)

The following words are defined at the bottom of the pupil's page.

cima (4)
grieta (4)
amuleto (6)
atarugar (6)
penumbra (6)
sazonar (6)
susurrado (6)
trancazo (7)

debatir (7)
estrépito (7)
ventolera (7)
siniestro (7)
tenebrosa (7)
fangoso (7)
alzar (7)
cautelosamente (7)

Techniques for Handling the Reading

Although the setting will probably be unfamiliar to many of your students, this brief narrative should cause no problems for most readers. Point out that the footnotes and glossary words will help students who have trouble with unfamiliar vocabulary.

Most students will enjoy the vivid descriptions of the hurricane and of the author's family. Guide students to recognize that the piece can also serve as a model for their own writing. Have readers focus specifically on Santiago's use of vivid sensory images. Visual learners, in particular, can use clues from the text to illustrate the interior of Doña Ana's house and the yard as the eye of the hurricane passes overhead.

Literatura y ciencia
(Literature and Science) (page 8)

Los huracanes (Hurricanes)

Here are some additional facts about hurricanes that you may wish to share with students:

- To be officially classified as a hurricane, a storm must have winds of 73 miles or more per hour.
- Tropical storms in the Pacific are called typhoons. In the Indian Ocean, where they can be just as severe, they are called cyclones.
- In 1992, in the United States, 26 people were killed by hurricanes, 84 were killed by floods, and 39 by tornadoes.
- Each year the National Weather Service assigns names for hurricanes in alphabetical order. The names alternate between male and female, so in 1996, storms were called Arthur, Bertha, Cesar, Dolly, etc.

Crea significados
(Making Meanings) (page 9)

Repaso del texto (Reviewing the Text)

a. **¿Dónde se refugian la narradora y su familia durante el huracán?** The family finds refuge next door, at Doña Ana's small but sturdy cement house.

b. **Menciona tres cosas que hacen los vecinos mientras esperan a que pase el huracán.** The men play dominoes; Papi listens to the radio; the women cut up chickens, cook, wash dishes, brew coffee, and tend babies; the children play among themselves and snatch bites of food.

c. **¿Quién sale a ver cómo ha quedado el patio?** As the eye of the storm passes over, the men go out to investigate the yard.

d. **¿Qué destrozos ha causado el huracán?** The high winds have littered the yard with branches, pieces of lumber, a tin washtub, and the carcass of a cow.

Primeras impresiones (First Thoughts)

1. **¿Temiste que les pasara algo a la narradora y a sus amigos y familiares durante el huracán? ¿Por qué?** Some students will say that they were afraid for the narrator and her friends and family, especially since she begins her narrative by mentioning the radio announcement warning that the storm was a severe threat. Other students, however, may have felt more confident that the group would ride out the storm without any serious injury or damage.

Interpretaciones del texto
(Shaping Interpretations)

2. **¿Crees que el recuerdo del huracán es positivo o negativo para Santiago? ¿Por qué?** Students' answers will vary. Many will suggest that the hurricane was a positive experience overall. The narrator seems to have savored the excitement, as well as the family and neighborhood togetherness caused by the hurricane. She takes special delight in recalling the warmth of the thirty people inside Doña Ana's small but sturdy house. Although the men, women, and children take part in separate activities, the author conveys the feeling that all the groups are knit together cohesively by their mutual support.

3. **¿Como estrecha el huracán los lazos entre los miembros de la comunidad?** The hurricane brings community members together physically, as they all crowd into Doña Ana's house. It also brings them together emotionally, as they support one another by playing games, cooking, and conversing.

4. **Haz un cuadro que muestre la división de responsabilidades entre los hombres y las mujeres. ¿Te parece justo el reparto de tareas? Justifica tu respuesta.** Students' charts and responses will vary. In general, the men and women are portrayed in traditional roles: For example, the men nail sheets of plywood across windows, while the women are busy with bundling clothes, cooking food, and tending babies. Papi shares with Mami the task of bringing in bundles of food, clothes, blankets, and diapers. During the storm itself, the men seem less busy than the women. They play dominoes and listen to the radio. In the morning, the men go out to investigate the damage in the yard.

5. **¿En qué consisten las descripciones de Santiago una vez que pueden abrir la puerta? Enumera algunas *imágenes*—sensaciones de la vista, el oído, el olfato y el tacto— que utiliza la autora para convertir el periodo que le sigue al huracán en algo memorable y auténtico para el lector.** Students' answers will vary. They should point out that the mood of the description changes from warm and comfortable to apprehensive and awe-struck. Sensory images that make the storm's aftermath vivid and memorable include the following: *gotas grises y tenebrosas como vapor, la tierra esponjosa que se convertía en charcos fangosos donde sus pies se hundían, la niebla se colgaba sobre el patio, ramas y pedazos de madera, una tina de lavar ropa que parecía haber sido pisada por un gigante, una res muerta, los animales adentro lloraban suavemente.*

Conexiones con el texto
(Connecting with the Text)

6. **Recuerda una ocasión en la que el clima supuso un desafío para ti. ¿Cómo resolviste el problema?** Students' answers will vary. They might mention, for example, being caught in a heavy rainstorm, or having to compete in a sports event in either very cold or very hot weather. Encourage students to describe their thoughts and feelings at the time of the challenge.

Más allá del texto (Extending the Text)

7. **En la película The Wizard of Oz (El mago de Oz), un tornado se lleva por los aires la casa de Dorothy hasta dejarla caer en la tierra mágica de Oz. Cuando abre la puerta y sale al exterior, se halla ante un mundo completamente distinto. ¿Puedes recordar otras películas donde un escenario contraste intensamente con otro? ¿Te recuerdan en algo los métodos descriptivos de Santiago?** Students' answers will vary. Be sure that students recognize the striking contrast in the selection between indoors and outdoors. Then encourage them to provide as many details as they can about contrasting settings from movies. Write some of the details on the chalkboard, and have students discuss how the film scenes might relate to Santiago's descriptive methods.

Beyond the Selection

Opciones: Prepara tu portafolio
(Choices:
Building Your Portfolio) (page 10)

Cuaderno del escritor (Writer's Notebook)

1. Compilación de ideas para un episodio autobiográfico (Collecting Ideas for an Autobiographical Incident)

Encourage students to begin their notes with a specific situation. Have them list the location, the date or time of year, and the names of the people involved. Then suggest that they close their eyes and visualize the incident in as much detail as possible. After students jot down a few sensory images, recommend that small groups get together to share their notes. Questions and comments from peers should prove helpful to students in expanding their lists of images.

Investigación (Research)

2. Averígualo todo (All About Hurricanes)

If students are interested in researching hurricanes, suggest that they begin by getting an overview of the topic from an encyclopedia. Almanacs will provide names, dates, and other details of notable hurricanes. Tell students that they can use the words *huracán* and *lluvia torrencial* to search for magazine and newspaper articles in indexes or computer databases. Students interested in exploring aspects of Puerto Rican culture could consider one or more of the following topics: explorations by Columbus and Ponce de León; the struggle for independence; the island's role in the Spanish-American War of 1898; the great migration to the mainland between 1945 and 1965; cultural life in *El barrio*; sports; music; and the island's ecology and natural history. If students need more information about research techniques, suggest that they consult the MANUAL DE COMUNICACIÓN (Communications Handbook) (page 334).

Hablar y escuchar (Speaking and Listening)

3. Planea de antemano (Planning Ahead)
Consider having each student group appoint a Recorder (to keep notes on the meetings) and a Presenter (to summarize the group's results to the class as a whole).

Lengua y literatura
(Language and Literature) (page 11)

En busca de palabras precisas
(In Search of Precise Words)

In this lesson, students become aware of the need to use precise language in their writing. Students are asked to evaluate a sample letter and determine if it gives a clear picture of a hurricane. They are then asked to edit the letter by choosing words that are more precise. Students may want to return to the selection and find precise words that Esmeralda Santiago uses to describe a hurricane.

You might also provide general categories, such as *árboles,* and ask students to supply precise words in that category. You can illustrate this with sets:

Conjunto de árboles

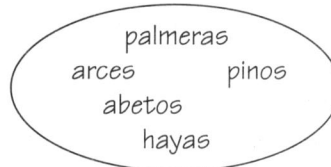

Conjunto de peces

Finally, you can ask students to edit their exercise on the OPCIONES page or, later in the collection, their autobiographical episode for the TALLER DEL ESCRITOR.

The exercise in the textbook uses Santiago's narrative as a springboard for a lesson on the use of precise words. Have students read the letters and discuss ways of making the writing more effective.

Answers:
Student responses will vary. Several sample responses follow:
tormenta fuerte:
borrasca de grandes dimensiones
torbellino de viento y lluvia
mucho viento:
sopla un viento racheado
el viento sopla a rachas violentas
cielo negro:
cielo encapotado y plomizo
olas grandes:
mar encrespado y furioso
olas gigantescas
todo mojado:
las lluvias intensas anegan casas y campos
muy feo:
deja un rastro de desolación y ruina

Vocabulario (Vocabulary)   (page 11)
Palabras que inspiran miedo
(Words That Cause Fear)
Students are asked to use the words in the story to create the scenario and plot for a movie. The word *guión* in Spanish refers to a basic description of a movie, not an actual script.

Trabajo de campo
(Field Work)

Rose Del Castillo Guilbault

page 13

Into the Selection

Summary
When the author was eleven, her family had no money for a summer vacation, so she and her mother decided to work the garlic harvest on the farm where they lived. Their first challenge was to convince Rose's father, who disapproved of his wife's working. However, he eventually agreed to intercede with the field-work boss, who consented to give Rose and her mother a chance.

The author then gives a graphic description of field work: the enormously heavy sacks that the pickers had to carry, the broiling afternoon sun, the pervasive odor of garlic, and the achingly sore muscles at the end of each day. On the final morning, the author almost caves in to exhaustion, but her mother gently reminds her that anything worth having is worth working for. Despite his own fatigue, Rose's father pitches in to help, and the family members complete their share of the harvest at sundown. At the end of the article, the author reflects on the rare and valuable family bond that they forged together.

Antes de leer (page 12)

Punto de partida

«¡No te rindas!» ("Don't Be a Quitter!")
Encourage students to draw on a broad range of situations and activities: at home, at school, or in the community. You might prompt discussion by volunteering some of your own ideas about when it is reasonable to quit something and when it is desirable to persevere.

Toma nota

Students' answers are likely to vary considerably. If students are willing to share their personal experiences, have them discuss their opinions in small groups.

Elementos de literatura

Tema (Theme)
Make sure that students understand the distinction between the *subject* of a piece of literature and its *theme*. The subject of a work is what it is about (for example, working in the fields harvesting garlic). The *theme* of a work is its overall message or underlying meaning about life or human behavior. Tell students that the theme is often the insight or opinion that the author wants us to take away from a work and think about, or to apply to our personal lives. Suggest that students can often find the theme of a work by (a) reviewing striking or memorable passages of the work carefully, (b) observing the changes the major character undergoes in the course of the work, and (c) examining the work's conclusion.

Estrategias para leer

(Becoming a Strategic Reader)
Pistas del contexto (Context Clues)
If you wish, have students preview the feature on context clues on page 28. Stress that the effective use of context clues depends on good observation.

Through the Selection

Aduéñate de estas palabras

nitidez (14)
costear (14)
incapaz (15)
mediar (15)
plazo (15)
capataz (15)
ceñir (15)
desalentador (16)

Techniques for Handling the Reading

This selection, which recounts a memorable incident in the author's life, offers a good companion piece for the excerpt from Esmeralda Santiago's *Cuando era puertorriqueña* (page 3). After students have been through the selection once, you might want to call on volunteers to link the piece with the collection theme of *desafíos* by listing the challenges the author faced and overcame. Students may mention, for example, that the author and her mother first had to confront the father's disapproval and win him over. Next, they had to persuade the field-work boss to take a chance on them. Then came the physical challenges of the field work itself: hauling heavy sacks, contending with the hot weather, and suffering from sore muscles. After students have summarized the selection in this way, proceed to CREA SIGNIFICADOS.

An audiocassette recording of the selection is available to supplement your reading and class discussion.

Crea significados (page 18)

Repaso del texto

a. **¿Qué es lo que más motiva a la familia a trabajar en la cosecha del ajo?** They want to make enough money to buy bus tickets for a vacation trip back to Mexico.
b. **¿Cómo se viste la familia para trabajar en los campos?** They wear layers of clothes—a T-shirt, a sweatshirt, and a windbreaker—to protect themselves from the early morning chill and to discard later when the afternoon sun becomes broiling hot. They wrap scarves around their heads and top them with knit caps.
c. **¿Qué hace Rose para que sea más fácil la labor de recoger los ajos?** She drags the sack with both of her hands to a certain spot and then runs back and forth, picking handfuls of garlic and depositing them in the bag.

d. **¿Qué es lo primero que decide Rose en la última mañana de la recolección?** Rose's muscles are so sore that she decides at first not to go picking in the field on the final day.

Primeras impresiones

1. **¿Sentiste lástima por la autora? ¿Por qué?** Students' answers will vary. Some students may say they felt sorry for the author because, as a girl of eleven, she had to endure such backbreaking labor. Other students, however, may suggest that at least the author and her family had a chance to work together and to create valuable family bonds.

Interpretaciones del texto

2. **En «Trabajo de campo» la autora define explícitamente más de un *tema*. Menciona uno de ellos.** Students' answers may vary. One theme they may mention is expressed by Rose's mother: Anything worth having is worth working for. Another important theme in the selection is that field work offered a rich environment for young people like Rose to learn about work, family values, and heritage.

3. **¿Cuál es el *momento crucial* del artículo, es decir, el lugar donde la narradora da un giro y cambia de rumbo? ¿Qué provoca este cambio de dirección?** The turning point occurs when Rose's father offers to help her and her mother finish the leftover work, despite his own exhaustion. This act of love causes the narrator to change her mind about working on the final day.

4. **Compara la experiencia de la autora con la de Esmeralda Santiago (página 3). ¿Cómo describe cada escritora a su familia y a su comunidad?** Students' answers will vary. In general, they may point out that both Santiago and Guilbault come from families with traditional values and strong bonds between parents and children. Although neither family is well-to-do, both are rich in love and mutual support. Santiago's community in Puerto Rico displays much solidarity and caring. Guilbault's portrait of her community, however, gives hints of conflict between Mexican-born workers and those born in the United States.

Conexiones con el texto

5. **Recuerda alguna experiencia que hayas tenido al trabajar en equipo. ¿Consiguió el equipo lo que se proponía? ¿Cómo se ayudaron mutuamente los miembros del equipo?** Students' answers will vary. Encourage them to offer examples of how teamwork can often make even the most difficult jobs seem easier.

Preguntas al texto (Challenging the Text)

6. **La madre le dice a Rose: «Merece la pena esforzarse cuando la recompensa es buena». ¿Estás de acuerdo?** Students' opinions will vary. Encourage them to support their responses with reasons and examples.

7. **¿Por qué crees que la autora decidió escribir sobre esta experiencia concreta y no sobre el trabajo agrícola en general?** Students' answers will vary. Guide them to recognize that a specific experience recounted in vivid detail is usually more effective at making an author's point or at expressing a general theme than an abstract analysis would be.

Beyond the Selection

Opciones:
Prepara tu portafolio (page 19)

Cuaderno del escritor

1. Compilación de datos para un episodio autobiográfico
Remind students that challenges can be physical, as with Rose's backbreaking work in the broiling sun. Challenges can also be mental or emotional: for example, solving a math problem or coping with a disappointment.

Redacción creativa (Creative Writing)

2. El placer del trabajo en el campo
(The Joy of Field Work)
For this activity, suggest that students choose a

paragraph like the one beginning *Después del almuerzo, el sol de la tarde me obligó a ir más despacio* (middle of the left-hand column on page 16). You might have students work in pairs, putting less proficient readers with more experienced ones. Suggest that students begin by listing all the sensory images in the passage they have chosen.

Hablar y escuchar

3. ¿Trabajo o placer? (Work or Pleasure?) Students will enjoy the opportunity to air their views. As speakers take turns, you may wish to create a chart on the chalkboard, listing the most important points on each side of the argument.

Investigación/Dibujo (Research/Drawing)

4. Producto de California (Made in California) Suggest that students first research some important crops like grapes and artichokes. Call on volunteers to share knowledge and ideas about the struggle for farm workers' rights in California and about prominent leaders such as Cesar Chavez and Dolores Huerta.

Elementos de literatura
(Elements of Literature) (page 20)

Autobiografías, biografías, ensayos y artículos
(Autobiographies, Biographies, Essays, and Articles) This feature introduces students to some fundamental distinctions between different types of writing—for example, the categories of fiction and nonfiction—as well as to some basic elements of critical thinking—for instance, the distinction between fact and opinion.

Make sure that students can answer the question asked in the text: Esmeralda Santiago's title hints that her work is an autobiography by implying the first-person pronoun in the verb form *era*.

You may wish to use the brief quiz below to test students' comprehension of the material.

1. **¿Cuál es la diferencia entre una biografía y una autobiografía?** (An autobiography is an account by a person of his or her own life, while a biography is an account of a person's life that is written or told by another person.)

2. **¿Qué es una *semblanza*?** (A firsthand biography is a brief report giving selected information about a person's life. It is written by someone who knows the subject personally.)
3. **Menciona ejemplos de textos sobre personas, acontecimientos o ideas que aparecen en los medios de comunicación.** (news articles, editorials, and essays)
4. **¿Cuál es la diferencia entre un hecho y una opinión?** (A fact is something that has happened or is true; an opinion is a judgment or a statement of belief.)
5. **¿Puede un escrito que no es ficticio utilizar las mismas técnicas de la ficción?** (Yes: Examples are plot, conflict, setting, characterization, and theme.)

de Negrita
(*from* Negrita)

Onelio Jorge Cardoso   page 22

Into the Selection

Summary
On the estate of Don Cristóbal, the ranch hand Bruno takes his two sons to the river to relax on Sundays. The boys love to dive to the bottom to find fresh mangoes that have dropped into the river. One morning, Bruno and his sons encounter Pedro, the hunter from the adjacent estate, at the river. Pedro explains that his master has ordered him to drown an unwanted female puppy, which he carries in a sack. Determined to save the little dog, Bruno grabs the sack and opens it, allowing the puppy to escape into the river. The puppy swims and splashes in the water. When Bruno's elder son sees it, he swims over and takes it in his arms. As the dog licks the child's face, Pedro smiles and agrees with Bruno that the dog knows more than humans do. Pedro acquiesces in Negrita's adoption, and the family members carry the puppy home in the net that they have brought to the river for fishing.

Antes de leer (page 22)

Punto de partida

Una mano amiga (A Helping Hand)
You may wish to have students hold small-group conferences to share recollections. Encourage group members to take turns telling about personal experiences. After each student has had his or her turn, the group should allow time for comments or questions.

Toma nota

Suggest that students freewrite for five to seven minutes without stopping. Assure them that the important goal is to get their ideas down on paper. Students should not worry about grammar, spelling, or mechanics. Tell students to save their notes.

Telón de fondo (Background)

The complete novel *Negrita* is published by Libros de Rincón, ERA, Mexico City (1992).

Elementos de literatura

Ambiente (Setting)
Tell students that setting involves specific details like the time of year or time of day and the geographical location of a narrative or play. Setting can be very important for the atmosphere or mood of a literary work, as well as for the plot. Ask students to recall movies or television shows in which the setting contributed to a certain mood: for example, suspense, sadness, holiday cheer, or a bittersweet yearning for the past.

Through the Selection

Aduéñate de estas palabras

remanso (23)	colindante (24)
follaje (23)	apesadumbrado (24)
gajo (24)	retozar (24)
montero (24)	atajar (25)

Techniques for Handling the Reading

Students should experience no particular difficulty with this straightforward, heartwarming narrative. To help emphasize the author's use of vivid images and details of setting, you might call on volunteers to read the first two paragraphs aloud. Remind students to use the footnotes and glossary word entries to identify the meanings of any unfamiliar words.

Crea significados (page 26)

Repaso del texto

a. **¿Qué les gusta buscar a los muchachos en el fondo del río?** They like to search for ripe mangoes.
b. **¿Qué piensa hacer Pedro?** He is planning to drown the puppy.
c. **¿Qué decide hacer Bruno?** Bruno decides to grab the sack and open it so that the puppy can escape into the water.
d. **¿Cómo llevan a casa los muchachos a Negrita?** They take her home in a net.

Primeras impresiones

1. **¿Qué sentiste cuando soltaron a Negrita del saco de Pedro?** Most students will acknowledge that they felt relieved.

Interpretaciones del texto

2. **¿Cómo da el autor intensidad y realismo al *ambiente*? Menciona algunos elementos que contribuyen a fijar el tiempo y el lugar.** Students' answers will vary. Among the details of setting that they may mention are the cascade falling into the pool of still water, the shade of the trees on the bank, the reflection of the green leaves on the water's surface, the occasional shafts of sunlight, and the boys' diving and searching for ripe mangoes on the bottom.
3. **¿Qué motivos crees que tiene Bruno para dejar en libertad a Negrita?** Students may suggest that Bruno wants to save the puppy's life.
4. **¿Cómo reacciona Pedro cuando Negrita recupera su libertad? ¿Por qué?** When Pedro sees the puppy licking the child's face, he smiles for the first time. He agrees with Bruno that the little dog, in her newfound freedom, exhibits an exuberance that makes the animal seem wiser than human beings.

Preguntas al texto

5. ¿Qué supones que habría pasado si Pedro no se hubiera conmovido y hubiera insistido en ahogar al cachorro?
Students' answers will vary. They may speculate, for example, that Pedro would have become hostile and grabbed the puppy back, or that he would have started a fight with Bruno.

Más allá del texto

6. Busca información sobre organizaciones como la aspca y la Liga de Rescate de Animales (*Animal Rescue League*). Estas organizaciones recogen animales abandonados o maltratados y buscan a alguien que quiera adoptarlos. Si te interesa, puedes colaborar.
Help students find telephone numbers, addresses, and general information for the organizations listed in the text and for similar groups.

Beyond the Selection

Opciones:
Prepara tu portafolio (page 27)

Cuaderno del escritor

1. Compilación de ideas para un episodio autobiográfico
Many students will be able to write notes from personal experience. For students who have never had a pet or wanted to own one, stress that they can still draw on knowledge that they have accumulated by watching television shows, visiting zoos, or hearing anecdotes about pets that belong to friends or family members.

Escribe el guión (Writing a Storyboard)

2. Negrita: la película (Negrita: the Movie)
Suggest that students examine the paragraphing of the narrative carefully. They will find that new paragraphs often correspond to transitions from one important scene to the next.

Redacción creativa

3. ¿Y después qué? (What Next?)
Divide the class into small groups and have group members brainstorm predictions about what might happen in a sequel to this chapter.

Hablar y escuchar (Speaking and Listening)

4. Negrita y Zlateh (Negrita and Zlateh)
Reassure students that they do not need to answer formal questions after reading "La cabra Zlateh." The selection is intended purely for enrichment. Interested students will enjoy pursuing connections, however—both with the collection theme and with the excerpt from *Negrita*.

Estrategias para leer (page 28)

Cómo utilizar pistas del contexto
(Using Context Clues)

Guide students to make inferences from context about the meaning of the underlined item in each example. For instance, the verb *detestaba* in the first sentence of the exercise should provide a clue to the meaning of *repugnaba*. The specific grocery items in the second sentence should serve as a clue for the meaning of *no perecederos*. The simile *como una hoja de papel blanco* in the third sentence should allow students to make an educated guess about the meaning of the word *lívida*. In the fourth sentence, the conjunction *pero,* signaling contrast, should alert students that the meaning of *arduo* contrasts with *fácil*. Finally, in the fifth item, the explanatory information in the second sentence should help clarify the meaning of *desconcertó* in the first sentence.

Escena cultural
(Cultural Scene) (page 30)

Comunicación animal
(Animal Communication)

Actividades para empezar
(Warm-Up Activities)

The purpose of this activity is to sharpen students' sensitivity to nonverbal communication. Remind students that whether or not animals can be said truly to possess "language," it is certain that they use many nonverbal channels to communicate with one another. Although we tend, from our human perspective, to regard these channels as inferior to spoken language, some of them are remarkably subtle and sophisticated.

Actividades de cierre (Wrap-Up Activities)
1. Encourage students to consider such communication channels as tone of voice (as opposed to the actual words used), gesture, and posture.
2. Suggest that students acquire an overview of the topic of bird song by consulting an encyclopedia article.
3. The honeybee dances are discussed in some detail by Donald R. Griffin in his books *Animal Thinking* and *Animal Minds* (see **For Further Reading**). The classic, full-scale exposition is by the Nobel Prize-winning ethologist Karl von Frisch in *The Dance Language and Orientation of Bees* (Harvard University Press: Cambridge, Mass., 1967).

For Further Reading
You may find these sources useful as background readings.
Bright, Michael. *Animal Language* (Cornell University Press, Ithaca, N.Y., 1984).
Griffin, Donald R. *Animal Thinking* (Harvard University Press, Cambridge, Ma., 1984).
———*Animal Minds* (University of Chicago Press, Chicago, 1992).
Hartshorne, Charles. *Born to Sing: An Interpretation and World Survey of Bird Song* (Indiana University Press, Bloomington, 1973).
Johnson, George. "Chimp Talk Debate: Is It Really Language?" *The New York Times* 6 June 1995: C1.
Kruuk, Hans. *The Spotted Hyena: A Study of Predation and Social Behavior* (University of Chicago Press, Chicago, 1972).
Linden, Eugene. "Can Animals Think?" *Time* 22 March 1993: 54–61.
Morton, Eugene S., and Jake Page. *Animal Talk: Science and the Voices of Nature* (Random House, New York, 1992).
Moss, Cynthia. *Elephant Memories* (Fawcett Columbine, New York, 1988).
Narins, Peter. "Frog Communication." *Scientific American* August 1995: 78–83.
Schaller, George B. *The Deer and the Tiger* (University of Chicago Press, Chicago, 1967).

Walther, Fritz R. *Communication and Expression Among Hoofed Mammals* (Indiana University Press, Bloomington, 1984).

A leer por tu cuenta
(No Questions Asked)
La cabra Zlateh
(Zlateh the Goat)

Isaac Bashevis Singer   page 34

Summary
It is Hanukkah time in a small village in Central Europe. Reuven the furrier has had a bad year, and after long hesitation he decides he must sell Zlateh, the family goat, to the town butcher in order to provide his family with the essential items for celebrating the holiday. He instructs his oldest son, Aaron, twelve, to take the goat to the town. Aaron and Zlateh, however, are caught in a blizzard and spend three nights in a haystack. Because the goat gives milk and provides warmth, the boy survives. After Aaron returns home with Zlateh and tells them how he survived, the family never again thinks of selling the goat. Because of the sudden snap of cold weather, the villagers need the furrier's services, and the family is able to celebrate a joyous Hanukkah.

Adueñate de estas palabras

vacilación (34)	terquedad (38)
acolchada (36)	sofocar (38)
pescuezo (36)	recompensar (38)
repentinamente (36)	caos (38)
graznar (36)	exhalar (38)
granizar (36)	irradiar (38)
ventoso (36)	

Techniques for Handling the Reading
You might introduce this story by asking students to brainstorm answers to this question: What animal has proved most valuable to human beings? Students will probably name domestic

animals such as horses, cows, and dogs, or mention creatures such as honeybees that provide food. Since the word *cabra* is in the story's title, call on volunteers to discuss how versatile goats are: They provide milk, cheese, meat, kid leather, and wool. They can be trained to pull carts, and they can be used to keep the grass clipped in a fenced yard. They also make good, albeit occasionally stubborn, pets.

Students should have few problems with this delightful story, in which we get to know not only a young boy's feelings at a time of challenge but also the amiable and trusting nature of Zlateh herself. The story's central conflict—the struggle to survive a force of nature—presents obvious parallels to the excerpt from Santiago's *Cuando era puertorriqueña* (see page 3). Even though the philosophy underlying the selections in A LEER POR TU CUENTA is to give students a chance to read freely, they may enjoy exploring parallels with the excerpt from *Negrita* (page 22) and connections with the cultural feature on animal communication (page 30).

Taller del escritor
(Writer's Workshop) (page 42)

La narración/Episodio autobiográfico
(Autobiographical Incident)

Presenting the Workshop

For a general overview of the writing process, see the MANUAL DE COMUNICACIÓN (page 324). Since this Writer's Workshop is the first extended writing assignment in the anthology, you may wish to devote part or all of a class session to reviewing the major aspects of each stage of the process.

Before students get started, encourage them to consider a range of springboards and models for an autobiographical incident. For example, point out that the first two selections in this collection are autobiographical, and draw attention to the authors' use of the first-person point of view.

Students will also recognize many of the features of autobiographical writing from everyday conversations with family members, friends, and classmates. This form of narration may also be familiar to students from television talk shows and from print interviews with local and national celebrities. There are thus many potential models and sources for students' ideas. The opportunities for self-discovery that this form of writing offers will also appeal to many students.

Antes de escribir (Prewriting)

Some of your students may be hesitant about the assignment because they feel that their own experiences are too insignificant to interest an audience of readers or listeners. Tell students that most autobiographical writing does not deal with dramatic issues or celebrities but with everyday, ordinary experiences that reveal some truth about a person, a place, or a relationship.

In addition to the prewriting strategies discussed in the text, point out to students that they may often be able to clarify their own memories by **interviewing** family members or friends. Suggest that students who conduct interviews should prepare a written list of questions in advance. You might also recommend that students experiment with **tape recording** some autobiographical anecdotes and then playing them back for a small group of friends and family members.

Early in the workshop, point out that the stages of the writing process are used merely as a convenient framework. Far from being distinct segments, the stages can often overlap. At various points during each stage, students may find it convenient to jump forward or backward, at least briefly, to tasks associated with another stage. Thus, they might want to consider publication or sharing formats as early as the prewriting stage, or in the revising stage they might find it necessary to go back and use a prewriting technique such as brainstorming or clustering to generate additional details. Likewise, many students will revise their paper somewhat during the drafting stage and then go over it more thoroughly during the revising and proofreading stages. Stress to the class that writing is cumulative and additive—truly a *process* that requires constant honing and polishing.

El borrador (Drafting)

If students use a computer to draft their autobiographical incident, make sure that they save each successive draft on disk so that nothing is lost.

You may wish to devote some class time to discussing how students can elaborate their narratives effectively with sensory images and figurative language. Remind students that all the selections in this collection can serve as models for the vivid use of language. Invite students to review some specific examples, such as the description of the hurricane's approach in the extract from *Cuando era puertorriqueña* (page 4) or the first paragraph of the *Negrita* excerpt (pages 23–24). Also point out that the explicit statements of theme in "Trabajo de campo" offer a model for reflections about the meaning of an experience.

Evaluación y revisión
(Evaluating and Revising)

When students have finished their first drafts, ask them to examine carefully the pair of models in the text (pages 45–46). Students may work independently, or you may wish to devote some time in a class session to analyzing and discussing this material. If you choose to have students work in class, call on volunteers to read the model drafts aloud. Then call on volunteers to comment on each draft. Make sure that students understand the reasons for the writing evaluations given in the text. Then encourage partners to exchange feedback. The guidelines for evaluation and revision on page 45 can be used by students whether they work in pairs or independently.

Bear in mind that students may need help in applying their notes and making workable alterations of their first drafts. On a purely mechanical level, for example, some writers may need a guided introduction to the basic proofreading symbols for insertion, deletion, and transposition. See the MANUAL DE COMUNICACIÓN (page 325).

Corrección de pruebas (Proofreading)

Emphasize the importance of refining and proofreading written work before publishing or sharing it. Proofreading or editing adds to the clarity, correctness, and presentation of an essay or story. Familiarity with the conventions of language and writing—spelling, punctuation, grammar, usage, capitalization, paragraphing, syllabification, accuracy of citations and graphics, and proper manuscript form—is an important part of being an effective writer.

Have students refer once more to the list of basic proofreading symbols given in the MANUAL DE COMUNICACIÓN (page 325). Then have partners exchange papers and proofread one another's writing. You may wish to circulate through the class, offering help when needed.

Publicación (Publishing)

In addition to the sharing opportunities mentioned in the text, suggest that students might like to read their narrative aloud to a class of younger students or publish it on a Web site for young writers on the Internet.

Reflexión (Reflecting on Your Writing)

Guide students to recognize that time set aside for reflection on the assignment is an investment in the growth of their writing skills. For example, if students had difficulty with the prewriting phase (trying to find a suitable topic for an autobiographical incident), they might want to get together with classmates in a small group to brainstorm topics for the next writing assignment. If they found that freewriting on the computer helped their ideas to flow more freely, they might want to use the computer regularly for writing assignments.

Reteaching

Students having difficulty evaluating and revising may work in pairs to read their narratives aloud. Encourage writers to focus on telling about their subject in chronological order and on using vivid sensory images and specific details.

Closure

Ask students to explain the difference between an autobiographical incident and a short story about the adventures of made-up characters.

Assessment Tools

As students work through the writing process, share the following assessment criteria with them, so they may use them in self- and peer evaluations.

Assessment Criteria

1 2 3 4 5 6
(needs   (superior)
improvement)

Content

- Beginning grabs reader's interest.
- Necessary background is supplied.
- Dialogue and sensory images are used to make the incident vivid and lively.
- Events are told in chronological order, and verb tenses are consistent.
- Personal thoughts and feelings are included.
- Outcome and meaning of the experience are clear.

Language Conventions

- Grammar and usage are standard.
- Paragraphs are indented properly.
- Words are spelled correctly.
- Quotation marks are used correctly.

Overall Rating: _____

Enrichment

Art Connection

Work with students to develop a class collage of items that they associate with challenges. Students should each contribute one small item: for example, a ticket stub, a concert program, a grocery shopping list, a journal entry about a babysitting assignment, an old newspaper article about a snowstorm, a photograph, a piece of sheet music, a tennis ball, and so forth. The item can represent either an individual challenge that has been met and overcome or a challenge met as a group (for example, a sports team). Visual learners can take the lead in arranging the items for display.

Taller de oraciones
(Sentence Workshop) (page 47)

Mil maneras de combinar oraciones
(A Thousand Ways to Combine Sentences)

This workshop introduces students to sentence combining, a strategy that is developed throughout the book. Sentence combining will help students use more complex sentence structures, avoid repetition, and show relationships between ideas. Sentence combining also aids students in comprehending difficult phrases and clauses.

The goals of the exercise are for students to practice editing repetitive and choppy sentences in their writing and for students to add transitional words to show the connection between ideas.

In this exercise, students are asked to read the sentences aloud to become aware of repetition and lack of coherence. Students can then combine the sentences by eliminating words and/or adding transitional words. Students will combine sentences differently and bring their own shades of meaning to the story. In the discussion you can ask these questions:

- **¿Cómo suenan las oraciones sin editar?** (Ask them to show particular places where sentences are repetitive or unconnected.)
- **¿Suenan mejor con los cambios? ¿Es posible combinar las oraciones de varias maneras?**
- **¿Qué sucede si las oraciones se combinan de maneras distintas? ¿Hay algo que sea muy distinto en la versión de tu compañero(a)?**

Finally, you can focus on transitional words that students have used and discuss the relationships they demonstrate. For further instruction, you can refer them to the GUÍA DEL LENGUAJE or ask them to find transitional words in a selection. Ask them to illustrate the use of transitional words in their personal dictionaries. In AL REVISAR TU TRABAJO, students apply what they have learned to their own writing.

A sample response to the sentence-combining exercise follows:

Yo había ido a la selva para encontrar a mi amigo Simón, que había marchado río arriba unos meses antes en busca de una especie de mono desconocida. Despúes de alcanzar los rápidos, llegamos a un lugar muy aislado donde vivía la tribu pacífica Txai, que seguramente tendría noticias de Simón.

Collection 2: SI TÚ SUPIERAS...

Collection Overview

The theme *Si tú supieras...* ("If You Only Knew . . .") is likely to appeal to sixth-graders, who usually have a keen appetite for the mysterious, the magical, and the dreamlike. Each of the selections, including the *adivinanzas,* or riddles in the form of poems, is a "tale with a twist" that ends with an ironic punch or a surprise.

The collection begins with a short story by Mexican writer Gregorio López y Fuentes. In "Una carta a Dios" ("A Letter to God"), a hard-working, pious farmer whose crops have been ruined in a hailstorm writes a letter asking for money from God. The post-office workers, sympathetic and admiring of the farmer's enduring faith, pool their money and come up with a little more than half of what he has requested. However, when the man receives the money, he writes back to God claiming that the thieving postal workers are not to be trusted. The story is accessible and amusing.

"El adivinador de máscaras" ("The Mask Diviner") by Antonio Robles is a creative and humorous story about Carnival, a central celebration in Spain, as well as in many other parts of the world. A clever boy plans to discover the identities of the masked revelers by comparing the shapes of their eyes to those of various animals in a book. He meets with success until one special reveler shows up.

"La casa de las tres viudas" ("The House of the Three Widows") by Pablo Neruda is taken from the Nobel Prize–winning poet's *Memorias* (*Memoirs*). Neruda recalls a trip during his student days when he unexpectedly visited three mysterious widows, who lived a timeless, dreamlike existence. Neruda's powers of observation and his poetic command of language are demonstrated in this challenging piece.

The final brief readings in this collection, under the heading A LEER POR TU CUENTA, are intended for enrichment. In "Adivinanzas" ("Riddles"), poet Nicolás Guillén offers three charming verse riddles that students can try to solve.

Throughout the collection, questions, exercises, and activities give students a wide range of opportunities to respond to the literature, both analytically and creatively. In ELEMENTOS DE LITERATURA (pages 58–59), a feature titled CUENTOS I: ARGUMENTO Y AMBIENTE introduces readers to two of the most important literary building blocks of the short story: plot and setting. This discussion will be continued with a treatment of characterization, point of view, and theme in Collection 3 (pages 110–111).

The integration of materials within the collection also extends to the opening assignments in OPCIONES: PREPARA TU PORTAFOLIO, which are designed to prepare students progressively for the writing assignment at the end of the collection in TALLER DEL ESCRITOR. Students will find numerous springboards and models within the literature itself for this assignment, which is to write an observational or descriptive essay. Further activities in OPCIONES challenge students to explore themes and ideas in a variety of modes, such as music, theater, or mask making. ESTRATEGIAS PARA LEER in this collection focuses on recognizing and analyzing cause-and-effect relationships, while LENGUA Y LITERATURA introduces students to word connotations. At the very end of the collection, in TALLER DE ORACIONES, students learn how to combine sentences and use noun modifiers.

Introducing the Collection

Encourage students to explore the theme of this collection by presenting them with a choice of opening activities. Possibilities include the following:
1. Have students freewrite about a time when something unexpected happened to them.

Tell them to write nonstop for four or five minutes, and assure them that their spelling and mechanics will not be checked. Was the surprise pleasant or unpleasant? How did they feel about it at the time? How do they feel when they look back on it now?

2. Divide students into small groups. Tell them to imagine what type of house might be found in the middle of a large forest. Who might live in this house? What would the rooms look like? What articles are found inside? Visual learners can take the lead in illustrating the exterior and interior of the house.

3. Write these three words on the chalkboard: *disfraz* (*disguise*), *secreto* (*secret*), and *sorpresa* (*surprise*). Then divide the class into small groups. Invite each group to choose one of the three words and write it in the center of a large piece of poster paper. Have group members brainstorm to create a cluster of associations for the word they have chosen. When groups have finished work, encourage them to share their clusters with the class as a whole.

Una carta a Dios
(A Letter to God)

Gregorio López y Fuentes

page 51

Into the Selection

Summary
Together with his family, a peasant farmer named Lencho happily greets the rain that will mean a good harvest of corn and beans. The rain, however, turns into a hailstorm, and the crops are destroyed. Lencho believes that his family's only hope is to trust in God, so he writes God a letter, requesting one hundred pesos to tide the family over until the following year, and mails the letter at the post office.

The postal employees, amused at the address on the envelope, show Lencho's letter to their boss. A kindly man who is impressed by the simple peasant's faith, the boss takes up a collection for Lencho. He is able to raise only sixty pesos, however. He places the money in an envelope addressed to Lencho and writes a letter, signing it "God."

The following Sunday, Lencho appears at the post office, receives his letter, and examines the contents. He immediately requests paper and ink so he can write a reply. After he places his letter in the mailbox and departs, the boss retrieves the envelope. Inside, Lencho informs God that he has received only sixty pesos. He earnestly requests the balance. However, he advises God not to trust the post office, because the employees are thieves.

Antes de leer (page 50)

Punto de partida

¿Qué te dice un título? (What Does a Title Tell You?)
Tell students that writers usually choose the titles of stories and poems to focus the audience's attention on an important feature of the plot, a major character, or the theme or overall message. The choice of a title, in turn, has an impact on the reader's expectations. As students consider the title of this story, you might call on volunteers to offer suggestions about the story's content and tone. Write some of their ideas on the chalkboard.

Comparte tus ideas (Think-Pair-Share)
Encourage students to jot notes about their predictions. They can save their notes and then review them when they have finished reading the story.

Diálogo con el texto
This feature serves to guide students in their reading of the first selection. Refer to DIARIO DEL LECTOR in **Through the Selection** for suggestions on how to extend this guidance.

Estrategias para leer

La relación de causa y efecto
(Understanding Cause and Effect)
Point out that the plots of many stories and movies can be analyzed in terms of cause and

effect. Stress that the events in a plot don't simply happen one after another in time; there is almost always a closer relationship in which causes logically lead to results, which in turn become the causes of further events, and so forth. At this time, you may want students to preview the full-page feature on cause and effect in this collection (see page 69).

Elementos de literatura

Ironía (Irony)
Sixth-graders often have a well-developed sense of irony, even though this literary term may be unfamiliar to some of them. Encourage students to offer some of their own examples of ironic situations from everyday life, and write a brief summary of each situation on the chalkboard. Tell students that irony in literature usually involves a surprise or a sudden reversal. Just like surprises in real life, irony can be light and amusing, or it can be dark and unpleasant in tone.

Through the Selection

Diario del lector (page 52)
The sample marginal annotations illustrate several helpful reading strategies, including questioning, summarizing, making inferences, and making predictions. If you feel your students will benefit, you can extend this activity, modeling similar annotations for the next page of the text or for the entire selection. Alternatively, you can pause at the end of each section, allowing enough time to monitor and discuss students' notes on an individual basis.

Adueñate de estas palabras
mortificado (52)   fortificar (54)
afligirse (54)   determinación (54)
conciencia (54)

Techniques for Handling the Reading
Remind students that they should use the glossary entries to find the meanings of unfamiliar words. Most of your students should have no trouble with this straightforward narrative, and they will enjoy the story's lightly ironic surprise ending. When readers have finished the selection, you might want to hold a quick brainstorming session, asking students to review and discuss the predictions they made in ANTES DE LEER about the story's contents and tone. Then call on volunteers to comment on how the story relates to the collection theme, *Si tú supieras...*

Crea significados (page 56)
Repaso del texto
a. **¿Con qué compara Lencho las gotas de lluvia?** Lencho compares the raindrops to new coins.
b. **¿Qué les pasa a los cultivos?** They are destroyed in the hailstorm.
c. **¿Por qué le escribe Lencho a Dios?** Lencho writes to God to request one hundred pesos. He needs this money to tide him and his family over until the next harvest.
d. **¿Qué hace por Lencho el jefe de la oficina de correos?** The boss takes up a collection and sends sixty pesos to Lencho, together with a letter signed "God."

Primeras impresiones
1. **¿Qué hará el jefe de la oficina de correos con la segunda carta de Lencho? ¿Por qué?** Students' answers will vary. Some students may suggest that the boss will do nothing, while others may suggest that he will write another letter signed "God," saying that the postal workers are honest.

Interpretaciones del texto
2. **¿Qué clase de hombre es Lencho? Describe su carácter en una o dos oraciones.** Students' answers will vary. In general, they will point out that Lencho is a simple, direct, hard-working farmer, and that he has an unwavering faith in God.
3. **¿Qué clase de hombre es el jefe de la oficina de correos? Describe su carácter en una o dos oraciones.** The boss is kind and unselfish, and he admires Lencho's religious faith. He is also persistent, collecting as much money as he can for a good cause.

4. **¿Por qué es *irónico* que Lencho crea que los empleados de correos son unos ladrones?** Lencho's belief is ironic because it contrasts sharply with what we know to be the truth: Far from being thieves, the postal workers generously sent Lencho the money.

Conexiones con el texto

5. **Si trabajaras en la oficina de correos y hubieras recibido las cartas de Lencho, ¿qué habrías hecho?** Students' answers will vary. Many students will say that they would have contributed to the collection after the first letter, but that they might have felt insulted after the second.

Preguntas al texto

6. **¿Lencho es demasiado exigente o tiene una fe inquebrantable?** Students' answers will vary. Encourage students to support their responses with reasons.

Beyond the Selection

Opciones: Prepara tu portafolio (page 57)

Cuaderno del escritor

1. Compilación de ideas para un ensayo de observación
(Collecting Ideas for a Descriptive Essay)
Before students begin this activity, model the technique of collecting and presenting specific details by reviewing some portions of "Una carta a Dios" with the class: for example, the description of Lencho's house, the hills, the river, the corral, and the field in the first paragraph, or the paragraph that describes the first raindrops (*Fue durante la comida cuando...*). Point out the individual phrases that the author uses to help us visualize the setting. Then suggest that students think of the five senses—sight, hearing, smell, taste, and touch—as they jot down their notes.

Redacción creativa

2. Lo que quiero (What I Want)
Remind students that the content and tone of a well-written and appropriate letter depend very much on the audience, or addressee. For example, if they were writing to a member of the school board, the tone would be quite different from the informal approach they might use in a letter to a classmate or a close relative.

Redacción creativa/Teatro (Theater)

3. Hablemos claro (Talking It Out)
Students may find this activity easier if you suggest that they work in small groups. Tell them to remember that their dialogue should be consistent with the way that Lencho and the post-office boss are portrayed in the story. You might suggest, for example, that students review their answers to questions 2 and 3 in CREA SIGNIFICADOS (page 56).

Elementos de literatura (page 58)

Cuentos I: Argumento y ambiente
(Short Stories I: Plot and Setting)

Make sure that students can answer the questions about plot elements in various selections that the class has already read. For example, the **external conflict** in "Una carta a Dios" is Lencho's struggle to survive a natural disaster, the hailstorm. The **internal conflict** within the mind of Pedro, the hunter in *Negrita,* is the struggle between his duty to obey his master's orders and his compassion for the little puppy. An example of **foreshadowing** in "La cabra Zlateh" is the snowstorm that creates the need for Reuven's services; people need more fur garments in the cold weather.

You can also use the brief true-false quiz below to test students' comprehension of the material in ELEMENTOS DE LITERATURA.

1. **La acción en un cuento suele variar con respecto al tiempo y al espacio.** (F)
2. **Cualquier forma narrativa o dramática que cuenta una historia tiene un argumento.** (T)
3. **El nucleo de la historia está en el conflicto, que puede ser interno, externo o ambos simultáneamente.** (T)
4. **Al punto crítico de una historia se le llama resolución.** (F)
5. **El lugar donde se desarrolla una historia puede ser muy importante para crear su ambiente.** (T)

El adivinador de máscaras
(The Mask Diviner)

Antonio Robles — page 61

Into the Selection

Summary
At Carnival time, an ingenious boy named Tupé amazes all the villagers with his ability to identify the masked revelers by name. He confesses the secret of his success to his friend Manolín. Tupé has studied the eyes of each villager, correlating them with the look of a different creature in an illustrated book of animals. In a little notebook he has carefully listed the individual characteristics of ninety-nine villagers; for example, "Juan López (look of camel)" or "Lino García (look of bear)."

The following year, however, Tupé faces an unexpected challenge. An unfamiliar masquerader, stylishly dressed in a monkey costume, sits silent on the highway outside the village, returning the gaze of all the onlookers. Tupé is challenged to identify him. After some puzzlement, the boy confesses to defeat. The figure seems to have human eyes, but since Tupé has never met him in the village he must be a stranger. The masked reveler then rises and walks away in triumph down the highway.

The following day, the newspapers carry a story about a large monkey that has escaped from the zoo and has been seen walking down the road. Tupé realizes what has happened. He takes out his notebook and writes, "Large monkey (look of man)."

Antes de leer (page 60)

Punto de partida

¿Tienes buena memoria?
(Do You Have a Good Memory?)
Since some good observers do not perform well under time pressure, suggest that students who try this activity make the time limit flexible. The important objective is to see what kinds of information observers remember about the various objects.

Toma nota
This is a good time to stress the fact that keen observation does not necessarily have to focus on unusual or striking objects. On the contrary, everyday objects like a scarf, a pen, a clock, a leaf, or an apple can be wonderful subjects for observational writing.

Through the Selection

Aduéñate de estas palabras
joroba (61)
posterior (61)
estrafalaria (61)
impertinencia (62)
caprichosito (62)
incógnita (64)
fracasar (65)

Techniques for Handling the Reading
Direct students' attention to the footnotes and glossary words for some unusual forms and usages. Ask students to notice as they read the story how important the setting is to the atmosphere or mood. Point out that disguise and secrets are important motifs in the story and help to build suspense until the final revelation.

Literatura y tradiciones populares
(Literature and Social Customs) (page 66)

El Carnaval (Carnival)
Some of your students will be familiar with Carnival from community celebrations just before Lent or from news reports about the famous celebrations in Rio de Janeiro, Brazil, or the Mardi Gras festivities in New Orleans. Carnival blends many traditions, religious and secular, but one pervasive element is topsy-turvydom: the reversal, for a brief holiday interval, of the normal social order. In some districts of Mexico where the ancient Mayan calendar is still used, for example, the five lost days of the annual cycle are believed to occupy the interval of Carnival, when evil spirits roam and the world is turned upside down. Another sign of such topsy-turvydom is the custom of disguising oneself with a mask, thus altering (if only

temporarily) one's identity. Carnival parades and spectacles often feature lighthearted mockery of authority figures or institutions, and inhibitions are temporarily abandoned, as any visitor to New Orleans's Mardi Gras can testify. This is, of course, a most appropriate setting for an ironic tale with a twist, in which the expectations of the characters in the story and those of the readers are sharply reversed.

Crea significados (page 67)

Repaso del texto

a. **¿En qué época del año tiene lugar el relato?** The action takes place at Carnival time.

b. **¿Cómo identifica Tupé a las personas disfrazadas?** Tupé identifies the masked revelers by comparing their eyes to the shapes of the eyes of various animals in an illustrated book.

c. **¿Qué máscara es incapaz de identificar Tupé?** He is unable to identify the monkey mask.

d. **¿Quién resulta ser el que se oculta tras la máscara?** A real monkey, rather than a man masquerading as an animal, turns out to be behind the mask.

Primeras impresiones

1. **¿Pudiste adivinar que había un mono tras el disfraz o te causó sorpresa?** Students' answers will vary. Encourage those who guessed the monkey's real identity to describe how they foresaw the ending.

Interpretaciones del texto

2. **¿En qué se parece la conducta del mono a la de un ser humano?** The monkey gives every indication of being a human because of his size and his unusual "costume" at Carnival time. He sits silently in the road, returning the villagers' gaze.

3. **¿Cómo contribuye el giro inesperado del final a la *ironía* del relato?** The concluding twist of the story is ironic because no one in the story expected that the masked figure would turn out to be non-human. The ending reverses the expectations of characters and audience alike.

4. **¿Crees que Tupé se merece el título de «El adivinador de máscaras»? ¿Por qué?** Despite Tupé's chagrin toward the end, most readers will agree that the clever boy deserves the title, since he displays considerable ingenuity throughout the story.

Conexiones con el texto

5. **¿Crees que a veces los animales tienen expresiones o rasgos faciales similares a los de las personas? Por ejemplo, ¿sonríen los perros?** Students' answers will vary. Ask them to support their responses with reasons.

Más allá del texto

6. **¿Se te ocurre otra forma creativa de determinar la identidad de una persona disfrazada?** Students' answers will vary. In addition to scientific techniques such as fingerprinting and DNA analysis, students might suggest clues such as voice timbre, gestures, gait, or other distinctive mannerisms.

Beyond the Selection

Opciones: Prepara tu portafolio (page 68)

Cuaderno del escritor

1. Compilación de ideas para un ensayo de observación
Here you may wish to introduce the concept of spatial order to students: namely, an organizational method of describing objects according to their location (front to back, left to right, top to bottom, and so forth). Students might try making two lists to record details about the experience they recall: On the first list, they can note objects and their spatial relationships, while on the second they can list sense impressions.

Investigación/Redacción

2. Conviértete en crítico de arte
(Become an Art Critic)
You may want to suggest that students look at color reproductions of masks for this activity. A fine collection from all parts of the world has

been published by John Mack, ed., *Masks and the Art of Expression* (Harry N. Abrams, Inc., New York, 1994).

Redacción creativa/Música

3. Música de Carnaval (Carnival Music)
You may wish to have students work in small groups for this activity. If students need more inspiration, they can ask a librarian to assist them in locating Carnival pictures and songs.

Artesanía y trabajos manuales
(Arts and Crafts)

4. El arte de hacer máscaras (Mask Making)
Again, students may enjoy working in small groups for this activity. Try to ensure that each group contains at least one or two visual or kinaesthetic learners.

Estrategias para leer (page 69)

La relación de causa y efecto

This feature provides another good chance to emphasize that the plot of a story, novel, or drama is not just a series of events that happen one after another, but rather a carefully ordered sequence of incidents that are bound together in a logical relationship. For more discussion of plot, see ELEMENTOS DE LITERATURA in this collection (pages 58–59). Make sure that students can finish the cause-and-effect "formulas" for the plot of "Una carta a Dios." Answers will vary, but some sample responses follow:

a. *Efecto: Lencho necesita dinero para alimentar a su familia y comprar semillas.*
b. *Efecto: El jefe hace una colecta de dinero para Lencho.*
c. *Efecto: Lencho está defraudado y sospecha que los empleados de correos son unos ladrones.*

La casa de las tres viudas (*de* Memorias)

(The House of the Three Widows *from* Memoirs)

Pablo Neruda — page 71

Into the Selection

Summary

During his student days, Neruda was invited to a threshing ceremony at a remote location in the Chilean mountains. He rode for some distance on a trail near the Pacific, then turned off toward Lake Budi. As he traveled, he gloried in the spectacular scenery of the vast, lonely beaches and the forests of hazel trees and giant ferns. Toward evening, he glimpsed a group of fishermen before he moved inland. At twilight, however, he realized that he had lost his way. In the growing darkness, a solitary traveler whom he met on the road advised him to spend the night at a nearby house owned by three sisters. About nine o'clock that night, Neruda reached the house. He was greeted by a slender, white-haired woman dressed in black, who quietly but sternly examined him. After Neruda explained his situation, the woman welcomed him in and called her sisters. Conversing with them in a well-appointed room, Neruda felt as if he had fallen to the bottom of a lake. The atmosphere was dreamlike, even a bit ghostly.

His visit took a new, more genial turn, however, when he happened to mention the French poet Charles Baudelaire, whose verse he was starting to translate. This reference to French culture was like a spark to the women, who then told Neruda their family history. A servant announced dinner, and Neruda's hostesses conducted him to the dining room. There he enjoyed a sumptuous feast. The sisters' greatest pride, in fact, was their cookery. They disclosed that over the past thirty years they had entertained twenty-seven travelers at their remote house in the mountains. The sisters had kept a personal file for each visitor, with the date of the visit and the menu they had prepared on each occasion, so that in the event of a repeat visit not even a single dish would be duplicated.

Neruda retired to sleep after dinner and departed at dawn the next morning. He confesses that after forty-five years, he wonders what ever became of those three mysterious and marvelous women. Their fate, he speculates, was death and oblivion. Yet they live on in Neruda's admiring recollections—honored for their devotion to tradition and heritage.

Antes de leer (page 70)

Punto de partida

Personajes extraños y mágicos
(Strange, Magical Characters)
In addition to the activity described in the text, you may want students to brainstorm about the concept of tradition, which plays an important role in the selection. For example, you could have students write about three traditions or rituals that they or their family observe every year. Then you might have students freewrite a paragraph explaining why they might keep up these traditions or rituals if they moved to another country.

Elementos de literatura

Figuras retóricas (Figures of Speech)
Remind students that they have already encountered a striking metaphor in "Una carta a Dios," when Lencho calls the raindrops *monedas nuevas*. See if students recall that Esmeralda Santiago also uses a simile for raindrops toward the end of the excerpt from *Cuando era puertorriqueña* in Collection 1: "Estaba lloviznando, gotas grises y tenebrosas *como vapor*" (page 7). A more extended discussion of *figuras retóricas* appears in ELEMENTOS DE LITERATURA for Collection 6 (see pages 222–223).

Through the Selection

Adueñate de estas palabras

intermitencia (71)
acosada (72)
colosal (72)
rocío (72)
agredirse (72)
crepuscular (74)
pavor (74)
emerger (74)
sobriamente (74)
legua (74)
divisar (74)
vedar (74)
esquivar (74)
melancólico (75)
súbitamente (75)
taladrada (75)
aserrín (75)
hechizo (76)
desterrada (77)
sobrevenir (77)
impenetrable (77)

Techniques for Handling the Reading

Although the narrative is told in chronological order and the first-person point of view makes the story accessible, your students may find this selection quite challenging. Encourage students to slow their normal reading pace so that they can cope with the footnotes and glossary words. Students who need vocabulary reinforcement may benefit from being assigned a word or group of words to illustrate. You can use the illustrations as visual reminders and as flashcards for practice. If students are keeping a spelling log throughout the year, have them record correctly any of the vocabulary words from this selection that they misspell. Students should write a brief definition next to each word.

Aside from vocabulary, the selection may also puzzle some of your students on the level of content and theme. Point out that the atmosphere of mystery in the piece is closely linked to the wild, almost ghostly setting of the mountains and forests of Chile. You may wish to pair less proficient readers with more proficient ones for work on this selection. Suggest that pairs pause at the point where Neruda arrives at the three widows' house, some time after dark (bottom of page 74). Encourage students to share their ideas about how the young traveler must feel at this stage. Then have readers go on to find out how the author's feelings progress from apprehension and puzzlement, at the beginning of his visit, to warmth and admiration for his three elderly hostesses.

Crea significados (page 79)

Repaso del texto

a. **¿Adónde conduce Neruda su caballo en la primera parte del ensayo?** Neruda rides his horse high up in the mountains far from town and then along the shore of a lake.

b. **¿Quién orienta y da consejo a Neruda?** A peasant whom Neruda encounters at nightfall gives him advice and directions.

c. **¿Qué hacen las tres viudas por Neruda?** The three women invite him to dinner and put him up for the night.

d. **¿Cómo llevan las tres viudas la cuenta de sus visitantes?** The three widows keep a file on each visitor, together with the dinner menu, so that they will not repeat even a single dish should a traveler ever return.

Primeras impresiones

1. **¿Qué imagen del ensayo recuerdas con más claridad?** Students' answers will vary. Among the images students may mention are the following: the description of the rugged coastline, the description of the forest, and the details the writer gives about the widows' parlor and dining room.

Interpretaciones del texto

2. **¿Qué tiene de insólito el estilo de vida de las viudas?** The sisters, who are in the lumber business, have grown accustomed to the lonely, mountainous setting of their house. Their only regular contact is with peasants and country servants. Nevertheless, they maintain an extremely elegant standard of living.

3. **Encuentra en el ensayo un ejemplo de cada una de las tres figuras retóricas principales: *símil, metáfora y personificación*.** Similes students may mention include the following: *Aquél era un salón de otro siglo, indefinible e inquietante como un sueño* (page 75); *Fue como una chispa eléctrica* (page 75); *Sus transidos ojos y sus rígidos rostros se transmutaron, como si se les hubieran desprendido tres máscaras antiguas de sus antiguos rasgos* (page 75); *Me invadió una timidez extrema, como si me hubiera invitado la reina Victoria a comer en su palacio* (page 76); *Me fui a dormir y caí en la cama como un saco de cebollas en un mercado* (page 76); *Pero en mi recuerdo siguen viviendo como en el fondo transparente del lago de los sueños* (page 77). Metaphors students may cite include the following: *Las tres damas apagadas se encendieron* (page 75); *la mesa era para ellas el cultivo de una herencia sagrada* (page 76). Examples of personification include the following: *El Pacífico allí se desencadena y ataca con intermitencia las rocas y los matorrales del cerro Maule* (page 71); *El oleaje asaltaba con tremendos golpes los pedestales del cerro* (page 71); *Por el lado de los bosques me saludaban los avellanos de ramajes verdeoscuros y brillantes* (page 72); *La noche y la selva, que fueron mi regocijo, ahora me amenazaban* (page 74); *Quizá la selva devoró aquellas vidas y aquellos salones que me acogieron en una noche inolvidable* (page 77).

4. **¿Cuándo empieza a cambiar la atmósfera del ensayo?** The mood begins to change from mysterious and apprehensive to warm and animated when Neruda mentions the poet Baudelaire and the widows start to talk about their heritage. Neruda signals this change with the use of *figuras retóricas* that, significantly, connote light and warmth: *Fue como una chispa eléctrica. Las tres damas apagadas se encendieron* (page 75).

Conexiones con el texto

5. **Esto escribe Neruda de la casa de las viudas: «Me pareció haber caído al fondo de un lago y en sus honduras sobrevivir soñando, muy cansado». ¿Qué aspectos de su experiencia te recuerdan a un sueño?** Students' answers may vary. They may mention details such as Neruda's fatigue, the lateness of the hour, the wild setting, the appearance and behavior of the elderly widows, and the surprising discovery of such elegant surroundings in such a rugged and lonely location.

Preguntas al texto

6. **¿Pensaste en algún momento que las tres viudas eran fantasmas? ¿Qué**

podría haber pasado si lo fueran? Students' answers will vary. Encourage them to elaborate on their speculations with imaginative details.

7. **Neruda reconoce que, después de tantos años, el destino de las tres hermanas debe haber sido «la muerte y el olvido». En cierto sentido, ¿cómo desmiente el autor su propia afirmación?** Neruda proves his own statement wrong in the sense that he eloquently and vividly memorializes the women, so that they are not forgotten after all.

Beyond the Selection

Opciones:
Prepara tu portafolio (page 80)

Cuaderno del escritor

1. Compilación de ideas para un ensayo de observación
You may want to suggest that visual learners draw a sketch of the memorable person they recall. They can then add details in phrases for a caption.

Dibujo

2. El viaje de Neruda (Neruda's Journey)
This activity, like the previous one, is good preparation for the assignment in TALLER DEL ESCRITOR to write an observational essay (see page 84). You may wish to have students work in small groups.

Hablar y escuchar

3. Un archivo de personalidades
(A File of Personalities)
Suggest that students write their interview questions in advance. Remind them that "why" and "how" questions are likely to generate more information than questions that can be answered with a simple "yes" or "no." Also tell students to make sure that they write notes as soon as possible after each interview.

Hablar y escuchar

4. Recuerdos que perduran (Memories That Last)
Tell students to use a small tape recorder for their interviews if possible. They can also supplement their written versions with a photograph or sketch of the storyteller.

Lengua y literatura (page 81)

La sensación que producen las palabras
(The Feelings That Words Produce)

The exercise introduces the concept of **connotation** by asking students to examine their own reactions to words, both in general and in the selection "La casa de las tres viudas." The first part of the mini-lesson makes a distinction between denotation and connotation: Two words may have similar meanings but different connotations, as evidenced by the examples. In the second exercise, students work in a group to discover connotations upon which they all agree. The INTÉNTALO TÚ presents a comic scenario in which a writer does not understand negative connotations. This exercise helps to teach students the adverse effects of not being aware of connotations in their own writing.

Answers:
The words that have negative connotations, and alternative words or phrases with positive connotations, appear below:
  flaca → *delgada*
  tacaña → *ahorrativa*
  antipática → *seria, tranquila, callada*
  agresiva → *emprendedora*
  crema como el marfil → *blancos como la nieve*

Vocabulario (page 81)

El cuento casi sin fin
(The Story Almost Without End)

The words in the ADUÉÑATE DE ESTAS PALABRAS for this selection are very suggestive and rich in meaning. In this exercise, students use these words to construct their own story. The format for the never-ending story is a *retahíla*, a well-known form of popular Spanish children's literature. This form also exists among Spanish-speaking children in the United States.

A leer por tu cuenta
Adivinanzas
(Riddles)

Nicolás Guillén — page 82

Summary
In three verse riddles, the poet uses metaphor and personification to describe three familiar things: rain, sea, and river. The answers to the riddles are printed upside down below the poems.

Techniques for Handling the Reading
These riddles should pose no particular problems for readers. Students may enjoy discussing Guillén's use of *figuras retóricas,* and they may also be interested in making up other brief riddles with the same answers (rain, sea, and river).

Taller del escritor (page 84)

La descripción/Ensayo de observación
(Observational Essay)

Presenting the Workshop
Before students get started, encourage them to suggest and comment on some spring boards for an observational essay. Remind them that they have seen some excellent models of description in the literature of this collection, and call on volunteers to give examples, such as the descriptions of setting in "Una carta a Dios" and "La casa de las tres viudas." Point out that students can also derive inspiration from familiar sources such as newspaper and magazine articles, as well as science textbooks. Stress the creative possibilities in choosing a simple, everyday setting or ordinary object for description: Students will be able to observe their subjects directly, and by using imaginative figures of speech and vivid sensory language, they may be able to generate unexpected insights.

Antes de escribir
In addition to the prewriting strategies discussed in the text, point out to students that they can brainstorm subjects in small groups. Suggest that students share notes and ideas about foods, household objects (like recliner chairs and toasters), computers, hats, birds, trees, or events such as parades, concerts, or pep rallies. First, have student groups decide on a general category for investigation. Then suggest that each member of the group name an object or event within that category. Have the group appoint a recorder to list all the objects and events. Group members can then take turns contributing suggestions for specific details that could be used in a description of each object or event.

El borrador
If students use a computer to draft the essay, make sure that they save each successive draft on disk so that nothing is lost. You may wish to devote some class time to discussing how students can use figurative language effectively in their essays. First, suggest that students review Neruda's use of similes, metaphors, and personification in "La casa de las tres viudas" (note especially question 3 in CREA SIGNIFICADOS on page 79). Have students note the contexts in which Neruda uses figures of speech. Then you might want to write examples such as the following on the chalkboard:

Símil: Las hiedras de la selva eran *como* serpientes gigantes.
Metáfora: Las hiedras de la selva *eran* serpientes gigantes.
Personificación: Las hiedras de la selva se *enrollaban amenazadoras* en los altos árboles.

Discuss with students the distinctive features of each figure of speech. Call on volunteers to propose variations of these examples or to create their own similes, metaphors, and personifications.

Evaluación y revisión
When students have finished their first drafts, ask them to examine carefully the pair of models in the text (page 88). Students may work independently, or you may wish to devote some time in a class session to analyzing and discussing this material. If you choose to have students work in class, call on volunteers to read the model drafts aloud. Then call on volunteers to comment on each draft. Make sure that students

understand the reasons for the writing evaluations given in the text. Then encourage pairs to exchange feedback. The guidelines for evaluation and revision on page 87 can be used by students whether they work in pairs or independently.

Bear in mind that students may need help in applying their notes and making workable alterations of their first drafts. On a purely mechanical level, for example, some writers may need a guided introduction to the basic proofreading symbols for insertion, deletion, and transposition. See the MANUAL DE COMUNICACIÓN, page 325.

Corrección de pruebas

Emphasize the importance of refining and proofreading written work before submitting it for publication. Proofreading or editing adds to the clarity, correctness, and presentation of an essay, story, or report. Before they begin this stage, some students may need a guided review of the proofreading symbols used for editing and correcting errors in spelling and mechanics. Go over the list of symbols given in the MANUAL DE COMUNICACIÓN (page 325). Then have partners exchange papers and proofread each other's writing. You may wish to circulate through the class, offering help when needed.

Publicación

In addition to the sharing opportunities mentioned in the text, students might like to publish their essays on a computer chat line, or they might prepare them for oral delivery as a radio feature.

Reflexión

Guide students to recognize that time set aside for reflection on the assignment is an investment in the growth of their writing skills. The reflection starters on page 88 are intended only as illustrations. Encourage writers to reflect on a broad range of feelings or specific aspects of the assignment, including both challenges and satisfactions. Suggest that students keep their written reactions in their portfolios, together with the finished draft of the observational essay.

Reteaching

Students having difficulty evaluating and revising may work in pairs to read their essays aloud. Encourage them to identify the most interesting and vivid parts of each essay.

Closure

Ask students to explain the difference between an observational essay and an autobiographical incident.

Assessment Tools

As students work through the writing process, share the following assessment criteria with them, so they may use them in self- and peer evaluations.

Assessment Criteria

1	2	3	4	5	6
(needs improvement)					(superior)

Content
- Introduction clearly states the subject.
- Essay uses factual and sensory details, as well as precise words, to create a clear picture of the subject.
- Details are organized so that the essay reads smoothly and is easy to follow.
- Details contribute to a single main idea.

Language Conventions
- Grammar and usage are standard.
- Paragraphs are indented properly.
- Words are spelled correctly.
- Quotation marks are used correctly.

Overall Rating: _____

Enrichment

Science/Publishing Connection

Divide the class into small groups, and have each group choose one of the following categories: animals, birds, insects, volcanoes, coral reefs, rivers, wetlands, or trees. Then have group members focus on a specific example of the category they have chosen: for example, *abejas* for insects or *Río Grande* for rivers. Once group members have reached consensus, they should

work to prepare an illustrated pamphlet on their topic for younger children. Suggest that group members list the order of tasks, like this:
1. Identify the most important physical features that need to be described.
2. Identify questions for library research.
3. Decide how the subject will be explained and illustrated with photographs, drawings, or other graphics.
4. Write the text and match it to the illustrations.

When students have finished work, encourage each group to share its illustrated pamphlet with the class as a whole. If possible, arrange a sharing opportunity as well with a class of younger students at your school.

Taller de oraciones (page 89)

Dime con quién andas y te diré quién eres
(Tell Me Who Walks with You and I Will Tell You Who You Are)

This TALLER DE ORACIONES is the first of three workshops on combining sentences to create noun modifiers: adjectives (Collection 2), prepositional phrases (Collection 3), and appositives (Collection 4). Verb modifiers are covered in Collection 7. As the title suggests, the workshop in this collection shows that modifiers are necessary to provide important details in writing.

You may want to start this lesson by asking students to discuss the title, which is a popular *refrán*. Some of your students may already be familiar with it.

You may choose to assign the following exercise to demonstrate the concept of noun modifiers. Ask each student to bring an object from home. Place the objects in large opaque bags or boxes, and ask one student at a time to pick an object without showing it to the class and then to describe it. The other students should try to guess what the object is.

Ask students how they guessed each object's identity. Write on the board the words or phrases that they specify. Explain that these are modifiers. They are called *noun modifiers* because they describe nouns.

At this point, you may want to ask students to group the modifiers you have written on the board according to whether they are adjectives or prepositional phrases. This distinction will help students understand the difference between adverbs and prepositional phrases when they later study verb modifiers. You may also want to refer students to the GUÍA DEL LENGUAJE for a more detailed approach and/or more exercises using adjectives.

In the lesson, students focus on adjectives and the way they are used in writing. This instruction will be particularly useful to them when they write their descriptive essays in the TALLER DEL ESCRITOR. Adjectives are very powerful tools in Spanish, as shown by the Neruda piece.

In the first exercise, students examine the impact of adjectives in writing by manipulating an actual passage from the Neruda piece. In the second exercise, students learn how to turn short, choppy sentences into longer, descriptive ones. They are then asked to apply these skills to their own writing in AL REVISAR TU TRABAJO.

The INTÉNTALO TÚ builds on a motif that runs throughout the sixth-grade language strand. Students are asked to examine the use of adjectives in poetry and to develop their command of language by manipulating a poem, in much the same way as they manipulated the Neruda text. The Rubén Darío poem on page 157 lends itself well to this exercise, but you can also suggest others. Have students share the new poems they have written or present them as a *Poemario*, a book of poems.

Collection 3: ENFRENTARSE A LOS RIESGOS

Collection Overview

One proverb that might express the theme of this collection, *Enfrentarse a los riesgos* ("Confronting Risks"), is: *Barco que no anda, no llega a puerto* ("A ship that doesn't sail never reaches port"). Taking a chance can often be its own reward, even if one does not achieve immediate success.

The collection begins with a legend from northeastern Brazil, "El pescador y la Madre del Agua" ("The Fisherman and the Mother of Water"). Originally passed on by word of mouth, the tale was eventually written down in the seventeenth century. The version that appears here is by Santo Neiva. The legend tells of a village afflicted with famine by the wiles of the Mother of Water, a river creature who lures all the fishermen away with her fascinating song. One fisherman vows to save the hungry village and sets out alone to meet the Mother of Water. Most students will enjoy the suspense in this well-told legend.

In Gary Soto's short story "La bamba," Manuel, a fifth-grader with dreams of fame, volunteers to lip-sync Ritchie Valens's song "La bamba" in the school talent show. Although the performance does not go as planned, Manuel gains many admirers. Gary Soto's authentic and humorous portrayal of young people should appeal to your students.

The next selection, which is an excerpt from Sandra Cisneros's *La casa en Mango Street (The House on Mango Street)*, typifies this author's compelling, lyrical prose. In "Chanclas," a girl is encouraged by her uncle to dance and finds the courage to do so despite her shyness and awkwardness. The translation, by the renowned writer Elena Poniatowska, preserves the pace, lyricism, and colloquial speech of the original.

The final reading in this collection, under the heading A LEER POR TU CUENTA, is an excerpt from *La tierra que perdí (The Land I Lost)* by Huynh Quang Nhuong. This selection will introduce students to aspects of Vietnamese culture, particularly wedding customs. Huynh Quang Nhuong recalls a true story of a bride who was carried off by a crocodile and her husband's attempts to rescue her. The suspenseful tale concludes happily: The woman escapes from the crocodile and is reunited with her husband.

ELEMENTOS DE LITERATURA in this collection completes the discussion of short stories that began in Collection 2 (see page 58) with an analysis of three additional literary elements: characterization, point of view, and theme. The opening assignments in OPCIONES: PREPARA TU PORTAFOLIO are designed to prepare students progressively for the assignment in TALLER DEL ESCRITOR to write a short story. ESTRATEGIAS PARA LEER focuses on summarizing as an aid to reading comprehension. LENGUA Y LITERATURA focuses on word roots. At the end of the collection, in TALLER DE ORACIONES, students learn how to use prepositional phrases in their writing.

Introducing the Collection

To encourage students to explore the theme of this collection, give them a choice of opening activities. Possibilities include the following:

1. Invite students to name a number of careers, such as architecture, law enforcement, nursing, teaching, and sales. Write students' suggestions on the chalkboard. Then ask students to brainstorm "What if?" situations in which a person in each occupation might take, or be forced to take, a risk.

2. Invite students to create a cluster diagram on the theme *riesgos*. What are the associations they have with this word? You might help students to begin by modeling a few examples of risk-taking, such as performing

daredevil stunts in movies, giving a speech in public without notes, or making a certain play in football.

3. Ask students to clip newspaper or magazine stories about contemporary people who have shown great courage in meeting risks or challenges. Then have students gather in small groups to discuss their stories. Related news stories can be clustered on a bulletin board.

4. Point out that people have a wide variety of feelings about risks in real life. Some people, for example, do not enjoy taking risks, because they value certainty and security highly. Other people enjoy running risks for the thrill they get from uncertainty or danger. Still others have a more analytical attitude: If given the choice, they will run a risk only when the potential benefits from success are significant enough to outweigh the potential losses from failure. How would students classify their own attitudes toward risk? Invite students to write a paragraph or two in which they explain their outlook.

El pescador y la Madre del Agua

(The Fisherman and the Mother of Water)

Santo Neiva   **page 93**

Into the Selection

Summary

According to a legend from northeastern Brazil, fishermen used to live in the area where the canal of Tarumá is located now. There came a time, however, when the region was paralyzed by fear. Fishermen would no longer take their boats on the river, and people went to bed hungry. It was said that the mysterious Mother of Water used her beautiful voice to lure fishermen to their deaths.

In this retelling of the legend, a young fisherman makes a decision to save his village. He fishes secretly for three nights but catches nothing. Then a beautiful young woman appears, telling the fisherman she will spare the village for a month if he will bring her all the flour the people can make. For eight months, the agreement holds firm and the village prospers. On the ninth full moon, however, the Mother of Water tells the fisherman that she has become lonely. She urges him to abandon his village and live with her under the water. She warns him, however, that the villagers must break and bury all their weapons by the river shore. Then they must cover the shore with a long, white sheet. If he meets her demands, the fisherman's village will forever be under her protection.

The young fisherman, deeply troubled, pretends to comply with the woman's request, but he cannot resign himself to leaving the village. Deciding to break his part of the agreement, he carries a hidden knife to protect himself.

At the next full moon, the villagers follow the woman's instructions. The Mother of Water swims to the shore and approaches the young fisherman. However, a gleaming reflection from the knife's blade betrays the presence of the weapon. The woman turns pale, and a flood suddenly engulfs the entire region: Trees, mountains, animals, homes, and people are all destroyed.

Now the canal of Tarumá is silent, but those who visit it late at night when the moon is full may see the Mother of Water bathing and singing. Beside her is a young man who weeps.

Antes de leer   (page 92)

Punto de partida

De boca en boca (Word of Mouth)
For a fuller discussion of legends as well as of other narratives stemming from oral tradition, you can refer students to ELEMENTOS DE LITERATURA for Collection 7 (see page 254).

Remind students that oral tradition plays an important part in most people's everyday lives; for example, in the transmission of family stories from generation to generation.

Comparte tus ideas

You might want to trigger discussion by writing some or all of the following categories on the chalkboard: fairy tales, nursery rhymes, tall tales, humorous anecdotes, and ghost stories. All of these genres have strong links with the oral tradition.

Diálogo con el texto

This feature is intended to guide students in their reading of the first selection. For suggestions on how to extend this guidance, see DIARIO DEL LECTOR in **Through the Selection**.

Estrategias para leer

Resumir (Summarizing)
To give students practice in summarizing, divide the class into groups of four members each. Have each group decide on a favorite movie or story. Then have group members put into practice the four-step strategy for summarizing. One student can divide the material into three segments: beginning, middle, and end. A second student can identify the most important event in each segment. A third student can develop a paraphrase for each major event. The fourth student can suggest transitional expressions (*palabras de enlace*) to clarify the order and logical relationships of events and ideas.

Through the Selection

Diario del lector (page 94)

The sample marginal annotations exemplify several reading strategies, including questioning the text, drawing conclusions, speculating, making inferences, and making predictions. If you think some of your students will benefit, you can extend this activity, modeling similar annotations for the next page of the text or for the entire selection. Alternatively, you can pause at the end of each section, allowing enough time to monitor and discuss students' notes on an individual basis.

Aduéñate de estas palabras

varar (94)
internarse (94)
centellear (94)
desentonar (96)
deslizarse (96)
proa (96)
regir (96)
imperar (98)
paraje (98)
sepultar (98)

Techniques for Handling the Reading

Students should have no particular problems with this selection. Be sure that readers can identify the central conflict in the story. Point out that the legend presents this conflict as essentially an external struggle, although it also hints at divided feelings within both main characters. Remind students to use the footnotes and glossary words for unfamiliar vocabulary.

Crea significados (page 99)

Repaso del texto

Resume brevemente la leyenda de «El pescador y la Madre del Agua». ¿Cuáles son los acontecimientos principales? Students' summaries will vary but should include a list of events such as the following: (1) the Mother of Water strikes fear into the hearts of the villagers; (2) the young fisherman makes a bargain with the Mother of Water; (3) the woman becomes dissatisfied and demands that the fisherman go to live with her under the water; (4) the woman grows angry when she sees the fisherman's knife; (5) the village is destroyed by a great flood.

Primeras impresiones

1. **Si estuvieras en la situación del joven pescador, ¿qué harías?** Students' answers will vary. Many readers will say that the young fisherman did all he reasonably could to help his village. Clearly, the legend presupposes that the Mother of Water is vastly more powerful than human beings, at least when they are unarmed.

Interpretaciones del texto

2. **Al principio, ¿por qué decide la Madre del Agua perdonar la vida a este pescador?** She is impressed by his tenacity.

3. **¿Te parecen razonables las condiciones de la Madre del Agua? ¿Por qué?** Students' answers will vary. Some students may

feel that the first bargain, in which the woman demands food, is reasonable but that the second, in which she demands a human life, is not.

4. **¿Qué crees que le pasa al pescador al final?** Students' answers will vary. Most readers will assume that the fisherman has been supernaturally changed so that he can live forever with the Mother of Water under the waves, just as she had originally demanded.

Preguntas al texto

5. **El narrador describe a la Madre del Agua como una hermosa joven. ¿Puedes caracterizarla también de otra manera? ¿Cómo?** Students' answers will vary. The legend mentions that long ago the young woman had the form of a *surucurana* snake. Encourage students to discuss the possibilities for other transformations: for example, metamorphoses into sea creatures or mermaids.

6. **¿Por qué la Madre del Agua le tiene tanto miedo a los cuchillos? Comparte tus ideas.** Students' theories will vary. In myths and legends, there are many instances of powerful beings who have one vulnerable spot or weakness: for example, the giant Antaeus in Greek mythology, who could be defeated if he were separated from the earth, or the hero Achilles, who could be vanquished only by a wound to the heel. Perhaps the Mother of Water's vulnerability to knives may be connected ultimately with the use of knives and hooks in fishing.

Más allá del texto

7. **Esta leyenda sobre el *igarapé de Tarumá* quizá explique una mala temporada de pesca o una serie de desastres naturales. El hambre y la escasez son problemas graves en muchas partes del mundo. ¿Cómo combate la gente estos problemas?** Students' answers will vary. Encourage students to be as specific as they can in their responses.

Beyond the Selection

Opciones:
Prepara tu portafolio (page 100)

Cuaderno del escritor

1. Compilación de ideas para un cuento
(Collecting Ideas for a Short Story)
You may wish to have students work in pairs or groups for this activity. Remind students that the assignment has two important parts: (a) identifying a situation that centers on a promise or agreement, and (b) isolating the conflict or tension that results from feelings that pull in different directions.

Hablar y escuchar

2. Lectura fragmentada (Jigsaw Reading)
Remind students that a springboard for this activity can be the lists of events they prepared for REPASO DEL TEXTO.

Arte (Art)

3. Un mural (A Mural)
You may find it helpful to have students look at reproductions of narrative murals so that they acquire a sense of the possibilities for representation, sequencing, and color in this art form.

Lengua y literatura (page 101)

Las palabras que pesca el pescador
(Words That the Fisherman Catches)

This mini-lesson on word roots is an introduction to several features on word formation. In Collection 4, the ESCENA CULTURAL covers the origins of Spanish words; in Collection 5, the LENGUA Y LITERATURA covers prefixes and suffixes; in Collection 8, the VOCABULARIO covers words of Arabic origin in more detail. The aim of these mini-lessons is to develop strategies for understanding words and building vocabulary.

The reading offers an opportunity for exploring word formation. In Guaraní, words for fish always have the morpheme *pira*. By generating Guaraní words with *pira*, students will see that words are composed of parts. Each part has an individual meaning. By putting together parts, one creates words with new meanings.

Finally, students are taught to group Spanish words in families according to roots, as a strategy for vocabulary building. They practice this strategy in the INTÉNTALO TÚ.

Answers:
Guaraní:
Pira means "fish."
Piraverá, Pirayaguá, Piraguasú.
Piraña is a word that Spanish incorporated from Guaraní.

For the familia de palabras:
compañero(a), compañía

For the definitions:
Acompañamiento—le hacen de fondo, le tocan la música…
Compañerismo—el ser compañeros, el hacer las cosas juntos…

Suggested activities on the Guaraní:
- locate territory on map
- listen to songs by Atahualpa Yupanqui

Suggested activities on language:
You might ask students to complete some of the following activities:
- Explore common Greek and Latin roots, such as *son* (sound), *morfo* (shape), *hidro* (water), *filo* (love), *fobia* (hate), *tele, cefa, cultor, grafía*.
  Examples: *algodón hidrófilo, gato hidrófobo, telégrafo, anglofilia, encefalitis, acéfalo, cultura, agricultor, culto, filosofía, geografía, bolígrafo*.
- Create more *familias de palabras* by using the dictionary to find words that start with the same root.
- Explain compound words such as *paraguas, lavavajillas, sacacorchos, portafolio, correveidile, astronave, aeropuerto, cuentagotas, minifalda, lanzatorpedos, saltamontes, baloncesto, puercoespín, garrapata, rompecabezas, guardaespaldas,* and *salvavidas*.
- Create your own compound words.

Suggested reading:
Alegría, Ciro. "El tigre negro y el venado blanco," in *Fábulas y leyendas americanas* (Espasa Calpe, Madrid, Spain, 1982.)
This Guaraní fable examines an unlikely relationship between a jaguar and a deer. Although they get off to a good start, their mutual fears lead to an unexpected and absurd ending. The story is an allegory about friendship.

Bibliography:
Guasch, Antonio. *El idioma guaraní: gramática, lecturas, vocabulario doble* (Joaquin Torres Editor, Buenos Aires, Argentina, 1947).
Bejarano, Ramón Cesar. *Indígenas paraguayos, Época colonial (Para uso de escuelas y colegios)* (Editorial Toledo, Asunción, Paraguay, 1980).

La bamba

Gary Soto — page 103

Into the Selection

Summary
Eager to impress a girl in his fifth-grade class, a boy named Manuel volunteers to take part in the talent show at school. In his act, Manuel plans to lip-sync Ritchie Valens's popular song "La bamba." The day before the show, however, Manuel begins to regret his decision. His nervousness grows during the rehearsal, when the record player malfunctions and he drops the record. Fortunately, the record does not break. Mr. Roybal, who is in charge of the talent show, tries to reassure Manuel that everything will go smoothly.

At length, the big night arrives. As Mr. Roybal introduces the talent of John Burroughs Elementary School, Manuel nervously waits his turn backstage. The acts include a pair of children dressed as a toothbrush and tooth, a violin duo, and a karate demonstration. Then it is Manuel's turn. At first he is dazed by the sight of the audience, but the sound of their applause encourages him. During his performance the record gets stuck, and Manuel is forced to repeat the same phrase of the song again and again. Manuel cannot believe his bad luck, but the audience believes the mistake is intentional and they clap wildly. At the end of the show, everyone showers Manuel with praise. When his father asks him how he managed to make the record stick so ingeniously, Manuel answers with an offhand quip. As he crawls into bed that night, he considers the possibility of volunteering for next year's show.

Antes de leer (page 102)

Punto de partida

No era lo que te esperabas
(It Wasn't What You Expected)
You might ask students to give some examples of the unforeseen in everyday life. On the chalkboard, list some of the situations that they mention. Then invite students to discuss the emotional outcome of each situation. What effects did the unforeseen changes in events produce: disappointment, anger, joy, amusement, surprise, sadness?

Una rueda de cuentos
(A Round Robin of Stories)

You might wish to divide the class into groups of five storytellers each. Every member of a group can spend three minutes or so freewriting his or her installment of a story.

Comparte tus ideas

Students might expand on one of the situations they recalled in PUNTO DE PARTIDA. Remind students that the events they tell their partners might form the nucleus for a short story. If students wish, they can make notes and save them for review in the prewriting stage of TALLER DEL ESCRITOR (see page 126).

Elementos de literatura

La anticipación (Foreshadowing)
Make sure that students recognize the close relationship between the two literary elements of foreshadowing and suspense. Foreshadowing helps to establish suspense because it induces a reader to make predictions. The uncertainty or tension that we feel as we wonder if our predictions will be fulfilled keeps us turning the pages of a novel or story.

Through the Selection

Aduéñate de estas palabras
ceder (103)
atorarse (104)
ademán (104)

Techniques for Handling the Reading

The realistic setting and straightforward presentation of this story should cause few problems for students. You might point out that Manuel's principal conflicts in this story are internal rather than external. In fact, Gary Soto emphasizes internal conflict as early as the first two paragraphs, where he highlights Manuel's divided feelings about volunteering for the talent show. Students' enjoyment and appreciation of the story may be enhanced if you can locate a recording of Ritchie Valens's hit song "La bamba" and play it in class.

Crea significados (page 108)

Repaso del texto

a. **¿Por qué se ofrece como voluntario Manuel para la función de la escuela?** Manuel yearns for the limelight, and he also wants to impress Petra López, the second-prettiest girl in his class.

b. **¿Qué experimento de Manuel resultó un fracaso?** When he was in first grade, Manuel wired together a C battery and a bulb and told everyone he knew how a flashlight worked. He gave so many demonstrations to the neighborhood kids, however, that when it was time to show the class his science project, the battery was dead and the bulb did not respond.

c. **Describe otro número de la función.** Among the acts that students may mention are the following: the girl dressed as a toothbrush and the boy dressed as a dirty tooth; the violin duo; the first-grade girls jumping rope; the karate kid; and Benny's trumpet number.

d. **¿Qué pasa en medio de la actuación de Manuel?** The record gets stuck, and Manuel has to repeat the same phrase from the song again and again.

Primeras impresiones

1. Si tú fueras Manuel, ¿participarías de nuevo en la función de la escuela al año siguiente? ¿Por qué? Students' answers will vary. Many students will say that despite Manuel's nervousness and the unexpected problem with the record, everything worked out for the best. The applause and praise that Manuel received might have strengthened his self-confidence so that he will feel better prepared to participate in another talent show.

Interpretaciones del texto

2. ¿Consigue Manuel lo que desea? ¿Por qué? Most students will agree that Manuel has succeeded. He has captured the limelight, albeit somewhat accidentally. The teachers, the parents, and the popular students at school all give him compliments after the talent show.

3. ¿Dónde usa el autor la *anticipación* para insinuar que la actuación de Manuel no va a salir como se espera? The author foreshadows the unexpected twist in the plot at several places in the story. The first clue occurs when the record player malfunctions and Manuel drops his record during the rehearsal. The second example of foreshadowing is Manuel's recollection of his ill-fated science demonstration when he was in first grade.

4. Dibuja la silueta de una cabeza. En su interior, traza símbolos, imágenes y palabras que ilustren lo que piensa Manuel, sus emociones y expectativas. Intercambia dibujos con los demás estudiantes. Students' interpretations will vary. Have students identify specifics in the story's text for each item in their diagrams.

Conexiones con el texto

5. ¿Has pasado alguna vez en público por una situación bochornosa? Compara tu reacción con la de Manuel. Students' answers will vary. You may wish to allow students to answer in writing or to discuss moments of embarrassment orally with a small group of peers.

Preguntas al texto

6. ¿Qué crees que habría pasado si la gente se hubiera burlado de Manuel por su actuación? Explica el giro que habría dado el cuento. Students' answers will vary. In general, students should recognize that this change would create a completely different outcome and tone for the story. Point out to students that the author may be fleetingly evoking the possibility of such an outcome when he describes the turmoil in Manuel's emotions as he stands backstage, waiting for the show to finish. See the paragraph on page 106 that begins *Manuel permaneció solo tratando de contener sus lágrimas*.

Beyond the Selection

Opciones:
Prepara tu portafolio (page 109)

Cuaderno del escritor

1. Compilación de ideas para un cuento
Point out that students should use chronological order for their narratives. Suggest that writers devote one paragraph to describing their expectations and a second paragraph to recounting what actually occurred. They can then write a concluding paragraph that discusses their emotions and reactions.

Teatro/Arte

2. Un taller de talentos (A Gallery of Talents)
Students will enjoy this opportunity to plan their own talent show. After you suggest a few organizational guidelines, permit students to do as much of the planning as they wish. Suggest that they allow for a variety of formats: for example, showcasing small groups as well as individuals and including a variety of media.

Hablar y escuchar

3. Una entrevista con la estrella
(An Interview with the Star)
To get interviewers started, hold a classwide brainstorming session in which you invite stu-

dents to propose questions for Manuel. Suggest that students can use clues in the text as springboards for their questions. Possibilities include the following:

When did you get interested in music?

Why did you choose "La bamba" as the song for your act?

Are any of your six brothers and sisters musical?

Do you play a musical instrument?

What other interests do you have?

Elementos de literatura (page 110)

Cuentos II: Caracterización, punto de vista y tema (Short Stories II: Characterization, Point of View, and Theme)

Point out that the material in this feature complements the discussion of plot and setting in short stories in Collection 2 (see page 58).

Students' answers to the questions in the text about theme will vary. In general, they may point out that the title of Antonio Robles's story (see page 61) focuses attention on the principal character. Concerning "La bamba," students may suggest that Manuel has learned that sometimes even unlucky events can be turned to one's advantage. Finally, students may point out that the last sentence in Isaac Bashevis Singer's "La cabra Zlateh" highlights the story's theme of love.

You may wish to use the quiz below to test students' comprehension of the material.

1. **¿Qué tipo de caracterización suelen preferir los escritores, la *directa* o la *indirecta*?** (indirect)
2. **¿Qué punto de vista emplea Pablo Neruda en «La casa de las tres viudas» (página 71)?** (first-person point of view)
3. **¿Qué punto de vista emplea Gary Soto en «La bamba» (página 103)?** (third-person limited point of view)
4. **¿Qué diferencia hay entre el mensaje y el tema de una obra literaria?** (The theme of a work is the main idea or message about life that the author expresses, while the subject is what the work is about.)

Chanclas

Sandra Cisneros — page 113

Into the Selection

Summary

In this brief sketch, the narrator, Esperanza, describes the scene at a baptism party for one of her relatives. Self-conscious and awkward, Esperanza is reluctant to dance at the party. Although her mother has bought her a new dress, Esperanza feels she looks foolish and clumsy in a pair of old saddle shoes. When her cousin asks her to dance, she declines. But then her uncle Nacho persuades her to dance with him, telling Esperanza that she is the prettiest girl at the party. Esperanza's mood changes from gloominess to exultation as all the partygoers, including her adolescent cousin, admire her dancing.

Antes de leer (page 112)

Punto de partida

Correr un riesgo (Taking a Chance)
You might wish to write the following proverb on the chalkboard and use it as a springboard for discussion: *Barca que no anda, no llega a puerto.* Ask students if they can think of any similar sayings in English or Spanish (for example, "Nothing ventured, nothing gained").

Toma nota

Suggest that students freewrite for five to seven minutes without stopping. Assure them that the important goal is to get their ideas down on paper—they should not worry about grammar, spelling, or mechanics. Tell students to save their notes.

Through the Selection

Adueñate de estas palabras
empinar (114)
presumir (115)

Techniques for Handling the Reading

Although this selection is brief and accessible, you may wish to preview several parts of the apparatus before students begin to read the assignment. For example, question 7 in CREA SIGNIFICADOS (page 116) indicates that Cisneros does not identify dialogue with dashes in the narrative. Point out that the author's decision to run the dialogue into the text requires readers to examine the text a bit more carefully than usual. Invite students to speculate, as they read, on what some of the advantages of this stylistic decision might be. Also draw students' attention to activity 2 in OPCIONES (page 117), which concerns Cisneros's artful manipulation of pace and rhythm in this vignette. Suggest that students read the selection aloud in order to appreciate the links between the author's syntax and the mood or atmosphere of the piece. Alternatively, you can play the audiocassette rendition of "Chanclas" and have students follow along in their texts.

Crea significados (page 116)

Repaso del texto

Escribe una lista corta de los acontecimientos del cuento en el orden en que suceden. Students' lists of events will vary but should include most or all of the following: (1) Mama returns home with the new clothes but has forgotten to buy shoes; (2) Uncle Nacho picks up the family in his car and takes them to the baptism party at Precious Blood Church; (3) Mama dances, laughs, and feels ill; (4) Esperanza feels embarrassed about her appearance and refuses to dance with her cousin; (5) Uncle Nacho persuades Esperanza to dance, and everyone looks on admiringly, including Esperanza's cousin.

Primeras impresiones

1. **Escribe dos palabras que describan las emociones de Esperanza al final del cuento.** Students' answers will vary. Among the adjectives they might choose are the following: *excitado, feliz, lleno de gozo, orgulloso, extático, jubiloso, radiante*.

Interpretaciones del texto

2. **¿Cuál es el *conflicto* del personaje principal?** Esperanza's internal conflict springs from her self-conscious feelings of awkwardness and shyness about her appearance.

3. **¿Cómo expresa este conflicto la opinión que Esperanza tiene de sus «chanclas», sus movimientos y su cuerpo?** Esperanza feels that her shoes are clumsy and that her feet are big and heavy "like plungers" (*como chupones*). Her movements feel awkward to her.

4. **¿Cómo le ayuda su tío a superar el conflicto?** By insisting that she dance with him, Uncle Nacho helps Esperanza to solve her conflict.

5. **¿Cómo describirías la relación de Esperanza con su familia?** Students' answers will vary. In general, most readers will agree that Esperanza has a close and affectionate relationship with her family.

Conexiones con el texto

6. **Piensa en una ocasión en la que alguien te animó a dar un paso adelante y correr un riesgo de verdad. ¿Qué pasó?** Students' answers will vary. Encourage students to refer to the freewriting notes they made in ANTES DE LEER (page 112).

Preguntas al texto

7. **En el primer párrafo, Cisneros no utiliza rayas para señalar las partes de diálogo. En su lugar, intercala el diálogo en la narración. Repasa de nuevo la narración y señala los lugares en los que te parece que hablan los personajes. Utiliza rayas para indicar las citas. Por ejemplo, el primer renglón debería quedar así:**
   —Soy yo, Mamá —dice Mamá.
   Students should identify the following dialogue in the story: *¿Y los zapatos? Los olvidé. Ya es muy tarde. Estoy cansada. ¡Ufa! ¡Uf, híjole!* (page 113).

Más allá del texto

8. **En español, *Esperanza* es, además de un nombre propio, una actitud. ¿Refleja el nombre de la narradora su actitud en**

CHANCLAS 37

el texto? Students' answers will vary. In general, they should point out that Esperanza's pessimism and self-consciousness about her looks in the first half of the story are not especially consistent with the meaning of her name. When Uncle Nacho asks her to dance, however, Esperanza's attitude changes. By the end of the story, she radiates happiness and might indeed be called "hopeful." **¿Se te ocurren otros nombres propios (quizá el tuyo o el de un amigo) que signifiquen algo?** Students' answers will vary. You may want to write some of their suggestions for significant names on the chalkboard.

Beyond the Selection

Opciones:
Prepara tu portafolio   (page 117)

Cuaderno del escritor

1. Compilación de ideas para un cuento
Remind students that an imaginary character can be based on a single person or on a combination of people from real life.

Redacción creativa

2. Ritmo narrativo (Narrative Rhythm)
You may wish to allow students to work in small groups for this activity. Suggest that students listen to the audiocassette recording of the selection. Hearing the recording will help students appreciate Cisneros' skillful use of grammar and syntax to control the pacing of the narrative.

Hablar y escuchar

3. Un poema improvisado (An Improvised Poem)
Students' choices will vary. You might suggest that they focus on words and phrases for feelings, specific details, and sensory images. Encourage students to experiment with arranging their words and phrases in different sequences in order to create various rhythmical and/or atmospheric effects.

Estrategias para leer   (page 118)
Los resúmenes nos ayudan a recordar
(Summarizing Helps Us to Remember)
Stress that a good summary does not only contain the essential events or main ideas of a text or speech. It also clarifies chronological, spatial, or other logical relationships between these events and ideas; for example, cause and effect, comparison or contrast, and so forth. To highlight this important feature of summaries, have students take turns identifying the transitional words and phrases in the sample summary of "Chanclas" on page 119. Be sure that students are able to spot words and phrases such as *antes de la fiesta, pero, porque, al final, al principio, mientras,* and *después del baile.*

A leer por tu cuenta
de La tierra que perdí
(*from* The Land I Lost)

Huynh Quang Nhuong   page 120

Summary
In this episode, which is titled "Muy cerca" ("So Close"), the narrator recalls visiting Mrs. Hong's house with his mother when he was a youngster. While the two women chatted, the narrator would talk with Mrs. Hong's daughter Lan, who was engaged to be married to the next-door neighbor, a young fisherman named Trung.

Trung and Lan had been inseparable playmates since childhood. Their mothers, both widows, were friendly, and they arranged for the young couple's marriage. At last the wedding day arrived. All the proper wedding traditions were observed, even though the houses of the bride and groom were next to each other. First, Trung and his friends and relatives came to Lan's house for prayers and a luncheon. After lunch, Lan stepped out of her house and was ceremonially escorted to the house of the bridegroom. A welcome dinner there ended the day's celebrations.

Late in the evening of the wedding day, Lan went to the river to bathe. Even though the villagers took precautions against crocodiles, the girl was carried off by a wily crocodile that sneaked up on her from behind.

After Trung and the villagers found traces of the incident, no one except the bridegroom believed that Lan had survived. Trung was positive that he heard Lan's voice on the wind, calling his name. Despite the discouragement of his relatives, Trung refused to give up hope. After hours of tearful vigil and prayer at the river, Trung suddenly glimpsed a shape waving at him from an island about six hundred meters away. It was Lan! Miraculously, she had survived her encounter with the crocodile. First she had fainted, and then she had played dead. After tossing her in the air numerous times, the beast finally abandoned his victim and went to the river to drink. Lan climbed a tree and then started to call for Trung. Although badly bruised, Lan had suffered no serious injury. Trung took his exhausted bride home and put her to bed. After she recovered, the mothers of the bride and groom decided to celebrate their children's wedding a second time, because Lan had come back from the dead.

Adueñate de estas palabras

infestado (122)	oscilante (122)
talar (122)	alucinación (123)
taimado (122)	descartar (123)
esquivar (122)	incoherente (124)

Techniques for Handling the Reading

Even though the philosophy underlying the selections in A LEER POR TU CUENTA is to give students a chance to read freely, they may enjoy exploring connections between the story and the collection theme. How would students describe the risks taken by each of the two major characters, Lan and Trung? Other possible discussion points are the marriage customs that the author describes, as well as the natural history of crocodiles.

Taller del escritor (page 126)

La narración/Cuento
(Short Story)

Presenting the Workshop

For a general overview of the writing process, see the MANUAL DE COMUNICACIÓN (page 324). You may wish to devote part or all of a class session to reviewing the major aspects of each stage of the process.

Before students get started, encourage them to consider a range of springboards and models for a short story. Students who completed the prereading activities for "La bamba" (see ANTES DE LEER, page 102) may already have a head start on their prewriting notes. Remind the class that conflict is the mainspring of most successful short stories. You can focus on conflict in a brief review session by having students identify the most important conflict in each selection in this collection. Review the concept that conflicts may be external or internal: for example, the external struggle between the young fisherman and the Mother of Water in "El pescador y la Madre del Agua," or the internal struggles within Manuel in "La bamba" and Esperanza in "Chanclas."

Antes de escribir

In addition to the prewriting strategies discussed in the text, students can talk to family members and friends to get story ideas. Students might want to read a brief selection such as "Chanclas" aloud to a group of family members. Then they might ask if the story they have read reminds any of the listeners of a similar experience. Remind the class that even though short stories are a type of fiction, many stories are based on events and characters from real life. Thus, an autobiographical incident might legitimately serve as the basis for a short story.

El borrador

If students use a computer to draft the short story, make sure that they save successive drafts on a disk so that nothing is lost.

You may wish to devote some class time to discussing how students can elaborate their stories effectively with sensory images and figurative language. Remind students that all the selections in this collection can serve as models for the vivid use of language. Invite students to review some specific examples, such as the description of the baptism party in "Chanclas" (page 114) or the narrative of Lan's struggle with the crocodile in *La tierra que perdí* (page 124).

Point out that word choice can be a very important factor in creating mood, or atmosphere, in a story. Remind writers of the impact that the connotations of words—their overtones or emotional associations—can have on the reader. You can suggest, for example, that students reread a paragraph or two from the opening pages of Pablo Neruda's "La casa de las tres viudas" (page 71) to see how the writer deliberately uses words that contribute to the mood of loneliness and the sense of nature's grandeur.

Evaluación y revisión

When students have finished their first drafts, ask them to examine carefully the pair of models in the text (pages 129–130). Students may work independently, or you may wish to devote some time in a class session to analyzing and discussing this material. If you choose to have students work in class, call on volunteers to read the model drafts aloud. Then call on volunteers to comment on each draft. Make sure that students understand the reasons for the writing evaluations given in the text. Then encourage pairs to exchange feedback. The guidelines for evaluation and revision on page 129 can be used whether students work in pairs or independently.

Small groups offer students a good chance to get feedback on how successfully their writing appeals to an audience. If you have students work in groups, tell them not to write on other group members' only copies. Instead, comments should be made on another sheet of paper or on self-sticking notes.

Remember that some students may need guidance in using their evaluation notes to revise their first drafts. On a practical level, for example, some writers may need a guided introduction to the basic proofreading symbols for insertion, deletion, and transposition. See the MANUAL DE COMUNICACIÓN (page 325).

Corrección de pruebas

Stress to students the importance of refining and proofreading written work before publishing or sharing it. Proofreading or editing adds to the clarity, correctness, and presentation of an essay or story. Familiarity with the conventions of language and writing—spelling, punctuation, grammar, usage, capitalization, paragraphing, accuracy of citations and graphics, and proper manuscript form—is an important part of being an effective writer.

Before they begin this stage, some students may need a guided review of the proofreading symbols used for editing and correcting errors in spelling and mechanics. Go over the list of symbols given in the MANUAL DE COMUNICACIÓN (page 325). Then have partners exchange papers and proofread each other's writing. You may wish to circulate through the class, offering help when needed.

Publicación

Remind students that publishing can take a variety of forms. In addition to the sharing opportunities mentioned in the text, suggest that students might, for example, get together to organize Reader's Theater productions of their stories. Another possibility is publication on a World Wide Web site for young writers.

Reflexión

The reflection starters on page 130 are intended only as examples. Encourage students to reflect on a broad range of feelings about specific aspects of the assignment. For example, you could ask students to review their work and identify their favorite piece of dialogue or the vivid details they like best. If students had trouble with the prewriting stage (trying to find a suitable story idea), they might want to get together with classmates in a small group to brainstorm topics for the next writing assignment. If they found that freewriting on the computer helped their ideas to flow more freely, they might want to use the computer regularly for writing assignments.

You may wish to offer students a choice between writing their reflections and delivering them orally. If students choose to write, suggest that they keep their reflections in their portfolios, together with the finished draft of the short story. Emphasize that by reflecting, students give themselves the chance to generate feedback on their own writing.

Reteaching

Students having difficulty evaluating and revising may work in groups to read their short stories aloud. Encourage listeners to identify the most interesting and important parts of each story.

Closure

Ask students to explain the difference between a short story and an observational essay.

Assessment Tools

As students work through the writing process, share the following assessment criteria with them, so they may use them in self- and peer evaluations.

Assessment Criteria

1 2 3 4 5 6
(needs   (superior)
improvement)

Content

- Beginning grabs reader's interest.
- The story presents a clear conflict.
- The plot leads up to a strong climax or turning point.
- The order of events is clear and easy to follow.
- The characters are lifelike and believable.

Language Conventions

- Grammar and usage are standard.
- Paragraphs are indented properly.
- Words are spelled correctly.
- Quotation marks are used correctly.

Overall Rating: _____

Enrichment

Music Connection

From the legendary songs of the Mother of Water to the talent show in "La bamba" and the baptism party in "Chanclas," music and dance are important motifs in this collection. Divide the class into small groups and have each group design and carry out a research or performance project of their choice on Latino music. For example, one group could research the origin and development of distinctive Latino dance forms such as merengue, salsa, cumbia, and samba. Another group might focus on the spectacular emergence of tejano music during the past decade. A third group might create a photo essay on a favorite performer, composer, or recording artist of Latino music. Give students a broad range of options for presenting their finished project to the class as a whole.

Taller de oraciones (page 131)

Palabras de enlace (Connecting Words)

Answers:

1. El lagarto de Miguel se metió en su guarida. (Students may also suggest this version: El lagarto que se metió en su guarida era de Miguel.)

2. Answers will vary. The paragraph in the example that follows contains clues to help students fill in the blanks.

   Los lagartos <u>con</u> **manchas** suelen ser venenosos. Tienen manchas para advertirles a los animales <u>con</u> **hambre** que no se acerquen. Aquel lagarto <u>de</u> **Miguel** tenía unos colores especialmente brillantes. En la guarida le esperaba una camada de pequeños lagartos <u>de</u> **cinco días**. Las crías eran <u>para</u> **venderlas**. ¡Sólo gente <u>sin</u> **miedo** se atrevería a comprarlas!

   The prepositions in the inserted phrases are underlined. Help students to see how the information in the prepositional phrases can alter the story.

3. Students can write their own comparisons based on the model.

Suggestions:

- Adjective clauses. Some students may suggest subordinate clauses instead of prepositional phrases. You may choose to do a further exercise using the same modifier as an adjective, a prepositional phrase, and a clause. Example: *mexicano, de México, que es de México.*

- Show students that a prepositional phrase is a preposition plus a noun phrase (a noun and its own modifiers).
- Find a poem that uses comparisons and encourage students to write their own poetry using comparisons.
- Make comparisons to exaggerate. Students will recognize that comparisons can be used in humor. Comparisons for exaggeration exist in regular speech: *como una casa, como una catedral, como tonto, como una foca, como por un tubo, como un angelito*....

Collection 4: UN MÁS ALLÁ

Collection Overview

The literature in this collection focuses on the unfamiliar. Each of the selections is about an uncommon place or a creature with striking or fantastic qualities. The theme *Un más allá* ("The Beyond") invites your students on some exotic adventures that they are likely to enjoy.

The collection begins with a selection by the Uruguayan writer Horacio Quiroga. Quiroga is known primarily for his short stories, particularly his dark and vivid tales of the jungle. "El cuendú" ("The Porcupine") describes a curious animal, a porcupine, which was given to the narrator. Quiroga portrays the porcupine with a naturalist's eye for detail, yet his account retains an innocent wonder at the existence of such a fantastic creature. Most students will enjoy learning about this unusual animal.

"Todo el verano en un día" is a translation of the much-anthologized story "All Summer in a Day" by Ray Bradbury, one of the masters of science fiction. With rich, imaginative detail, Bradbury tells the story of a group of children who live on the planet Venus, where rain falls incessantly and the sun shines only once every seven years. Margot, a child who remembers living on Earth, is taunted by the other youngsters because she is different from them and remembers the sun's beauty from her time on Earth. When the sun finally appears for one brief hour, Margot, a victim of childish cruelty, is denied the chance to see it. Although this story has an otherworldly setting, its issues are extremely relevant to children.

In the lyric poem "El trópico" ("The Tropics"), Rubén Darío beautifully renders the soothing, languid pace of a day in a tropical landscape. This Nicaraguan writer is one of the most esteemed figures in Latin American literature.

The collection continues with an article titled "La isla Sangalakki" ("Sangalakki Island") by Norbert Wu. Originally printed in the magazine *GeoMundo,* this article describes a sea turtle's quest to lay its eggs on a beach once threatened by poachers but now under protection. The richly detailed scientific descriptions of a marine habitat off the coast of Kalimantan (Indonesian Borneo) will introduce students to miraculous and bizarre creatures of the sea. The article is particularly relevant to the report of information that students will be asked to write in the TALLER DEL ESCRITOR.

The collection concludes with Nicolás Guillén's poem "La Osa Mayor" ("The Great Bear"), which is from the author's "fantastic zoo," a group of poems that brilliantly personify ideas, objects, and natural phenomena—in this instance, a constellation. Guillén is a celebrated Cuban poet known for his Afro-Cuban style, which draws on diverse elements of song, dance, and speech.

The ELEMENTOS DE LITERATURA in this collection is the first section of a two-part discussion of the elements of poetry. In POESÍA I: RECURSOS DE SONIDO E IMÁGENES, students are introduced to the following elements of poetry: rhyme, rhythm, repetition, parallelism, onomatopoeia, alliteration, and sensory images. The discussion of poetry concludes in Collection 6, where figures of speech such as simile, metaphor, personification, symbol, and hyperbole are explained (see page 222).

ESTRATEGIAS PARA LEER in this collection focuses on distinguishing facts from opinions. In ESCENA CULTURAL, students are introduced to some of the sources of Spanish words. In the collection as a whole, there is a strong cross-curricular connection to science, especially to animal behavior, marine biology, and astronomy. Students will find helpful commentary about some of these links in brief features titled LITERATURA Y CIENCIA (see pages 139, 152, 172).

The opening assignments in OPCIONES: PREPARA TU PORTAFOLIO are designed to prepare students progressively for the assignment in TALLER DEL

ESCRITOR to write a report of information. This assignment synthesizes many of the skills that students have been developing through reading and discussion in the collection as a whole. Further OPCIONES activities challenge students to explore themes and ideas through a variety of modes, such as research, creative writing, and art. Finally, in TALLER DE ORACIONES, students learn how to use apposition to combine sentences.

Introducing the Collection

To encourage students to explore aspects of the collection theme, give them a choice of opening activities. Possibilities include the following:

1. Have small groups of students compile a "Recommended List" of science-fiction stories, novels, films, and television series. For each item on the list, tell students to write a capsule summary and commentary, explaining why audiences are likely to enjoy the setting, plot, or characters.
2. Divide the class into small groups and have each group select an exotic country, island, mountain range, barrier reef, or other location that they would like to visit. Then work with students to develop a travel brochure that uses both text and illustrations to advertise their ideal travel destinations.
3. Have students skim through recent issues of magazines to identify some of the trailblazing discoveries or new areas of research in scientific fields. Possibilities include the *Galileo* probe of Jupiter in space exploration, pioneering experiments in gene therapy, and the remarkable discovery (in December 1994) of prehistoric cave paintings at Chauvet in France. Ask students to prepare oral reports summarizing their findings.

El cuendú
(The Porcupine)

Horacio Quiroga

page 135

Into the Selection

Summary

The narrator begins by describing the porcupine's habitat and strange appearance. According to popular belief, these creatures defend themselves by throwing their venomous spines at an enemy from a distance of eight or ten meters. One day, a settler brought the narrator a captive porcupine, enclosed in a bag inside a kerosene container. With great difficulty, the two men managed to place the animal in a cage, where the narrator could observe it at leisure.

Surprisingly, the animal had sweet and gentle eyes. The narrator says that as he observed his captive, the porcupine's delicacy and vulnerability impressed him more than its spines did. The porcupine became curious about the narrator, slowly grasping his hand and lifting a finger to its mouth. Since porcupines are nocturnal, the light bothered the animal greatly, and it passed the daylight hours on the bottom of the cage, with its face clasped in its paws, as if it were doing penance. In order to ease the burden of captivity, the narrator placed the porcupine in a summer house, together with two hawks and a magpie. But the porcupine could not get used to the birds' sudden movements and screeches. Finally, the narrator donated the porcupine to a zoological garden.

Antes de leer (page 134)

Punto de partida

Criaturas extrañas (Strange Creatures)
If students need additional inspiration, encourage them to skim issues of magazines dealing with history, wildlife conservation, or animals.

Toma nota

Reassure students that they need not worry about correct grammar, punctuation, or spelling.

The important goal is to record as many facts, ideas, and impressions on paper as possible. Students can jot notes or make lists, rather than write complete sentences.

Diálogo con el texto

The marginal annotations shown on pages 136–137 exemplify several reading skills: questioning, challenging the text, drawing conclusions, and making predictions. If you feel that some of your students will benefit, you can extend this activity through the entire text, modeling similar kinds of marginal annotations.

You can pause at the end of each paragraph, allowing enough time to monitor and discuss students' notes on an individual basis.

Estrategias para leer

Distinguir hechos de opiniones
(Distinguishing Facts from Opinions)
At this time, you may wish to have students preview the more extended discussion on distinguishing fact from opinion that appears later in this collection (see page 155). As an alternative, give them a few pairs of statements such as the following to discuss before they read the essay:

*Hecho: Los puercoespines son animales nocturnos.
Opinión: Los puercoespines tienen un aspecto monstruoso.*

Through the Selection

Adueñate de estas palabras

púa (136)	adherida (137)
sombría (136)	reanuda (137)
erizado (136)	huraño (137)

Techniques for Handling the Reading

Since Quiroga uses straightforward syntax and relatively brief paragraphs in this story, most of your students should not encounter any stumbling blocks. Encourage students to think about the author's tone, or attitude toward the subject matter, as they read the selection. Ask students to identify the points at which the narrator seems neutral or almost clinically detached. Then ask students to find places in the essay where the narrator shows wonder and sympathy for his captive. Listening to a recording of this selection, available on audiocassette, may help students to identify these subtle alterations in tone.

Literatura y ciencia (page 139)

El cuendú

The creature in Quiroga's story is *Coendou prehensilis,* the Brazilian porcupine, whose habitat also includes northeastern Uruguay. Adults of this species may weigh as much as twelve pounds but are far smaller than North American porcupines (*Erethizon dorsatum*), which may weigh as much as forty pounds and lack prehensile tails. The porcupine's spines are normally white or pale yellow at the base and tip and black or dark brown in the center. The animal is arboreal, nocturnal, and solitary in its habits, feeding on green or ripe fruits, seeds, tree bark, and leaves. Porcupines cannot, in fact, "throw" their spines, as Quiroga's narrator reports from popular tradition. However, the spines detach very easily when touched. Contact with an enemy thus results most often in injury to the enemy. The porcupine, which belongs to the rodent family, is thus equipped with superb natural defenses against far larger carnivores. Even the largest of the big cats, lions and tigers, are wary of porcupines in the wild, and there is only one carnivore known to kill porcupines regularly. This is the North American fisher, a large marten of the weasel family, whose strategy is to disable the porcupine with numerous bites to the face.

For a history of the porcupine's scientific name and its designation in Spanish, see the discussion in ESCENA CULTURAL in this collection (page 142).

Crea significados (page 140)

Repaso del texto

Dibuja al cuendú sentado en su jaula; utiliza lo que recuerdes de la parte de la narración en la que se describe esa escena. You may wish to allow students to work in pairs or small groups for this activity. Students' sketches will vary, but each one should exhibit some of the prominent details mentioned in the essay: for example, the porcupine's *actitud de penitencia* with its face in its paws.

Primeras impresiones

1. **Completa la siguiente oración: Si el cuendú pudiera hablar con el narrador, le diría _____.** Students' answers will vary. Basing their opinion on the animal's gentle and submissive behavior and its posture in the cage, many students will suggest that if it could speak to the narrator, the porcupine would ask to be returned to the wild.

Interpretaciones del texto

2. **¿Dónde usa Quiroga la *personificación* para describir al cuendú?** Among the uses of personification that students may point out are the mention of the sweetness of the porcupine's eyes, the description of the animal's bringing the narrator's finger to its mouth *por ver a qué sabía,* the paragraph about the porcupine's *actitud de penitencia,* and the speculation in the concluding paragraph that the porcupine *no dejaría de ser interesante en nuestro jardín zoológico.*

3. **¿Cómo es la actitud del narrador hacia el cuendú? ¿Lo alaba? ¿Tiene curiosidad? ¿Es cruel? Apoya tus respuestas con datos del texto.** Students' answers will vary. Most students will agree that the narrator is curious, since he takes considerable trouble to observe and describe the porcupine. Many students will point out that the narrator probably does not mean the references to the animal as a *monstruo* literally; this word is a humorous exaggeration, based on the popular tales about the porcupine's ferocity in attacking its enemies. On the whole, the narrator finds his captive to be sweet, timid, and inoffensive. Note the phrase *dulzura de pobre ser inofensivo y tímido* in the first paragraph on page 137. Most students will agree that the narrator is not cruel to the animal, since he takes some pains to ease its captivity, but some readers may criticize him for giving the porcupine to a zoo instead of returning it to the wild.

4. **¿Cuáles de las siguientes afirmaciones son *hechos* y cuáles son *opiniones*?** The first statement is a fact reported from direct observation. The second statement is an opinion giving the narrator's subjective judgment about the mood expressed in the animal's eyes. The third statement is a fact that is based on scientific observation.

Conexiones con el texto

5. **¿Crees que es aceptable enjaular a los animales? Si es así, ¿cuáles animales? y ¿en qué circunstancias?** Some students may say that it is acceptable to keep certain animals in cages as pets: for example, birds, hamsters, or rabbits. Some students may add to this list the wild animals that are kept in zoological parks, although they may point out that within the last thirty years these institutions have redesigned most of their exhibition areas so that animals can live in more natural surroundings. Other students may object that denying any animal its freedom and its natural habitat is cruel and unacceptable, even for educational or breeding purposes. Encourage students to support their opinions with reasons.

Preguntas al texto

6. **¿Crees que el narrador hizo lo correcto al dar el cuendú a un zoológico?** Students' answers will vary. The narrator comments somewhat whimsically on his action in the final paragraph, saying that the porcupine would doubtless find the zoo interesting. Many students will suggest that the narrator might just as easily have returned the porcupine to the wild, especially since this species is neither rare nor endangered.

Más allá del texto

7. **¿Qué motivos tiene la gente para cazar o poner los animales en una jaula?** Students' answers will vary. Among the reasons they may suggest for hunting animals are people's enjoyment of the outdoors, the challenge of a test of skill, or pride in winning a trophy. Among the reasons students may suggest for keeping animals in cages are scientific observation, educating the public about natural history, breeding rare or endangered species to

Todo el verano en un día

(All Summer in a Day)

Ray Bradbury — page 145

Into the Selection

Summary

After seven years of incessant rain on the planet Venus, the nine-year-olds in Margot's class look forward to the sun's brief appearance, which has been forecast by scientists. They have prepared for the event by reading about the sun and by writing essays, poems, and stories about it. Only Margot, however, really knows about the sun, because it has been only five years since she arrived on Venus from Earth.

The children dislike Margot for many reasons. She is a very frail girl who looks like an old photograph. She does not play games with the rest of the children, and she usually does not join in their singing. The children are also jealous of her because she remembers the sun on Earth and because she may return to Earth with her family the following year. She is, in short, different—and her classmates pick on her mercilessly.

A bully named William leads the teasing. Before the teacher arrives, William seizes Margot roughly and, together with the other children, locks her, pleading and crying, into a closet. Soon after the teacher arrives, the rain ceases and the sun comes out. The children tumble outdoors into the great jungle that covers Venus and revel in the sunshine. For two hours they run, play, and turn their faces to the sky. Suddenly, however, one of the girls wails. She holds out her palm to reveal a single raindrop. The sun fades behind a mist, a boom of thunder sounds, and the rains return.

The children rush back to their underground refuge. One of them suddenly remembers that Margot has been shut in the closet the whole time. Unable to meet one another's guilty glances, the children slowly walk down the hall and over to the closet door. In silence, they unlock the door and let Margot out.

Antes de leer (page 144)

Punto de partida

Lejos de la Tierra (Far from Earth)
You may wish to encourage students to brainstorm in small groups for this activity. Invite group members to take notes during their conferences.

Lluvia de ideas (Brainstorming)
Point out that some of the bulleted questions have a range of factual answers. For example, space probes have established a surface temperature for Venus in excess of 500 degrees Fahrenheit, and a Venusian day lasts about as long as 117 Earth days—a bit more than 58 days of light alternating with the same period of darkness. Other questions on the sample list, however, are far more subjective: for example, "What would you miss most about Earth?"

Elementos de literatura

Personaje (Character)
You may wish to remind students that the first four methods in the bulleted list are techniques of *indirect characterization,* while the last method is called *direct characterization.* Although only two characters in Bradbury's story—Margot and William—are named, tell students to look for ways in which the author characterizes Margot's classmates as a group.

Through the Selection

Aduéñate de estas palabras

marejada (146)
abalorio (146)
amainar (146)
desconcertada (147)
predecir (147)
amortiguado (147)
repercusión (149)
audición (149)
tumultuosamente (149)
estaca (150)

Techniques for Handling the Reading

Because Bradbury's uses of flashback, images, and figures of speech may make this selection relatively challenging for some of your students, you might want to call on student volunteers to take turns reading portions of the story aloud. Have students preview the text by discussing the

boost animal populations in the wild, and pleasure in keeping pets.

Beyond the Selection

Opciones:
Prepara tu portafolio (page 141)

Cuaderno del escritor

1. Compilación de ideas para un artículo informativo (Collecting Ideas for a Report of Information)
Before students begin this activity, you may want to write some information categories on the chalkboard, such as the following: *dimensiones físicas, peso, coloración, hábitat, dieta, periodo de gestación, longevidad, comportamiento social cuidados y alimentación de las crías.*

Investigación

2. Protección natural (Natural Protection)
Recommend that students begin their research by reading an encyclopedia article on the mammal, bird, insect, or fish that they select. Once they have an overview, students can do some more specialized research on the animal's defense mechanisms.

Redacción creativa

3. Libre al fin (Free at Last)
This activity will appeal to imaginative writers in the class, since it involves hypothesizing some changes in setting as well as writing from an animal's point of view. Before students plan their letters, recommend that they familiarize themselves with major aspects of porcupine behavior by reading an article in a reference source. Remind students that Quiroga's animal is one of the South American species, a group that differs significantly in size and social behavior from the porcupines of Africa and India and from North American porcupines.

Escena cultural (page 142)

El origen de las palabras del español
(The Sources of Spanish Words)

Actividades para empezar
Although the teams' explanations of word relationships will differ somewhat, make sure that students in each group are able to identify roots as follows: *mayor* (from Latin *mai* "larger"); *–ten–* (from Latin *tendere,* for "stre *sent(s)–* (from Latin *sentire,* for "feel" or "se and *historia* (from Latin for "history" and mately from Greek for "search" or "inquire"

Actividades de cierre

1. Answers are as follows: *iguana* < Ar *agutí* < Tupí-Guaraní; *capibara* < Portu and Tupí; *jaguar* < Tupí; *armadillo* < Latin.

2. Students' explanations of the original n ing of each word may vary somewhat. In eral, they should identify etymologie follows: *drama* < Greek *dran* ("to do"); *t* < Greek *theatron* ("theater"), in turn de from Greek *theasthai* ("to watch"); *poe.* Greek *poiein* ("to make"); *ensayo* < Fr *essai,* "trial" or "attempt"; *cuento*< Old Fr *conte* and Late Latin *computus,* "calcula reckoning."

3. The word *gringo* is an altered form of *gr* Its original sense of *lenguaje incomprensit* ironic, because the ancient Greeks use analogous deprecation for foreign ton that they could not understand, calling tl the languages of *barbaroi,* or savages.

For Further Reading

Corominas, Joan. *Breve diccionario etimológico la lengua castellana.*

Emmons, Louise H. *Neotropical Rainforest M mals* (University of Chicago Press, Chica 1990).

Gonzalez-Berry, Erlinda, and Shaw N. Gyn "Chicano Language," in Francisco A. Lon and Carl L. Shirley, eds., *Chicano Writers: F Series, Dictionary of Literary Biography,* vol. (Gale Research, Inc., Detroit, 1989) 30 308.

Lipski, John M. "Language," in Nicolás Kanell ed., *The Hispanic-American Almanac* (Gale R search, Inc., Detroit, 1993) 209–227.

McCrum, Robert, William Cran, and Robe MacNeil. *The Story of English* (Viking, Ne York, 1986).

Roze, Uldis. *The North American Porcupir* (Smithsonian Institution Press, Washingtor D.C., 1989).

title and looking at the illustrations. Then remind readers, as they follow along in the text, to consult the footnotes and the glossary entries for the meanings of any unfamiliar words. At the end of each page, pause to give students an opportunity to ask questions.

When the class reaches the bottom of the left-hand column on page 147, you might want to invite students to make predictions about what will happen in the story.

Literatura y ciencia (page 152)

¿Lluvia en Venus? (Rain on Venus?)

Recommend that students read a short encyclopedia article about Venus to get an overview of basic facts about the planet. They can also consult reference sources such as the *World Almanac*. Students might also be interested in researching the name of the planet. Like the other planets in our solar system (*Mercurio, Marte, Júpiter, Saturno, Urano, Neptuno, Plutón*), Venus is named for a Roman divinity, in this case the goddess of love.

Crea significados (page 153)

Repaso del texto

a. **¿Cómo es el clima en Venus?** Rain falls incessantly on Venus, with the sun appearing only once every seven years.
b. **¿Cómo luce Margot?** Margot is pale and fragile, with blond hair and light blue eyes.
c. **¿Cómo saben los niños que el sol está a punto de aparecer?** The scientists have predicted the event. When the children peer outside, they see that the rain is stopping.
d. **¿Qué hacen los niños cuando el sol aparece?** They romp ecstatically outdoors, running and turning their faces to the sky to feel the sun on their cheeks.

Primeras impresiones

1. **¿Qué crees que pasa inmediatamente después de que Margot sale del armario?** Some students may predict that Margot will shout angrily at the other children who tormented her, while other students may predict that Margot will continue to suffer in silence. Ask students if they think that the other children will apologize to Margot or will attempt now to make friends with her. Do students think that Margot would accept such overtures of friendship?

Interpretaciones del texto

2. **¿Por qué Margot es diferente de los otros niños? ¿Por qué se burlan de ella?** Margot is different because she has been on Venus a shorter time than the other children and because she remembers the sun far more vividly than they do. She is also different because she keeps to herself, refusing to join in the children's games and songs. She is the "odd child out" in the group. The other children instinctively sense Margot's difference, and they resent her for it.
3. **¿Por qué Margot no se relaciona con los niños, ni responde cuando la molestan?** Margot is truthful, creative, and independent, despite her frail appearance. She is unhappy and taciturn. She does not feel that she is part of life on Venus, and there is talk that her parents may take her back to Earth, despite the great financial sacrifice that such a journey would involve.
4. **¿Qué sienten los niños por Margot al final de la historia? Explica tu respuesta.** Students' answers will vary. Many students may agree that the children feel guilty about depriving Margot of one of the rarest, most enjoyable sights on Venus: the appearance of the sun. Whether the other children like Margot at this point, though, is debatable.

Conexiones con el texto

5. **¿Cuándo crees que es más fácil para un niño ser cruel con otro, cuando está en grupo o cuando está solo?** Students may point out that group dynamics play an important part in young children's unpleasantness to each other. When they are backed up by others, children seem to find it easier and more attractive to indulge in bullying or teasing.
6. **El narrador dice que los padres de Margot están considerando regresar a la**

Tierra, aunque esto signifique un gasto de miles de dólares. Tú qué escogerías, ¿ser rico en Venus o regresar a la Tierra? ¿Por qué? Students' answers will vary. Some students may say that if they had to endure Margot's experiences, they would be glad to return to Earth, whatever the cost.

Preguntas al texto

7. **¿Qué acontecimientos de esta historia pudieran suceder en un salón de clases en la Tierra? ¿Cuáles no?** Students' answers will vary. In general, they should point out that the children's bullying of Margot could happen in any classroom. The specific setting and plot events that involve the rare appearance of the sun, however, could happen only in science fiction.

Más allá del texto

8. **Los colonizadores y los exploradores, en la búsqueda de nuevas tierras, han tenido que enfrentarse a situaciones desconocidas y peligrosas. ¿Por qué la gente persiste en la búsqueda de nuevas tierras? ¿Qué compensaciones encuentran ahí? Analiza tus puntos de vista. Si lo deseas, puedes hacer en la biblioteca una investigación sobre los colonizadores en los Estados Unidos y en otros países.** Students' speculations about the rewards and motives of pioneers will vary. Some students may hazard that facing hardships is worthwhile because exploring frontiers gives people new experiences, more opportunities, and alternative places to live. Other students may counter that it is better to invest effort in making our own planet, or our own neighborhood, more habitable.

Beyond the Selection

Opciones:
Prepara tu portafolio (page 154)

Cuaderno del escritor

1. *Compilación de ideas para un artículo informativo*
Recommend to students that they use encyclopedias and almanacs to carry out their research at the school or local library.

Arte

2. *Propiedades fabulosas* (Hot Property)
You may want to recommend that students work in small groups for this activity. Students can pool their knowledge of science-fiction stories, real-estate advertising, and specific facts about the planet Venus.

Dramatización (Dramatization)

3. *El monólogo de William* (William's Monologue)
Have students work in pairs for this activity. The student who takes the role of Margot can also contribute to the writing of the dramatic monologue.

Estrategias para leer (page 155)
Distinguir hechos de opiniones
Recommend that students work in pairs to analyze editorials or Op-Ed columns for the activity in INTÉNTALO TÚ. These types of persuasive or analytical essays usually contain a number of facts as well as opinions.

El trópico
(The Tropics)

Rubén Darío

page 157

Into the Selection

Summary
The speaker in this poem exults in the freshness and languid pace of a day in the tropics. In the morning, a girl grinds corn on a stone. A young hunter strides along the path with his game bag, and a farmer searches for his cow to milk it beside the corral. At noon, the light in a clear sky sharply defines the hills. The cattle munch the leaves, and golden and vermilion beetles shine in

the green field. A cowboy sounds a curved horn, and evening's glowing light brightens the golden marks on the hocks and forehead of a white bull.

Antes de leer (page 156)

Punto de partida

Pintar un paisaje (Painting a Landscape)
Some students may need some more specific orientation to "the tropics." The technical definition of this region is the zone between the Tropic of Cancer (23° 26' north latitude) and the Tropic of Capricorn (23° 26' south latitude). A more informal definition would be any very warm, attractive location with abundant fauna and flora. You might list some of the following locations to prompt students' associations: *India, Tailandia, Indonesia, Australia, Tahití, Hawai, América Central, Puerto Rico, Brasil, África Central.* Students may wish to review notes they made for the second introductory activity for this collection.

Planes de viaje (Travel Plans)

Encourage students to take advantage of information resources such as atlases, travel magazines and brochures, guidebooks, and airline schedules.

Elementos de literatura

Aliteración (Alliteration)
Tell students that they will be able to *hear* many examples of alliteration if they read the poem aloud, as slowly and expressively as they can. You may wish to have students work in pairs, with each partner taking turns reading one stanza aloud.

Through the Selection

Adueñate de estas palabras

mozo (157)
carmín (157)

Techniques for Handling the Reading

Students will best appreciate the rhythm, rhyme, sound effects, and imagery of this poem if they read it aloud or listen to the recording on the audiocassette. Remind readers to consult the footnotes and glossary entries for the meanings of unfamiliar words. Ask readers to compare and contrast this selection with other poems they have read. You may also wish to have students preview ELEMENTOS DE LITERATURA (page 161) before they read the selection.

Crea significados (page 159)

Primeras impresiones

1. **¿Te gustaría vivir o ir de vacaciones a un lugar como el que se describe en el poema? Explica tu respuesta.** Students' answers will vary. Many readers will agree that the setting Darío describes is attractive, even beautiful. Some students, however, may object that they would not find much to occupy them in this setting. Encourage students to support their answers with reasons.

Interpretaciones del texto

2. **Identifica tres ejemplos de *aliteración* en el poema. ¿Qué ambiente enfatiza la aliteración?** Among the examples of alliteration students may mention are the following: *me agarra el aire por la nariz* (line 2); *muele el maíz* (line 4); *un mozo trae por su sendero/sus herramientas y su morral* (lines 5–6); *por las colinas la luz se pierde* (line 10); *sonando un cuerno curvo y sonoro/viene el vaquero* (lines 15–16). The alliteration contributes to the mood of serenity and natural beauty.

3. **¿Cuánto tiempo transcurre en el poema? ¿Cómo lo sabes?** The poem seems to cover the span of one day. In the first stanza, it is morning. In the third stanza, the first two lines imply that it is noon (*un cielo claro y sin fin*), while in the final stanza, the golden light (line 18) and the actions of the vaquero imply that it is evening.

4. **Escribe tres palabras que describan la actitud del narrador.** Students' answers will vary. Among the words they might choose are the following: *feliz, sereno, sosegado, comprensivo, extático, pasmado.*

Conexiones con el texto

5. **¿Puedes recordar un lugar en el que hayas disfrutado mucho? Completa la**

EL TRÓPICO 51

siguiente oración: **Yo creo que _____ es el lugar más hermoso que he visto porque _____.** Students' answers will vary. Encourage students to support their responses as specifically as possible.

Preguntas al texto

6. **¿Cómo cambiaría este poema si la mañana hubiera sido lluviosa y sin sol? Describe el mismo lugar bajo estas circunstancias.** Students' answers will vary. In general, they should point out that the weather plays a very important role in establishing the poem's mood. If the morning had been cloudy and rainy, for example, the outdoor activities the poet mentions—such as those of the hunter, the farmer, the cattle, and the *vaquero*—would probably have lost much of their charm. Some of these activities, in fact, would seem like a struggle rather than a pleasure.

Beyond the Selection

Opciones:
Prepara tu portafolio (page 160)

Cuaderno del escritor

1. Compilación de ideas para un artículo informativo
You may suggest that students work in small groups for this activity. Recommend that notetakers focus on processes, such as how something works or how to do something.

Arte

2. Pintar el trópico (Painting the Tropics)
This activity is likely to appeal to your visually oriented students. As an alternative, you may want to encourage students to skim through old magazines and collect interesting photographs of tropical scenes.

Elementos de literatura (page 161)

Poesía I: Recursos de sonido e imágenes
(Poetry I: Sound Effects and Imagery)

Be sure that students can answer the questions embedded in the text of this feature. For example, the repetition of the *s* sound in Nicolás Guillén's riddle onomatopoeically suggests both a snake and the "swish" sound of a river. In the stanza from Ana María Fagundo's "La canción del árbol," students should be able to identify images appealing to sight (lines 1–2), touch (lines 3–4), and hearing (lines 5–6).

Use the quiz below to test students' comprehension of the material in ELEMENTOS DE LITERATURA.

1. **¿Qué diferencia hay entre *rima asonante* y *rima consonante*?** (In *rima consonante*, both vowel and consonant sounds exactly match each other, while in *rima asonante*, only the vowel sounds are repeated.)
2. **¿Qué es el *verso libre*?** (poetry without regular rhyme or rhythm)
3. **¿Qué es el *paralelismo*?** (the use of balanced phrases that are similar in structure or in meaning)
4. **¿Se usan las imágenes literarias tanto en prosa como en verso?** (yes)

La isla Sangalakki
(Sangalakki Island)

Norbert Wu

page 164

Into the Selection

Summary
The author begins this informative article by describing an aged green turtle returning to lay its eggs on the hot sand of a tropical island. The turtle patiently waits until evening to approach Sangalakki Island off the east coast of Kalimantan, or Indonesian Borneo. Surrounding it are its neighbors in the bustling community that is a coral reef. Wu compares this entire reef to a city, likening certain sections of it to *barberías* (barbershops), where groupers, parrotfish, and

angelfish assemble and are cleaned of parasites by brilliantly colored shrimp. As night falls, the sea creatures and a multitude of other animals make for their places of resting or feeding.

The turtle awakens and begins its march toward land. Slowly and tortuously, it traverses the beach until it finds a suitable place to dig a hole and deposit its eggs.

The author then describes the development of Sangalakki Island by Ron Holland and his partners. Their company, "Divers of Borneo," is engaged in a novel project: developing a paradisiacal resort while trying to conserve the environment. Besides the attraction of diving to see the reef and the manta rays, the huge aggregations of green tortoises offer visitors a wonderful spectacle. In the new spirit of conservation, islanders like Papa Tambuli guard the turtles' eggs rather than harvesting them. The newborn turtles are marvelous to see, although they meet many dangers in infancy. One morning, the author reports, he glimpsed the prints of twenty baby turtles leaving a nest in the direction of the sea. The tracks ended halfway from the nest to the water, where a hungry monitor lizard had intercepted and eaten the young turtles.

Although it may seem like a tropical paradise, Sangalakki Island does not lack problems. Many islanders are displeased that the corporation has bought the tortoise-egg concession, and the Indonesian government seems to be yielding to the islanders' pressure. It is still beyond question, however, that Sangalakki Island is an important attraction for natural history enthusiasts.

Antes de leer (page 163)

Punto de partida

Bajo las olas (Beneath the Waves)
You may wish to hold a classwide brainstorming session on topics in marine biology and oceanography. Give students a chance to free-associate about a variety of subjects, and write some of their data, questions, or anecdotes on the chalkboard.

Toma nota

Stress that students need not worry about spelling, grammar, or punctuation for this activity. The important goal is for writers to get their ideas down on paper.

Elementos de literatura

Las imágenes (Imagery)
Emphasize that all good writers of prose, as well as poetry, use images to present their subjects vividly and concretely. You may wish to give students an illustration of the importance of imagery by reading the first paragraph of the selection aloud. Ask students to raise their hands or write a note as they recognize each sensory image in the paragraph.

Through the Selection

Adueñate de estas palabras

adherir (166)
parásito (166)
al unísono (166)
diurno (166)
opaco (166)
fosforescencia (168)
caparazón (168)
semejar (168)
estela (168)
tramo (168)
ecosistema (168)
surtir (168)
incubar (169)
acechar (171)
carecer (171)

Techniques for Handling the Reading

The unfamiliar subject matter and relatively complex structure of this article may pose challenges for some of your students. You may wish to have students work in pairs, teaming less proficient readers with more experienced ones. Have partners pause at the end of each page to summarize the author's main points and to clear up any confusions. Remind students to use the footnotes and glossary entries. A recording of the selection, available on audiocassette, dramatizes the beauty and danger of the island and may help students overcome some initial difficulties with the text.

Literatura y ciencia (page 172)

Tortugas marinas (Sea Turtles)

Ironically, the green turtle (*Chelonia mydas*) is protected in almost every country in the world except Indonesia, where it is quite common. Green turtles are vegetarians that feed on seagrass. One mystery surrounding them is why the females nest only on certain beaches. Experts speculate that two important factors in this choice may be the degree of protection each site affords against the prevailing winds and the saltiness of the moisture in the sand.

Crea significados (page 173)

Repaso del texto

a. **¿Dónde pone la tortuga marina sus huevos?** It lays them in a hole that it digs in a shady spot on the beach behind some trees, where the eggs will stay warm but not become too hot.

b. **¿Qué son las «barberías»?** They are places on the reef where groupers, parrotfish, and angelfish are cleaned of their parasites.

c. **¿Qué es «Buzos de Borneo»?** This is the company founded by Ron Holland and his partners to develop a resort on Sangalakki Island.

d. **¿Por qué no alcanzan a llegar al mar muchas de las tortuguitas?** Many babies are eaten by predators such as monitor lizards.

Primeras impresiones

1. **Describe en una oración una cosa nueva que hayas aprendido en este ensayo.** Students' answers will vary. Be sure that each response states a single specific fact in a complete sentence.

Interpretaciones del texto

2. **Nombra tres *imágenes* memorables del ensayo.** Again, students' answers will vary. Among the many images they may cite are the following: the aged female waiting in a cave of dark coral for night to fall, the description of the *barberías*, the seabird turning in the wind, the jumps of small fish in unison, the parrotfish spitting a cocoon of mucus, the phosphorescence caused by the turtle's splashing, the prints that resemble the tracks of a tractor, the "lake of the jellyfish," Papa Tambuli patrolling the beach, the great female turtle that invaded the kitchen, and the prints of the baby turtles on the sand.

3. **¿Con qué compara el autor el arrecife? ¿Por qué?** The writer compares the coral reef to a city with a large number of inhabitants, buildings, and activities. Almost every available surface is covered with creatures, each one occupying a distinct niche.

4. **¿Por qué crees que Papa Tambuli pasó de ser recolector de huevos de tortuga a ser protector de los mismos?** Students' answers will vary. They may speculate that Papa Tambuli was converted from harvesting turtle eggs to protecting them because he recognized the value of conservation to the tourist business. They might suggest that he is paid by the proprietors of the resort as well.

5. **¿Crees que el autor describe específicamente una tortuga marina o su conocimiento general de las tortugas? ¿Por qué?** Students' answers will vary. Many students will suggest that the generic quality of the description—for example, no specific dates or times are mentioned—hints that the author is drawing on his knowledge of sea turtles in general, rather than describing one specific individual.

Preguntas al texto

6. **¿Cómo crees que el autor reunió su información para el ensayo? En grupo, mencionen todos los métodos de investigación que pudo haber usado.** Students' answers will vary. They may suggest that the author combined firsthand observation with interviews, library research on sea turtles and coral reefs, and study of publications such as tourist brochures, newspapers, and government documents.

7. **¿Por qué crees que el autor empezó su ensayo con la tortuga marina, en vez de iniciarlo inmediatamente con el proyecto «Buzos de Borneo»?** Students' answers will vary. In general, they may point out that beginning with the vivid picture of the sea turtle captures the audience's attention with a graphic, striking image. This kind of introduction is more effective than a comparatively dry, abstract account of the "Buzos de Borneo" project.

Beyond the Selection

Opciones:
Prepara tu portafolio (page 174)

Cuaderno del escritor

1. Compilación de ideas para un artículo informativo
Suggest that one good way to discover topics is for group members to skim volumes of an illustrated encyclopedia.

Redacción

2. Desde el punto de vista de la tortuga
(A Turtle's-Eye View)
Remind students that the first-person point of view requires using pronouns such as *yo, mí, mi,* and *mío.* Encourage students to use clues in the text to visualize the scene and then to give their imaginations free rein.

Dibujo

3. Un diagrama del océano (An Ocean Diagram)
You may wish to have students work in pairs for this activity.

A leer por tu cuenta
La Osa Mayor
(The Great Bear)

Nicolás Guillén page 175

Summary
The speaker playfully describes the constellation *Ursa Major* (containing the Big Dipper) in the night sky. The lines of this brief lyric whimsically combine allusions to modern technology, in the form of a Russian space satellite, and to age-old beliefs that attribute the shapes of animals to the constellations.

Techniques for Handling the Reading
Although this selection has no formal apparatus, students may enjoy speculating about ways in which this brief, amusing poem exemplifies the collection theme, *Un más allá.*

Taller del escritor (page 176)

La exposición/Artículo informativo
(Report of Information)

Presenting the Workshop
See the MANUAL DE COMUNICACIÓN (page 324) for a general overview of the writing process. You may wish to devote all or part of a class session to reviewing the major aspects of each stage of the process.

Before students begin the assignment, suggest that they review the collection for some springboards and models. For example, you can point out that Horacio Quiroga's story "El cuendú" gives both factual information and subjective impressions about the behavior of an unusual animal. Norbert Wu's article "La isla Sangalakki" is also a stimulating model for informative writing, since it combines vivid imagery with specific, objective data about an exotic locale.

You can also encourage students to explore informational writing in familiar formats from everyday life: for example, news articles, science textbooks, instruction manuals, and magazine columns.

Antes de escribir
In addition to the prewriting techniques discussed in the text, you may wish to model the technique of brainstorming with small groups of students. Students can exchange notes about hobbies, after-school jobs, and interesting projects from shop class or home economics class. When ideas start to flow, remind students to focus on the steps of a process and the materials required for accomplishing a specific task.

Another prewriting technique that you can recommend is interviewing. Students can question family members or store owners in their neighborhood on a variety of topics: for example, how to run a pharmacy or how to plan a street fair. Suggest that students prepare a list of specific questions in advance. Also tell students to use a tape recorder, if possible, when they conduct their interviews.

Stress to the class that an important part of informative writing is the presentation of facts in an interesting way. Urge students to review Norbert Wu's style in "La isla Sangalakki." Point out that Wu combines a lot of factual information with vivid imagery. Remind students, too, that Horacio Quiroga blends information with personal reactions in his story "El cuendú." Although an informative article should be relatively formal in style and tone, you may recommend to students that they include some personal touches revealing their own thoughts and feelings about their subject.

El borrador

If students elect to describe a process in an informational article, chronological order is probably the most effective method of organization for their report. However, not all reports of information are "how-to" papers. If students have chosen to write a different kind of report, urge them to consider how to organize factual material logically and clearly. The importance of transitional words and phrases cannot be overemphasized. You may wish to refer students to the discussion of paragraph development in the MANUAL DE COMUNICACIÓN (page 325).

Make sure that students appreciate the examples in the text of how to avoid wordiness, repetitiousness, and monotonous sentence structure. If necessary, hold a brainstorming session to give students practice in finding synonyms. Remind the class that they can consult reference books such as a Spanish *diccionario de sinónimos y antónimos*.

Evaluación y revisión

When students have finished a first draft, ask them to examine carefully the pair of models in the text (pages 179–180). Students may work independently, or you may wish to devote some time in a class session to analyzing and discussing this material. If you choose to have students work in class, call on volunteers to read the model drafts aloud. Then call on volunteers to comment on each draft. Make sure that students understand the reasons for the writing evaluations given in the text. Then encourage pairs to exchange feedback. The guidelines for evaluation and revision on page 179 can be used whether students work in pairs or independently.

Bear in mind that students may need help in using their notes to make workable revisions of their first drafts. On a purely mechanical level, for example, some writers may need a guided introduction to the basic proofreading symbols for insertion, deletion, and transposition. See the MANUAL DE COMUNICACIÓN (page 325.)

Corrección de pruebas

Emphasize that proofreading or editing adds to the clarity, correctness, and effective presentation of an essay. Familiarity with the conventions of language and writing—spelling, punctuation, grammar, usage, capitalization, paragraphing, syllabification, accuracy of citations and graphics, and proper manuscript form—is an important part of being an effective writer.

Before they begin this stage, some students may need a guided review of the proofreading symbols used for editing and correcting errors in spelling and mechanics. Go over the list of symbols given in the MANUAL DE COMUNICACIÓN (page 325). Then have pairs exchange papers and proofread each other's writing. You may wish to circulate through the class, offering help when needed.

Publicación

In addition to the sharing opportunities mentioned in the text, students might like to use their article as the basis for a radio script or for a "how-to" brochure aimed at younger students.

Reflexión

Guide students to recognize that time set aside for reflection on an assignment is a helpful investment in the growth of their writing skills. For example, recognizing that one aspect of the project was especially challenging means that students can seek special assistance for their next effort.

Reteaching

Students having problems with evaluating and revising may work in pairs to read their reports of information aloud. Encourage listeners to identify the most interesting and important parts of each report.

Closure

Ask students to explain the difference between a report of information and a persuasive essay such as an editorial or a letter to the editor.

Assessment Tools

As students work through the writing process, share the following assessment criteria with them, so they may use them in self- and peer evaluations.

Assessment Criteria

1   2   3   4   5   6
(needs   (superior)
improvement)

Content

- Introduction captures reader's interest.
- Topic is clearly identified and main idea is stated.
- Required materials are identified.
- Unfamiliar terms are defined, and steps in a process are given in correct order.
- Main idea and/or value of process are restated in a strong conclusion.

Language Conventions

- Grammar and usage are standard.
- Paragraphs are indented properly.
- Words are spelled correctly.
- Quotation marks are used correctly.

Overall Rating: _____

Enrichment

Folklore Connection

Work with students to develop illustrated reports on legendary creatures such as the Loch Ness monster (Scotland), the yeti or Abominable Snowman (Tibet), the yowie (Australia), and the sasquatch (Pacific Northwest). Students can use magazines and encyclopedias in the school library or local library as reference sources. When students have finished, encourage them to share their reports in small groups.

Taller de oraciones (page 181)

La aposición: Un segundo nombre
(Apposition: A Second Name)

In this exercise students get practice in recognizing appositive phrases, punctuating them, and combining sentences by placing one of the ideas within an appositive phrase. More information on noun phrases is in the GUÍA DEL LENGUAJE.

Answers:

1. Las tortugas, incansables viajeras, llegan todos los años a las playas vírgenes de Sangalakki, una isla del Pacífico.
2. Las crías salen hacia el mar, su futuro hogar, donde pasarán la mayor parte de sus vidas.
3. Las gaviotas, voraces predadores, son uno de los mayores peligros para las tortugas en sus primeros instantes de vida.

Collection 5: LA CONVIVENCIA

Collection Overview

How do people get along together? What solutions do they find for problems in their neighborhoods or communities? The selections grouped under the theme of *La convivencia* ("The Community," or "Living Together") address issues posed by social living and diversity in a fashion that will be immediately accessible to sixth-graders. In a short play and two amusing poems, practical advice on living with others is mingled with imaginative humor.

Two of the selections can be traced back ultimately to the fables of the ancient Greek writer Aesop (sixth century B.C.). For his brief one-act play "Los dos labradores" ("The Two Farmers"), José María Osorio Rodríguez drew on a narrative by the Infante Don Juan Manuel, a famous fourteenth-century Spanish writer, who was in turn indebted to one of Aesop's fables. The central story is framed by a classic problem-solution situation: A count who finds himself criticized on all sides seeks advice on how to govern. The moral of his adviser's response is dramatized when a farmer and his son are shown traveling to a fair with their donkey. Whether the father or the son rides the donkey, they are criticized by the passersby. Two other ideas bring the same result: Both father and son ride on the donkey's back, and both try walking beside the animal. The count's adviser draws the moral: Since you can never please all the people, let your conscience be your guide.

Lope de Vega is the renowned playwright and poet of the *Siglo de Oro,* the Golden Age of Spanish literature that actually extended for more than a century, from about 1500 to 1680. In "Los ratones" ("The Mice"), Lope de Vega retells in verse Aesop's fable "Belling the Cat." The mice face another familiar problem: what to do about a threat to the community from the outside. The jaunty rhythm and clever rhyme in this short poem are likely to appeal to your students.

The final reading in this collection, which appears under the heading A LEER POR TU CUENTA, offers another point of contact with the collection theme. In her poem "Se cayó la luna" ("The Moon Fell"), Emma Pérez describes with whimsical humor how the sun solves the problem of the moon's accidental "fall" into a well. Many students will have fun solving the riddle that the poem poses, and they will intuitively enjoy Pérez's clever use of metaphor and personification.

Throughout the collection, questions, exercises, and activities give students a wide range of opportunities to respond to the literature. The instructional material also encourages readers to relate the literature to their own lives and to respond emotionally and imaginatively as well as analytically.

ELEMENTOS DE LITERATURA, a feature on the literary and performance elements of drama, is intended to complement students' reading of "Los dos labradores." A cultural feature focusing on Latino sports offers students different and equally accessible angles on the collection theme, since sports events serve as an important mechanism for knitting society together in contemporary cultures.

The integration of materials also extends to the opening assignments in OPCIONES: PREPARA TU PORTAFOLIO, which are designed to prepare students progressively for the assignment, in TALLER DEL ESCRITOR, to write a problem-solution essay. This assignment synthesizes many of the skills that students will develop as they read and discuss the selections in the collection. Further activities on the OPCIONES pages challenge students to explore themes and ideas through a variety of modes, such as drama and problem-solving. Finally, in TALLER DE ORACIONES, students look at conventions of punctuation and learn how to use different forms of punctuation in their own writing.

Introducing the Collection

To encourage students to explore some of the themes of this collection, give them a choice of opening activities. Possibilities include the following:

1. Have students explore the theme *La convivencia* by making a collage or three-dimensional display of photos, posters, and other significant objects from their neighborhood. Tell students to be prepared to explain how each object illustrates an aspect of neighborhood life.
2. Tell students that many animals (*leones, elefantes, gorilas, lobos, hienas, abejas*) live in social groups, while others (*tigres, osos panda, jaguares, mapaches*) are more solitary. What are some of the advantages of each lifestyle? What are the disadvantages? Have students work in small groups to do some research. Then have them present their results in oral reports to the class. After each report, allow time for a discussion. Can students draw any conclusions about human society from the facts they have learned about animal behavior?
3. How would students define the words *neighbor* (*vecino*) and *neighborhood* (*vecindario*)? Have them write a paragraph on a specific person who exemplifies the qualities of a good neighbor. As an alternative, they can write a paragraph describing their neighborhood. Invite students to share their paragraphs by reading them aloud to the class. Then encourage students to identify some of the strengths and problems in their community.

Los dos labradores
(The Two Farmers)

Basado en una obra del
Infante Don Juan Manuel

Adaptación de
José María Osorio Rodríguez

page 185

Into the Selection

Summary

As this brief play begins, Count Lucanor and his adviser Patronio are seated in the foreground. The count wearily confides that although he strives to serve his people day and night, he is always criticized by those he governs. What should he do? Patronio responds with a story. Two farmers, father and son, were traveling along a road with a donkey to a fair.

At this point, actors impersonating the characters of the father and son enter to dramatize the remainder of the story in a series of vignettes, while Patronio acts as narrator. In the first tableau, the father is mounted on the donkey, while the son walks alongside. A man criticizes the father for being so inconsiderate of his poor child. The father then insists that his son take his place on the donkey's back. Once they have reached a second town, however, another passerby is equally critical, wondering how the son could be so inconsiderate as to ride while his poor old father must walk.

Both farmers now mount the donkey, only to be criticized in a third town by an onlooker who says they have no compassion for animals. Accordingly, both dismount and walk alongside the donkey, but at a fourth town they are mocked for their stupidity. Finally, the son ruefully tells the father that the only alternative they haven't explored is for them both to carry the donkey on their shoulders! After the crestfallen farmers exit, Patronio draws the moral for the count: It is not possible to govern to the liking of all. The best course is to rule according to one's conscience.

Antes de leer (page 184)

Punto de partida

«Quien no oye consejo, no llega a viejo» ("He Who Doesn't Listen to Advice Doesn't Live Long")
To stimulate responses, ask students if they have ever read advice columns in the newspapers. Remind students that in everyday life people give and receive advice in many ways: for example, writing letters, listening to radio call-in shows, telling personal anecdotes to friends, quoting proverbs, studying with classmates for a test, or planning strategies with a coach for a sports event. As students brainstorm about how people give and receive advice, you may want to write some key phrases on the chalkboard.

Toma nota

To get students started, you may wish to focus a brief discussion on the first example of a *refrán*: *Quien no se arriesga no gana.* Call on volunteers to suggest other real-life situations from their own experience that support or contradict the saying.

Diálogo con el texto

Stress the importance of students' trying to *visualize* the action on stage as the play unfolds. Since the physical relationship of the two farmers and the donkey is such an important visual element in the play, you may want to encourage students to draw their own sketches to illustrate each incident.

Elementos de literatura

Drama

If necessary, have students preview the discussion of dramatic plot in ELEMENTOS DE LITERATURA (page 192). Remind them that the elements of drama are structurally identical to the elements of a short story (see pages 58–59). For review, write this diagram on the chalkboard:

Then call on volunteers to choose a short story they have read recently (for example, Ray Bradbury's "Todo el verano en un día" in Collection 4, page 145) and identify the plot elements.

Estrategias para leer

Hacer predicciones (Making Predictions)

If you wish, have students preview the feature ESTRATEGIAS PARA LEER (page 202) at this point. This material provides a specific, step-by-step description of the process of making predictions.

Through the Selection

Diario del lector (page 186)

The sample marginal comments exemplify several reading skills in practice: making inferences, questioning, noting details, and speculating. If you feel that some of your students may benefit, extend the activity by modeling similar kinds of marginal annotations. Then allow enough time to monitor and discuss students' notes on an individual basis.

Adueñate de estas palabras

prudencia (186)   pollino (186)
dictar (186)   ronzal (187)
desasosegado (186)

Techniques for Handling the Reading

Most of your students will find this short play accessible. You may wish to play the audiocassette recording for the class, urging students to envision the drama taking place on a stage while they listen.

Once the students understand the framing device—whereby Patronio's *cuento* is actually dramatized onstage—they will easily grasp the repetitive plot structure of the four vignettes involving father and son. Urge students to use the glossary notes, which explain a few unusual words and grammatical forms.

Point out to students that this brief drama offers a clear, concise illustration of the similarities between the elements of a *cuento* or *fábula* and the elements of a *drama*. The playwright accom-

60 LA CONVIVENCIA

plishes this by dramatizing Patronio's story as a play-within-a-play. Guide the students to understand that Count Lucanor's central conflict (he is distressed because he is criticized on all sides, no matter how he governs) precisely parallels the conflict of father and son (they are criticized no matter how they travel to the fair). The climax of the play-within-a-play occurs when the son realizes that no matter what he and his father do, *me parece que no daremos gusto a la gente*. The climax of the main play occurs immediately thereafter, when Patronio says to the count, *no es posible gobernar a gusto de todos*.

This play also offers a good opportunity for groups of students to put on their own productions. To stage the drama, which requires virtually no scenery or props, all you need is a performance space and a group of thirteen imaginative performers: eight for the speaking parts, four for the silent characters in each pair of critics who enter from backstage, and one actor who is willing to play the donkey! If one student wishes to volunteer as director, encourage him or her to focus on the actors' tones of voice for the delivery of their lines, as well as on appropriate gestures and movements.

Crea significados (page 189)

Repaso del texto

a. **¿Por qué problema necesita consejos el conde Lucanor?** Although Count Lucanor works night and day to serve his people by governing them well, they are never satisfied.

b. **¿Por qué son criticados el padre y el hijo a lo largo de toda la historia?** No matter how the father and son ride, the passersby criticize them for their lack of consideration—of each other and of the donkey. Finally, when both farmers dismount and walk alongside the donkey, they are criticized for stupidity.

c. **¿Cómo reaccionan el padre y el hijo a los comentarios de cada transeúnte?** They yield to their critics immediately, even though doing so involves shifting to a completely opposite course.

d. **Al final de la historia, ¿qué propone el hijo?** The son ironically suggests that the only course left is to carry the donkey on their shoulders—but they still wouldn't please the people.

Primeras impresiones

1. **¿Crees que Patronio le da buenos consejos al conde Lucanor? Justifica tu respuesta.** Students' answers will vary. Many students will suggest that it is important for leaders or governors to steer a steady course, after they have consulted with their advisers and with the people as a whole. Continual shifts and reversals in response to the slightest criticism or displeasure are likely to result in weak leadership or even chaos. To this extent, Patronio's advice is wise.

Interpretaciones del texto

2. **¿Qué problema sobre su condición de gobernante pone al descubierto la pregunta del conde?** Count Lucanor's question reveals that he wants to take the best course for his people, but that he also wants to be liked by them. He is well-meaning and hard-working; on the other hand, he is ultra-sensitive to criticism.

3. **¿Por qué cuenta Patronio una fábula para explicar un problema, en lugar de simplemente decirle al conde Lucanor lo que debe hacer?** Students' answers will vary. Many students will suggest that Patronio—as a subordinate to the count—wants to phrase his advice as diplomatically as possible for fear of offending his master. Thus he tactfully uses the indirect format of a story.

4. **¿Qué conflictos hay en este *drama*?** Students should single out at least two conflicts: Count Lucanor's struggle to please his people and the two farmers' efforts to avoid being criticized. Some students may subdivide Lucanor's conflict into an external struggle (the count vs. his subjects) and an internal struggle (the count's motivation to serve his people well vs. his dislike of their criticism).

5. **¿Por qué le pueden importar al conde dos hombres y un burro? ¿Qué tiene que ver la fábula con el gobierno de un pueblo?** Students' answers will vary. In general, their responses should demonstrate an understanding that the story about the two farmers and their donkey is intended as a moral lesson. The fable relates to ruling and serving a kingdom, because it points to the impossibility of pleasing all the people. As the final comment of the son implies, efforts to achieve such a goal can lead only to absurdity.

Conexiones con el texto

6. **¿Cuál es el mejor consejo que te han dado? ¿Y el peor?** Students' answers will vary. This question offers a good opportunity for students to share anecdotes—serious or humorous—with their classmates. Call on volunteers, after assuring them that they should choose to share only any personal matters they feel comfortable about. Remind them that if they are going to tell a brief story, like Patronio, they should use chronological order. When the students label advice as the "best" and the "worst," encourage them to support their responses with reasons.

Más allá del texto

7. **En la literatura se usan a veces personajes tradicionales, como por ejemplo Patronio en «Los dos labradores». Se trata de un tipo de personaje fácil de reconocer que le permite al lector concentrarse en el argumento y la moraleja. ¿Por qué se llama «Patronio» el consejero de esta historia? Consulta en el diccionario las palabras «patrón» y «padre» para obtener la respuesta.** Students' answers will vary. In general, they should recognize that Patronio's name signals the playwright's use of him as a wise "father figure." You might wish to remind students that the history of drama (especially comedy) is full of characters with names that suggest significant aspects of their appearance or personality. See if students can name some examples from films or television shows.

Beyond the Selection

Opciones:
Prepara tu portafolio (page 190)

Cuaderno del escritor

1. Compilación de ideas para un ensayo sobre problemas y soluciones (Collecting Ideas for a Problem-Solution Essay)
Encourage students to use a variety of sources for this activity. For example, instead of consulting print media, students can interview a parent, an older relative or friend, a local businessperson, or a law-enforcement officer. Or they might visit the public-relations office of an important community institution, such as a hospital or museum.

Redacción

2. ¿Qué me aconsejas? (What's Your Advice?)
If you wish, allow students to use the questions and answers in newspaper advice columns as models for this activity. Students may also get some ideas from radio call-in shows.

Dramatización

3. ¡En vivo! (Live!)
If you do not have sufficient class time to devote to this activity, a convenient alternative may be to develop a student performance of "Los dos labradores." See **Techniques for Handling the Reading.**

Lengua y literatura (page 191)

Cómo se construyen las palabras
(How Words Are Constructed)

This mini-lesson builds on the skills learned in LENGUA Y LITERATURA in Collection 3. Students use their knowledge of word roots to learn about prefixes and suffixes.

The first task is to break down a word into its three parts: *desa-soseg-ado* (prefix-root-suffix). This word's root is the same as *sosiego,* or "peace, calm." You may want to have the students practice breaking down other words such as *desconocido, descosido,* etc.

The second paragraph introduces the concept of **prefixes. Des-** means "without." To be *desa-sosegado* is to be anxious or confused (lacking peace). You may want to teach other prefixes such as the ones that appear in the following chart.

PREFIXES	
De origen griego	
a-:	sin. Ejemplo: ateo = sin dios
anti-:	contra. Ejemplos: antigas = contra el gas; antítesis
peri-:	alrededor. Ejemplo: periferia = los alrededores de una cosa, como una ciudad
tele-:	lejos. Ejemplos: televisión = visión desde lejos; telediario; telégrafo; teléfono
De origen latino	
bis- o **bi-:**	dos. Ejemplos: bimotor, bicicleta
des-:	sin. Ejemplo: descafeinado = sin cafeína
ex-:	fuera o más allá. Ejemplos: expatriado, exmarido, extraño, excéntrico
multi-:	muchos. Ejemplo: multicolor

The next paragraph introduces **suffixes**. Two suffixes that indicate a profession are **-ero** and **-ista** (for example, *oficinista*). The suffix that indicates a shop is **-ería**. Suffixes that indicate size, such as **-iño, -ico, ón, -uca, -eta, -ín,** differ according to region. Encourage students to create other words using these suffixes. The INTÉNTALO TÚ exercise introduces more difficult Greek and Latin prefixes, as in the following chart:

SUFFIXES	
De origen griego	
-algia:	dolor. Ejemplo: gastralgia = dolor de estómago
-filo:	amigo. Ejemplo: francófilo = que ama el francés
-grafo:	dibujar, escribir. Ejemplos: bolígrafo, escenógrafo
-itis:	inflamación. Ejemplos: gastritis, otitis
De origen latino	
-cida:	que mata. Ejemplo: insecticida
-cultor:	que cultiva. Ejemplo: agricultor
-fugo:	que hace huir (*de fuga*). Ejemplo: vermífugo = que ahuyenta a los gusanos
-voro:	que se alimenta de. Ejemplo: carnívoro

Some suffixes indicate parts of speech. For example, in *desasosegado* **-ado** indicates that the word is an adjective.

Suggested activities:
- Have students go through a chapter they have studied in a science textbook and locate prefixes and suffixes in scientific terms.
- Have students look at previous ADUÉÑATE DE ESTAS PALABRAS and look for prefixes and suffixes.
- Have students look at a newspaper article and find words whose roots, prefixes, or suffixes they recognize.

Vocabulario (page 191)

Un lenguaje antiguo (Archaic Language)

This exercise explains the unusual language of "Los dos labradores." Students are introduced to words that have fallen out of common usage. By referring to the selection, students may realize that these difficult words were once used in ordinary conversation. Students should also notice differences in syntax and in the feel of medieval Spanish, particularly if they read sections of the play aloud.

Elementos de literatura (page 192)

Drama

Be sure that students can answer the questions in the text that relate to "Los dos labradores." For example, they should identify the father and son's conflict as similar to that of the count: No matter how the two farmers act, they provoke criticism from one passerby or another, just as Count Lucanor is criticized no matter how hard he works to govern his subjects properly. At the climax of the play, the two farmers leave the stage, with the son pointing out that even if they should make the absurd choice of carrying the donkey on their shoulders, they would still invite criticism.

Use the quiz below to test students' comprehension of the material in ELEMENTOS DE LITERATURA.

1. **¿Cuáles son los tres componentes fundamentales de cualquier representación dramática?** (actors, audience or spectators, and a performance space such as a stage)
2. **Nombra varias de las técnicas que contribuyen a dar vida a los personajes sobre el escenario en una representación dramática.** (sets, lighting, costumes, and make-up)
3. **¿De qué elementos depende un dramaturgo para desarrollar la acción?** (dialogue, or the conversation between the characters, and stage directions)
4. **¿Cómo se reconocen las acotaciones escénicas en el guión de un drama?** (They are normally printed in italics.)
5. **¿Qué es la utilería?** (Props are important objects used by the characters in a play.)

Los ratones
(The Mice)

Lope de Vega — page 195

Into the Selection

Summary
Alarmed by the threat that the cat poses to their survival, the mice hold a solemn and urgent meeting. After a long discussion, they agree that the best course is to put a bell on the cat so that they will be warned of his approach. This consensus having been reached, an elderly mouse soberly addresses the gathering, asking which member of the assembly will dare to put the plan into action.

Background
Lope de Vega was not the only European writer to adapt Aesop's ancient tale. The French poet Jean de La Fontaine (1621–1695), whose fables have become classics of the genre in world literature, adapted the same story as *Conseil tenu par les Rats* (*Fables* II.2). If you have any students who speak or read French, tell them they might want to look up La Fontaine's version. A Spanish translation appears below.

¿Quién pone el cascabel al gato?

Durante muchos años, los ratones han padecido constantemente la terrible amenaza de su enemigo: el gato. Un día convocaron un consejo para buscar la mejor forma de resolver su problema. Se propusieron y se rechazaron muchos planes.

Al final, un ratón joven se levantó. «Propongo» —dijo con aire de importancia— «colgarle al gato un cascabel del cuello, de modo que cuando se acerque siempre podamos sentir su presencia y escapar a tiempo».

El joven roedor se sentó en medio de una gran ovación. Su idea se sometió al voto de los allí presentes y fue aprobada por unanimidad.

Pero entonces, un ratón viejo que había estado callado todo el tiempo, se levantó y dijo: «Amigos míos, sólo una mente joven sería capaz de idear un plan tan ingenioso y tan simple, al mismo tiempo. Con un cascabel atado al cuello del gato, siempre sabremos donde se encuentra y estaremos a salvo. No tengo más que una pregunta para los partidarios de este plan: ¿quién de vosotros pondrá el cascabel al gato?»

Moraleja: Una cosa es proponer y otra ejecutar.

Antes de leer (page 194)

Punto de partida

La lección de las fábulas
(The Lesson of Fables)
Be sure that students understand that a fable is a brief narrative that is told to teach or emphasize a practical lesson. As with the stories of Aesop,

fables often feature animal characters, who are personified and given very human traits. Some students may be familiar with fables from a wide range of cultures. Native American oral traditions are rich in fables, as is the folklore of South Asia (the Indian *Panchatantra*) and East Asia (folk tales of China, Japan, and Korea).

Resuelve un problema (Solve a Problem)
When students have finished writing their notes, call on volunteers to give their ideas. You may want to create a chart on the chalkboard, writing students' suggestions in two columns headed "Individual Solutions" and "Group Solutions."

Elementos de literatura

Rima (Rhyme)
Students should have no trouble picking out the rhymes in Lope's poem. You can encourage analytically minded students to draw up a rhyme scheme showing Lope's sequence of end rhymes (*abba, cddc, effe, bggb*). Aural learners can be encouraged to suggest other words that rhyme with the last word in each verse: for example, *romano* and *mexicano, podrían* and *sabían*, or *opiniones* and *reacciones*. Have students note the ingenuity of Lope's rhyme in lines 6 and 7: *cascabel* and *con él*.

Through the Selection

Adueñate de estas palabras
cascabel (195)
encrespar (195)
culto (195)

Techniques for Handling the Reading

Because the poem presents some unusual vocabulary items and relatively complex syntax, you may wish to call on a proficient student reader to recite the poem as other class members follow along with their texts. Make sure that students note the gloss explaining the allusion to the Roman senate in line 12.

Call attention to some of the devices Lope uses to present the tale with such piquant humor. For example, the poem is precisely divided into two balanced, parallel sections of eight lines each: The first describes the decision of the mice, while the second leads up to the question of the old "senator." You might also point to the humorous echoes of the word *ratón* in *rato* (lines 3 and 13), as well as to the way Lope uses syntax to create suspense in the second half of the poem. Call on volunteers to explain why the allusion to the Roman senate (line 12) is verbally ironic. Ask students how they think Lope's use in lines 13 and 16 of the same two rhyming words *rato* and *gato*—this time in reverse order from their occurrence at the beginning of the poem in lines 2 and 3— subtly contributes to the poem's meaning and humorous effect.

Finally, you may want to discuss why Lope de Vega, unlike Aesop and Jean de La Fontaine in their versions, chose not to conclude with an explicit moral or lesson. Do students think the poem would have been enhanced by an explicit moral? Or would adding a moral have detracted from the poem's pithy effect? Encourage students to support their answers.

Crea significados (page 196)

Repaso del texto

Students' answers will vary to some extent. Sample answers might run as follows:

The problem faced by the mice is how to protect themselves from the cat. The solution proposed is to put a bell on him so that the mice will be warned of his approach. The leader of the mice asks who will dare to put the bell on the cat. The new problem is that the proposed solution is not practical.

Primeras impresiones

1. **¿Qué te pareció este poema: gracioso, serio o una mezcla de ambas cosas?** Many students will answer that they found the poem humorous. Some readers may suggest, however, that Lope's irony points to a serious theme: It is all too easy to offer advice, but it is hard to put the advice into practice.

Interpretaciones del texto

2. **¿Por qué no va a funcionar la solución de los ratones?** The solution won't work

because no mouse is bold enough to bell the cat.

3. **¿Cómo podrías resumir la *moraleja*, es decir, la lección de esta fábula en una oración?** Students' answers will vary. A sample statement of the moral might run as follows: Proposing a solution to a problem is one thing, but implementing it is quite another.

Preguntas al texto

4. **Lope de Vega describe a un ratón viejo y barbudo, pero no describe a los demás. ¿Cómo te los imaginas? ¿En qué se diferenciarían del ratón anciano?** Students' answers will vary. They may suggest that many of the mice are young and inexperienced, in contrast to the older, wiser mouse.

Más allá del texto

5. **¿Recuerdas un problema de la vida real similar al de los ratones? ¿Cómo podría resolverse?** Students' answers will vary. Encourage them to support their responses with specific details and strategies.

Beyond the Selection

Opciones:
Prepara tu portafolio (page 197)

Cuaderno del escritor

1. Compilación de ideas para un ensayo sobre problemas y soluciones
If you wish, allow students to work in small groups for this activity. Remind group members that, while having a personal interest in topics may spur them to write a good persuasive essay, choosing a topic that affects a number of people is also important. Students should avoid problem-solution topics that are too narrow, such as matters of personal taste, individual disputes, and so forth. You might illustrate the distinction between suitable topics and unsuitable ones by giving students the following example:

Problem: Too much pasta in lunch menus. I like vegetables better.
(Limited potential for essay)
Problem: Lunch menus could provide better nutrition. One solution would be to include more fresh vegetables.
(Broader application)

Solución de problemas (Problem Solving)

2. Tu propio invento (Your Own Invention)
If you wish, have students work in small groups for this activity. Make sure that each group contains someone who can illustrate the inventions suggested by members.

Hablar y escuchar

3. Detengan al gato (Stop the Cat)
Suggest that groups appoint a recorder, a graphic artist, and a presenter. The remaining students in each group can serve as members of the "strategy panel."

Escena cultural (page 198)

Deportes latinos (Latino Sports)

Actividades para empezar
Many students will enjoy talking about their favorite sport or team and offering a dramatic description of the all-time greatest play they have seen. Although this activity may motivate students to read the feature in the textbook, the potential drawback is that athletes or sports enthusiasts will dominate the discussion. Encourage the athletes among your students to involve nonathletes by discussing *why* they get excited about sports and *how* sports offer a valuable way for students to practice their competitive skills and solve problems together.

Actividades de cierre

1. Tell students that sources for their biographical sketch can include newspaper and magazine articles, entries in annual sports almanacs, and biographical dictionaries. Although the assignment here is shorter, you may also want to have students preview TALLER DEL ESCRITOR for Collection 6 (page 232) on writing a *semblanza*.

2. This activity should appeal to many of your students, and the main problem may be get-

ting them to agree on which game or match to advertise. Encourage them to practice their interview skills by obtaining brief quotes from team members.
3. Interested students will be able to find many research sources on this issue, which is the subject of a continuing national debate. If they wish, students can widen the field by researching the status of women's sports at colleges and universities.
4. Many publications have delved into this issue. Tell students that librarians can help them locate interesting articles on the question. Encourage students to combine research with their own opinions and reasons when they write their notes.
5. You might suggest that students begin this activity by watching or listening to some sportscasts on television or radio. Then ask them to envision what the daily schedule of a sports journalist might be like, both in and out of the office.

For Further Reading

You may want to research the following sources for further ideas on Latino sports.

Aliotta, Jerome J. *The Puerto Ricans* (Chelsea House Publishers, New York, 1991).

Amdur, Neil. "Pancho Gonzalez, U.S. Tennis Champion, Dies at 67." *The New York Times* 5 July 1995: D9.

Brown, Bruce. "Cuban Baseball." *The Atlantic* June 1984: 109–114.

Dwyer, Christopher. *The Dominican Americans* (Chelsea House Publishers, New York, 1991).

Kanellos, Nicolás. "Sports," in Nicolás Kanellos, ed., *The Hispanic-American Almanac* (Gale Research, Inc., Detroit, 1993) 697–716.

Katel, Peter. "The Best Team Money Can't Buy." *Newsweek* 8 June 1992: 62–63.

Mamaed, Amalia R. "Baseball Memories." *Hispanic* April 1994: 28–29.

Perez, Louis A., Jr. "Between Baseball and Bullfighting: The Quest for Nationality in Cuba, 1868–1898." *Journal of American History* September 1994: 493–507.

Reisges, Tess. "Carlos Baerga." *Sports Illustrated for Kids* July 1995: 40.

Samuelson, Marnie Crawford. "Rodeo Women." *Ms. Magazine* July/August 1993: 47–51.

"Team USA: Pioneros del otro sueño americano." *Gol USA Internacional* 31 de julio–6 de agosto de 1995: 16–17.

Verducci, Tom. "Martínez Mania." *Sports Illustrated* 24 July 1995: 26–30.

Wulf, Steve. "Of Major Interest: Baseball." *Sports Illustrated* 17 August 1992: 52.

Estrategias para leer (page 202)

Hacer predicciones

Stress that good predictions, which are opinions, always have a basis in facts or—even more important—in *patterns* of information or events. For the exercise on "Los dos labradores," you can have students work in small groups.

A leer por tu cuenta
Se cayó la luna
(The Moon Fell)

Emma Pérez — page 203

Summary

This brief poem opens with a dialogue between two speakers. Who will rescue the moon, now that it has fallen into a well? The wind has left the forest for the sea; the owl has flown away in alarm. Will the sun come to the rescue? Indeed, says the speaker, when the sun begins to shine, the face of the moon dissolves in the well water.

Adueñate de estas palabras
alumbrar (203)

Techniques for Handling the Reading

This poem gives a playful twist to the theme *La convivencia* by imagining an "emergency" in which the moon needs to be rescued after it has "fallen" down a well. The sun solves the "problem" nonchalantly by using his rays to dissolve the moon's reflection in the well water. Although this selection is intended solely as enrichment, students may enjoy commenting on the poet's uses of personification, by which the moon, the wind, the forest, the owl, and the sun are given human qualities.

Taller del escritor (page 204)

**La persuasión/
Ensayo sobre problemas y soluciones**
(Problem-Solution Essay)

Presenting the Workshop

For a general overview of the writing process, see the MANUAL DE COMUNICACIÓN (page 324). You may wish to devote all or part of a class session to reviewing the major aspects of each stage of the process. Stress that students may have to move back and forth among the steps of the writing process: for example, from the evaluating and revising stage back to the prewriting stage to collect more supporting details for the main idea. Before students get started, encourage them to suggest and comment on some springboards for problem-solution writing. For example, point out that newspaper editorials and Op-Ed columns often discuss important problems and offer solutions for them. Students can bring some editorials to class and use them as the basis for a brainstorming session.

Antes de escribir

Stress that students should choose a problem of manageable size for discussion in their essay. For example, the problem of how best to conserve the environment on a national scale is far too broad. It would be better instead to focus on one aspect of conservation at the community level. Also point out that problems resulting from personal likes or dislikes can spark a strong essay, but the writer should base his or her argument on less subjective reasons.

Give students a chance to comment on the prewriting chart on page 205 of the text. Invite them to add to the lists of possible solutions, strengths, and weaknesses. If students need further practice on how to explore a problem, you may wish to lead a class discussion on one of the topics listed in the text. For example, for neighborhood safety problems, the class might discuss solutions ranging from an increase in law-enforcement officers to civilian safety watches to curfews for teenagers. As students identify the advantages and disadvantages of each solution, write key points on the chalkboard.

Another prewriting technique students can use to identify problems and possible solutions is interviewing. Point out, for example, that the writer of Draft 2 (page 208) refers to a class poll.

Finally, stress that since problem-solution writing is a form of persuasion, students need to support the solution they recommend with convincing evidence. If necessary, give students some concrete examples of the distinction made in the sidebar box between fact and opinion. For example:

Fact: The Golden Gate Bridge links San Francisco with the southern tip of Marin County.
Opinion: The Golden Gate is one of the most graceful suspension bridges in the world.

El borrador

Tell students that their chief goal at this point should be to get their ideas flowing. Assure writers that they need not worry now about grammar, punctuation, and spelling. They will have the opportunity to correct mistakes in mechanics later, in the evaluating and revising stage.

You might want to suggest that students use a computer to draft their essays, since this may enable them to get their thoughts down faster. They can easily adjust or expand ideas as they input them. Tell them to choose a title for each draft they create and to save the drafts separately on disk so that nothing is lost.

Evaluación y revisión

Suggest that peer readers not make any comments until they have read the entire draft. Tell them to feel free to go beyond the questions listed in the text and to make sure that their suggestions are as specific as possible. The guidelines for evaluation and revision on page 207 can be used whether students work in pairs or independently.

When students have finished their first drafts, ask them to examine carefully the pair of models in the text (pages 207–208). Students may work independently, or you may wish to devote some time in a class session to analyzing and discussing this material. If you choose to have students work in class, call on volunteers to read the model drafts aloud. Then call on volunteers to comment on each draft. Make sure that students understand the reasons for the writing evaluations given in the text. For example, the third sentence of Draft 1 repeats the first sentence. The writer of Draft 2 captures the reader's interest by using a specific quotation and setting it in context. Ask students to suggest some alternative techniques for starting this essay with an attention-grabbing introduction.

Keep in mind that students may need help in applying their notes and making workable alterations of their first drafts. On a purely mechanical level, for example, some writers may need a guided introduction to the basic proofreading symbols for insertion, deletion, and transposition. See the MANUAL DE COMUNICACIÓN (page 325).

Corrección de pruebas

Emphasize that proofreading or editing adds to the clarity, correctness, and effective presentation of an essay or story. Familiarity with the conventions of language and writing—spelling, punctuation, grammar, usage, capitalization, paragraphing, syllabification, accuracy of citations and graphics, and proper manuscript form—is an important part of being a good writer.

Before they begin this stage, some students may need a guided review of the proofreading symbols used for editing and correcting errors in spelling and mechanics. Go over the list of symbols given in the MANUAL DE COMUNICACIÓN (page 325). Then have pairs exchange papers and proofread each other's writing. You may wish to circulate through the class, offering help when needed.

Publicación

In addition to the sharing opportunities mentioned in the text, suggest that students interested in the same or similar problems organize a round-table discussion. Give students some guidance on procedure: For example, have each group appoint a moderator, and tell the group to agree in advance on an agenda of topics and on a time limit for each panelist's presentation.

Another publication option might be to have a student panel orally present their solutions to several problems with a panel of older students as the audience. The older students can then comment on each solution's validity from the vantage point of more experience.

Reflexión

Guide students to recognize that real-life problems usually resist "quick fixes," but that progress can be made when solutions that are fair and practical are identified. Since the best solutions often involve some sort of compromise, persuasion plays a vital role in the problem-solving process.

Reteaching

Students having difficulty evaluating and revising may work in groups to read their essays aloud. Encourage readers to pause at the end of each sentence or paragraph to allow time for questions or suggestions.

Closure

Ask students to explain the difference between a report of information and a problem-solution essay.

Assessment Tools

As students work through the writing process, share the following assessment criteria with them, so they may use them in self- and peer evaluations.

Assessment Criteria

1   2   3   4   5   6
(needs   (superior)
improvement)

Content

- Introduction captures reader's interest.
- Problem is presented clearly, and its extent and importance are shown.
- Possible solutions are presented, together with their strengths and weaknesses.
- The best solution is identified and then supported with facts, reasons, examples, expert opinions, or other evidence.
- Writer restates the best solution in a strong conclusion.

Language Conventions
- Grammar and usage are standard.
- Paragraphs are indented properly.
- Words are spelled correctly.
- Quotation marks are used correctly.

Overall Rating: _____

Enrichment

Art Connection
Work with students to design posters on the theme of *La convivencia*. Suggest that posters might advertise a neighborhood block party or street fair, or they might serve as announcements for a pan-Latino festival in the community. Possible attractions are parades, music, dancing, craft exhibits, and food stalls. Arrange to exhibit students' posters.

Taller de oraciones (page 209)

Una norma para poder leer
(A Rule to Help in Reading)

This is the first of two workshops focusing on punctuation. The exercise provides a history of punctuation and ties in with the selection by Don Juan Manuel in its medieval subject matter. The workshop should help students discover that punctuation arose to fill a specific need.

The first exercise reveals that much of our current punctuation was borrowed from Gregorian chants. Reading aloud was not a common practice in medieval times, but it was a common task for monks who sang the chants. As a result, singers of Gregorian chants developed punctuation for pauses and intonation. Our modern question mark was a horizontal mark indicating a rising tone. The practice of running words together, rather than separating them, posed a special problem for readers whose Latin vocabulary was not extensive. Other difficulties that students may point out include lack of lowercase letters, lack of periods, and lack of commas.

The second example shows the chronological development of punctuation as a way of addressing these problems. The example used is an old Roman saying intrinsic to the development of writing. In the fourth paragraph, students are asked to edit the monk's eulogy. Students may then turn their attention to punctuation in their own writing.

In the INTÉNTALO TÚ, students are asked to look at more complex punctuation conventions: punctuation in the *acotaciones*. They have studied stage directions in the ELEMENTOS DE LITERATURA on drama and now have an opportunity to construct their own *acotaciones*. You may want to discuss the use of the parenthesis in prose and the placement of the period with a parenthesis: inside if the statement is an independent sentence and outside if the parenthetical statement is part of a sentence.

Bibliography:
Goodman, Yetta, and Carolyn Burke. *Reading Strategies: Focus on Comprehension* (Richard C. Owen Publishers, New York, 1980).

Collection 6: EL PAISAJE DE LA AMISTAD

Collection Overview

The theme *El paisaje de la amistad* ("A Landscape of Friendship") comes from the concept that friendships can arise from unusual circumstances and, in the realm of literature, need not be exclusive to humans. The selections, which comprise three short poems and a biographical sketch, present friendships between a tree and a bird, a book and a child, a sister and a brother, and a young child and her grandmother.

The collection begins with "La canción del árbol" ("The Song of the Tree") by the contemporary Spanish poet Ana María Fagundo. The poem's language, rhythm, and rhyme will be easily accessible to your students. Many readers will be moved by the haunting sadness of Fagundo's lyric.

The selection that follows, "El ruego del libro" ("The Request of the Book"), offers several points of comparison and contrast with the first: for example, in structure, tone, theme, and the prominent use of personification. In this beautiful lyric, a book speaks to a child, promising a relationship full of wonders and secrets. Chilean poet Gabriela Mistral won the Nobel Prize for literature in 1945.

The well-known African American poet Maya Angelou has written a series of autobiographical books and five collections of poetry. The selection in the textbook is an excerpt from *Yo sé por qué canta el pájaro enjaulado* (Spanish translation of *I Know Why the Caged Bird Sings*). In this passage, Angelou captures the essence of her older brother, Bailey, whom she adored. This selection is an excellent model of biographical writing to prepare students for the assignment to write a *semblanza* in TALLER DEL ESCRITOR.

The final reading in this collection, under the heading A LEER POR TU CUENTA, is "Las manos de la abuela" ("The Hands of Grandmother") by Spanish poet Cristina Lacasa, which presents another angle on the theme of friendship. The poem's speaker recalls how during her childhood she feared the wind's unfriendly hands scraping around the walls of the house. She then vividly remembers the loving, comforting hands of her grandmother, who would come and soothe her.

Throughout the collection, questions, exercises, and activities give students a wide range of opportunities to respond to the literature, both analytically and creatively. In ELEMENTOS DE LITERATURA: POESÍA II, a feature on *figuras retóricas* (simile, metaphor, personification, symbol, and hyperbole) complements the earlier discussion in Collection 4 of sound devices and imagery in poetry (see page 161). Each figure of speech is clearly defined and illustrated. You may wish to encourage your students to find additional examples of these *figuras retóricas* in the collection's three lyric poems.

The integration of materials within the collection also extends to the opening assignments in OPCIONES: PREPARA TU PORTAFOLIO, which are designed to prepare students progressively for the assignment in TALLER DEL ESCRITOR to write a first-hand biographical sketch. This assignment is especially appropriate to the collection theme of friendship, since many of your students may select a classmate, best friend, or family member as their subject. Further activities in OPCIONES challenge students to explore themes and ideas in a variety of modes, such as creating a collage or speaking and listening. In TALLER DE ORACIONES, students learn how to recognize and correctly punctuate run-on sentences.

Introducing the Collection

Encourage students to explore some of the themes of this collection by presenting them with a choice of opening activities. Possibilities include the following:

1. Have each student interview a classmate on the nature of friendship. Tell students to make a list of at least four questions in advance, such as "What qualities do you look for in a friend?" or "How do friends make a difference in your life?" Students should be encouraged to take notes on their partners' responses. After five minutes of questions, have students switch roles, with the interviewer becoming the interviewee.
2. Write the word *amistad* on the chalkboard. Then have students form word associations and call them out so you can write these terms on the board in a cluster. Call on volunteers to suggest where lines can be drawn to connect the terms to illustrate similarities and relationships.
3. Write the collection theme on the chalkboard: *El paisaje de la amistad*. Guide students to recognize that this phrase is a metaphor. (If necessary, preview the definition of metaphor in ELEMENTOS DE LITERATURA: See page 222). Ask students to suggest what kinds of people or objects they would expect to find in a "landscape of friendship."

La canción del árbol
(The Song of the Tree)

Ana María Fagundo   **page 213**

Into the Selection

Summary
A tree laments the departure of its beloved friend, the nightingale. Without the beauty and inspiration of the bird's song, the tree's branches wither. No grass grows around the tree's base, and it cannot feel the caress of the breeze on its foliage. It feels lonely and bereft.

Antes de leer   (page 212)

Punto de partida

Los amigos nos ayudan a crecer
(Friends Help Us Grow)
Since the nightingale is seen (or more often, heard) in Europe, Asia, and Africa rather than in North America, you may wish to share some information about it with your students. Nightingales are small birds related to thrushes, chats, and robins. They have a wingspan of about ten inches and are colored a warm reddish-brown. Nightingales are migratory, traveling up to 3,500 miles from northern Europe to spend the winter in the warmer climates of Africa and the Middle East. Celebrated for their beautiful songs, they are active at night; in fact, the first word in their scientific name (*Luscinia megarhynchos*) refers to their popular image as "heralds of dawn." Because of their singing ability, nightingales have been celebrated in mythology and poetry for thousands of years. For example, the nightingale inspired one of the most famous lyric poems in the English language, John Keats's "Ode to a Nightingale." In several popular folk legends, the nightingale was associated with tragedy as well as ecstasy, for it was said to die from its own love of music.

El árbol de la amistad (Friendship Tree)

Suggest that on the branches of their friendship tree, students write the names of groups of friends whom they think of together or whom they see on the same occasions or in the same locations.

Diálogo con el texto

You may wish to point out that Fagundo often uses *rima asonante o parcial* in the poem. If necessary, suggest that students review the discussion of rhyme and rhythm in ELEMENTOS DE LITERATURA: POESÍA I (see Collection 4, page 161).

Through the Selection

Diario del lector   (page 214)
The sample marginal comments exemplify several reading skills in practice: questioning, making inferences, summarizing, and identifying a significant detail or pattern. You may wish to extend

the activity by calling on volunteers to offer additional annotations.

Aduéñate de estas palabras
alentar (214) amapola (214)
marchita (214)

Techniques for Handling the Reading
Most of your students will find this short poem very accessible. Point out that the poem's title signals the central personification, in which the tree is presented as a person lamenting the sudden departure of a friend. If you wish, have students preview the discussion of personification in ELEMENTOS DE LITERATURA: POESÍA II (page 222).

Reading the lyric aloud will give students a better appreciation of the poet's effective use of repetition, parallelism, and sound effects. Be sure that students notice, for example, how the repetition of lines in the first and third stanzas contributes to the melancholy tone.

Crea significados (page 215)

Repaso del texto
Students should list the following effects: the tree's branches wither; no grass grows around the tree's base; the breeze no longer caresses the tree's foliage; the poppies no longer sing of love.

Primeras impresiones
1. **¿Cómo te imaginas el árbol? ¿Qué clase de árbol es?** Students' answers will vary. From the description of the tree's specific parts such as the top, the branches, the base, the foliage, and the sap, students may infer that the tree is tall, well-proportioned, and deciduous: Perhaps it is a birch or a maple.

Interpretaciones del texto
2. **Describe los sentimientos del árbol hacia el ruiseñor.** Students' answers may vary. The tree's feelings for the nightingale may be described as tender and admiring. The tree loves the nightingale's beautiful song and enjoys providing the bird with a home.
3. **¿En qué época del año crees que el árbol canta su canción? ¿Por qué?** Although students' answers may vary, they should recognize that the description of the tree's withering branches hints at autumn as the time of year. The departure of the nightingale (possibly because of its need to migrate to a warmer climate for the winter) and the fact that the grass no longer grows also support this inference.

Preguntas al texto
4. **¿Por qué crees que se fue el ruiseñor? ¿Crees que volverá? ¿Por qué?** Since nightingales are migratory, the bird may have left in the autumn to spend the winter in a warmer climate. It is therefore quite possible that the nightingale will return in the spring.

Beyond the Selection

Opciones: Prepara tu portafolio (page 216)

Cuaderno del escritor
1. *Compilación de ideas para una semblanza* (Collecting Ideas for a Firsthand Biography)
Encourage students to list as many sensory details as they can think of when they make their notes. For example, draw attention to the mention of *pelo negro rizado* and *camisetas de color púrpura chillón* in the sample notes. Ask students to suggest other vivid details that the student writer might have listed, such as Dorotea's favorite foods or clothing fabrics.

Redacción
2. *Haz que el ruiseñor regrese* (Bring Back the Nightingale)
Assure students that their poems need not rhyme. Suggest that since nightingales are migratory, the setting for a poem about the bird's return might be springtime.

Arte
3. *Conserva tus recuerdos* (Save Your Memories)
Encourage students to give their collage a title in order to convey an overall theme or message. Students might use the title of Collection 6, *El paisaje de la amistad,* as a model for experimenting with metaphorical titles.

El ruego del libro
(The Request of the Book)

Gabriela Mistral

page 218

Into the Selection

Summary
A book speaks to a girl, professing its friendship for her. In return, it asks only that the girl treat it with tender care. The book's knowledge may be slight, but it can offer the child a vision of new worlds and can unleash the power of her imagination. In return, the book wants only a little bit of the child's love.

Antes de leer (page 217)

Punto de partida

El poder de los libros (The Power of Books)
You may want to tell students that because of the expansion of technology in the "information age," essayists and commentators have seriously debated the "end of books." Ask students to describe some of the advantages of using books, as opposed to getting information or entertainment from other media.

Comparte tus ideas
You might recommend that students think of a specific story that they have read and also seen on film or television. You could also suggest that pairs discuss how well particular types of communication (such as poetry) are suited to different media such as print or film.

Elementos de literatura

Tono (Tone)
To check on students' comprehension of tone, ask them to suggest adjectives that describe the tone of "La canción del árbol" by Ana María Fagundo (page 213). Responses might include the following: *triste, nostálgico, afligido, arrepentido, lastimero.*

Through the Selection

Aduéñate de estas palabras
recobrar (219)
liviano (219)

Techniques for Handling the Reading
As with most verse selections, an oral reading of this poem will enable students to appreciate elements such as stanza form, rhyme, rhythm, sound effects, tone, and theme more fully. A recording of the selection is available on audiocassette. You might also call on volunteers to read a stanza each. Encourage students to try to express the meaning of the lines through changes in their volume, rate, and pitch. At the end of each stanza, you may wish to pause so that students can ask questions or offer comments.

Crea significados (page 220)

Primeras impresiones

1. **¿Qué clase de personalidad parece tener el libro?** Students' answers may vary. In general, they may describe the book's personality as friendly, tender, and modest.

Interpretaciones del texto

2. **¿Dónde crees que tiene lugar la charla del libro con la niña?** Students may suggest that the speech takes place in a school or library, since the girl seems to be using the book in the same place on a regular basis. This suggestion might be supported by the book's mention of *labor* (line 6).
3. **¿Qué recompensas ofrece el libro a la niña?** The book offers the girl rewards such as knowledge of nature, history, and religion, as well as the pleasures of the imagination.
4. **¿Cuál es el *tono* del poema: despreocupado, cómico, serio, amistoso?** Students' answers will vary. Many readers will describe the tone as serious and dignified.
5. **En la sexta estrofa, el libro le dice a la niña que su conocimiento es liviano y que le puede enseñar el mundo. ¿Qué quiere decir el libro con esto?** The book

74 EL PAISAJE DE LA AMISTAD

modestly refrains from setting itself up as a final authority. It asserts, however, that it has the power to enlarge the girl's knowledge and imaginative vision. Even one book can broaden a reader's horizons.

6. **¿Es el libro del poema un libro en específico, o es una voz que habla por muchos libros? Explica tu repuesta.** The voice in the poem may be speaking for many books because of the variety of subjects mentioned in the seventh and eighth stanzas.

Conexiones con el texto

7. **Si pudieras llevarte un solo libro a una isla desierta, ¿cuál elegirías y por qué?** Students' responses will vary. Encourage them to support their opinions with reasons and specific references to the books they select.

Más allá del texto

8. **¿Has oído alguna vez la frase «más puede la pluma que la espada»? ¿Se te ocurre algún ejemplo, de la historia o de tu propia experiencia, en el que un libro haya influido de manera importante en la gente?** Students' answers will vary. One landmark book that might be included in the discussion is *On the Origin of Species (El origen de las especies)* (1859) by Charles Darwin. For more than a century, Darwin's theory of evolution has aroused intellectual controversy in religious and scientific circles.

9. **En «The Fun They Had», un cuento futurista de Isaac Asimov, los niños aprenden con computadoras en vez de con libros. Las computadoras funcionan como maestros y los niños aprenden por su cuenta en vez de en un aula con otros compañeros. Cuando uno de los personajes encuentra un libro, los otros imaginan con tristeza lo mucho que los niños se debían haber divertido en el pasado. Comenta las ventajas y las desventajas de un mundo sin maestros humanos ni libros.** Students' answers will vary. In general, they may observe that a teacherless and bookless environment would have the disadvantage of being without social contact, role models, and friendship—even though such an environment might have the advantage of being more efficient or productive.

Beyond the Selection

Opciones:
Prepara tu portafolio (page 221)

Cuaderno del escritor

1. Compilación de ideas para una semblanza
Because direct quotations can bring a biographical sketch to life, stress the importance for this activity of noting the friend's exact words. Students can interview their friends to get quotations. Remind writers that the quotations they list don't have to be profound, but the words should reveal something important about the speaker's personality. Point out, for instance, that Laura's words in the sample notes show her qualities of spirit and energy.

Redacción

2. Diálogo con el libro
(Dialogue with the Book)
Suggest that students prewrite by considering clues offered by the text of the poem: for example, the reference to making marks in the book (stanza 3) or the mention of childish stories and gossip (stanza 5).

Arte

3. Juzgar un libro por su portada
(Judging a Book by Its Cover)
Model this activity by passing around some book jackets in class. Go over the separate parts of each jacket: for example, book title, art, blurb, and critical comments.

Elementos de literatura (page 222)

Poesía II: Figuras retóricas y de estilo
(Poetry II: Figurative Language and Style)

This discussion of *figuras retóricas* complements the earlier treatment of poetic sound effects and imagery that appeared in Collection 4 (see page 161). To check that students have mastered the definitions of simile, metaphor, and personification, call on volunteers to locate an example of each device in the first four lines of "Las manos de la abuela" by Cristina Lacasa (page 231). Possible responses are as follows:

  simile: *como un alma en pena* (line 4)
  metaphor: *las tejas, tímidas alas de arcilla* (line 2)
  personification: *el viento con sus manos largas, ariscas* (line 1)

In Lacasa's poem, the wind might symbolize danger, fear, or pain, while the grandmother's hands might symbolize tenderness, reassurance, gentleness, or love.

You can also use the quiz below to test students' comprehension of the material in ELEMENTOS DE LITERATURA.

1. **¿Son las figuras retóricas exclusivas de la poesía?** (No, they can appear in prose as well.)
2. **¿Qué diferencia hay entre un símil y una metáfora?** (A simile uses an explicit word of comparison such as *como* or *igual*.)
3. **¿En qué consiste la personificación?** (It gives human feelings or thoughts to an object or animal.)
4. **¿Puede un símbolo tener más de una interpretación?** (yes)
5. **¿Qué efectos puede crear una hipérbole?** (irony, humor)

de Yo sé por qué canta el pájaro enjaulado
(*from* I Know Why the Caged Bird Sings)

Maya Angelou — page 224

Into the Selection

Summary

In this excerpt from her autobiographical memoir, Angelou tells three anecdotes to explain why her older brother, Bailey, was the greatest person in her childhood world. She first recalls how Bailey loyally defended her when their elders made unkind comments about her features. Next, she describes Bailey's mischievous theft of two pickles from Uncle Willie's store. Finally, Angelou gives a description of Bailey's energy and imagination as the children play their after-school games. Summing up Bailey's significance, Angelou writes that her handsome brother was her "Kingdom Come," for he served as the embodiment of hope for her when she was a lonely, self-conscious youngster.

Antes de leer (page 224)

Punto de partida

«La persona más admirable»
("The Greatest Person")
After having read the details in this description, do students feel they know someone like Bailey? Ask students to predict how Bailey might behave in certain specific situations—such as waiting to get a test back in school or discovering that he is the victim of a practical joke.

Toma nota

You may wish to prescribe a definite time limit, such as five or seven minutes, for students' writing. Stress that the important goal is for students to get their thoughts flowing. Tell them not to worry about spelling, punctuation, and mechanics. If you wish, allow writers to use modified outline form or lists.

Telón de fondo

Maya Angelou published her first volume of autobiography (*I Know Why the Caged Bird Sings*) in 1970. The title of this work came from a poem titled "Sympathy" by the African American writer Paul Laurence Dunbar (1872–1906), which appears in Spanish translation on page 229 of the textbook. Angelou's subsequent memoirs include *Gather Together in My Name* (1974), *Singin' and Swingin' and Gettin' Merry Like Christmas* (1976), and *The Heart of a Woman* (1981).

Angelou's collected poems are available in paperback (Bantam Books, New York, 1986), as is the poem she composed and recited for the 1993 presidential inauguration, *On the Pulse of Morning* (Random House, New York, 1993). Angelou has also published a book of short essays titled *Wouldn't Take Nothing for My Journey Now* (Random House, New York, 1993).

Estrategias para leer

Hacer deducciones (Making Inferences)
Remind students that the technique of *caracterización indirecta* requires readers to make inferences about characters' personalities (see ELEMENTOS DE LITERATURA, page 110). Evidence for such inferences often includes details of physical appearance, characters' direct speech or thoughts, and other characters' remarks and actions. You may want to recommend that students preview the feature on making inferences in ESTRATEGIAS PARA LEER (see page 230).

Through the Selection

Aduéñate de estas palabras

proponer (226)	afrentosa (226)
afable (226)	maña (226)
alabar (226)	substraer (226)
facción (226)	integridad (227)
vestigio (226)	infalible (227)

Techniques for Handling the Reading

This selection should present no particular problems for students, although you may want to remind them to consult the footnotes and the glossary for the meanings of any unfamiliar words. Many members of your class will probably identify with Bailey or with the narrator, depending on their personalities or their experiences with siblings. Be sure to allow time for students to give their reactions to the two personalities that Angelou characterizes so vividly in this piece: Bailey and the young Angelou herself. Because the writing assignment in TALLER DEL ESCRITOR for this collection is a biographical sketch or profile (see page 232), you will also want to encourage students to notice the techniques Angelou uses to create such a lifelike portrait of her brother. Tell students to look for specific examples of the following: sensory images in the description of Bailey's physical appearance and movements; direct quotations that reveal Bailey's personality traits; anecdotes told in chronological order; *figuras retóricas* such as simile or metaphor; and a summary of Bailey's significance for the writer.

Crea significados (page 228)

Repaso del texto

a. **¿Por qué era rara la ocasión en la que se castigaba a Bailey?** Bailey was rarely punished because he was the family's pride and joy.

b. **¿Qué roba Bailey de la tienda de su tío Willie?** Bailey stole two fat pickles from the store.

c. **Nombra uno o más de los juegos infantiles que Angelou menciona.** The games are *el escondite* (hide-and-seek), *seguir a la madre* (follow-the-leader), and *el látigo* (crack-the-whip).

d. **De acuerdo con Angelou, ¿cuál es la necesidad «que debe satisfacerse, para que haya esperanza, esperanza de integridad...»?** The need is described as *la infalible necesidad de un Dios inconmovible*.

Primeras impresiones

1. **¿Te gustaría conocer a Bailey? ¿Por qué?** Students' answers will vary. Most students will probably say that they would like to meet Bailey because of his cheerful, outgoing, fun-loving personality.

Interpretaciones del texto

2. **¿Cuál consideras que es la característica más destacada de Bailey?** Students' opinions will vary. Many readers will single out qualities such as cheerfulness, gregariousness, and capacity to enjoy life.

3. **¿De qué manera demuestra Bailey que tiene buen corazón, a pesar de que su comportamiento sea a veces «escandaloso»?** Students' answers will vary. In general, Bailey shows that his heart is in the right place when he uses humor to defend his sister from her critics among the adults. Bailey is also able to laugh at himself, and he is a natural leader who can create interesting and daring things for the other children to do.

4. **Angelou llama a Bailey su «Reino de Dios en la Tierra»; ¿qué quiere decir**

con esto? By calling Bailey her *Reino de Dios en la Tierra,* Angelou means that Bailey gave her hope and provided her with an invaluable role model.

5. **De tu lectura de las descripciones que Angelou hace de Bailey, ¿qué *deducciones* puedes hacer sobre el carácter de Angelou? ¿Es tímida, atrevida, maleducada, traviesa? Explica tu opinión en una o dos oraciones.** Students' answers will vary. In general, they may infer that Angelou felt shy and awkward and lacked confidence when she was a child.

Conexiones con el texto

6. **¿Crees que Angelou está celosa de Bailey? ¿Por qué?** Students' answers will vary. In general, Angelou praises her brother's handsomeness, his agility, and his capacity for avoiding punishment. She offers no hint that she was jealous of him during their childhood. Students may suggest, however, that she might have envied Bailey somewhat, especially for his good looks and popularity.

Preguntas al texto

7. **¿Por qué una niña solitaria como Maya Angelou podría encontrar consuelo en «la infalible necesidad de un Dios inconmovible»?** Students' answers will vary. In general, they may observe that all lonely children need some kind of consolation, which may be offered by religious belief.

Beyond the Selection

Opciones:
Prepara tu portafolio   (page 229)

Cuaderno del escritor

1. Compilación de ideas para una semblanza
Recommend that students use chronological order when they write about their incident. If you wish, have students work in pairs or small groups for this activity. When they finish writing, they can ask peers for responses and comments.

Redacción

2. Bailey habla (Bailey Speaks)
Tell students that Bailey's outlook on the incident should be consistent with the character portrait that Angelou gives in the selection. Incidents might reflect Bailey's love and support of his sister, his need to be with other people, his cheerful outlook, and his mischievous and fun-loving nature.

Hablar y escuchar

3. El origen del título
(The Origin of the Title)
Suggest to students that by referring to a well-known poem, an author can evoke mood, meaning, and setting, as well as broaden the implications of both works.

Estrategias para leer   (page 230)

Los detalles te ayudarán a hacer deducciones
(Details Help You Make Inferences)

Stress that inferences are *educated* guesses: They are most likely to be valid when they are based on specific evidence. Remind students that they use the critical thinking skill of making inferences when they try to identify the theme or message of a short story or poem.

A leer por tu cuenta
Las manos de la abuela
(The Hands of Grandmother)

Cristina Lacasa   page 231

Summary
The speaker in this brief poem recalls her sensations of loneliness and apprehension when she heard the sound of the wind during her childhood. She would bless herself three times in the night in an attempt to calm her troubled spirit. Then her grandmother would come to soothe her with the gentle touch of her hands.

Aduéñate de estas palabras

rústica (231)   sellar (231)   aplacar (231)

Techniques for Handling the Reading

In contrast to the other two poems in this collection, "Las manos de la abuela" is written in *verso libre* (free verse), with no regular rhythm or rhyme scheme. Nevertheless, the poem is extremely musical. Encourage students to read the selection aloud so they can appreciate Lacasa's use of sound effects and *figuras retóricas*. Then invite them to discuss how the poem relates to the collection theme, *El paisaje de la amistad*.

Taller del escritor   (page 232)

La descripción/Semblanza
(Firsthand Biography)

Presenting the Workshop

For an overview of the writing process, see the MANUAL DE COMUNICACIÓN (page 324). You may wish to devote all or part of a class session to reviewing the major aspects of each stage of the process.

Before students get started, encourage them to suggest and comment on some springboards for a firsthand biography. You may want to urge them to study Maya Angelou's portrait of Bailey with special care, since in many ways it is an excellent model for this assignment.

Point out, for example, that just as Angelou writes about a person she knew extremely well and admired (her older brother), students should select someone well known to them as the subject of their biography. You may also wish to note that Angelou approached her subject with a definite point of view: She loved and admired Bailey, feeling that he brought out the best in her.

Next, you may wish to remind students that Angelou uses sensory images to describe her subject's physical appearance. (See especially the first paragraph of the excerpt.) She structures her biographical sketch as a series of three brief anecdotes told in chronological order. Each story brings out an important feature of Bailey's personality: loyalty, mischievousness, and cheerful enthusiasm for games.

Angelou also uses direct, revealing quotations to characterize Bailey. When we read his exact words, we gain an even more vivid picture of him. Finally, Angelou sums up Bailey's significance for her in a personal, eloquent conclusion. To emphasize the importance of an effective conclusion in this type of writing, suggest that students reread the last paragraph of Angelou's biographical sketch.

Antes de escribir

In addition to the prewriting strategies discussed in the text, point out to students that they may often be able to interview their subject to acquire fresh impressions of his or her appearance or personality and write down exact quotations. Recommend that students write a list of questions before an interview. Remind them that "how" and "why" questions usually elicit more information than questions that can be answered simply "yes" or "no." If possible, students should record their interviews on tape. Urge them to write detailed notes about the interview as soon as possible after completing it.

El borrador

If students use a computer to draft their biographies, make sure that they save each successive draft on disk so that nothing will be lost.

You may wish to devote some class time to discussing how students can use figurative language effectively in their firsthand biographies. Call on volunteers to read aloud the examples of *figuras retóricas* given in the text on page 234. Then ask students to suggest their own examples of similes, metaphors, and personifications. Draw students' attention to Maya Angelou's use of similes in her descriptions of Bailey: for example, *con voz tan agradable como la grasa de cordero fría* (page 226), *olía como un barril de vinagre o como un ángel avinagrado* (page 226), or *salía girando como una peonza* (page 227).

Evaluación y revisión

When students have finished their first drafts, ask them to examine carefully the pair of models in the text (pages 235–236). Students may work independently, or you may wish to devote some time in a class session to analyzing and discussing this material. If you choose to have students work in class, call on volunteers to read the model drafts aloud. Then call on volunteers to comment on each draft. Make sure that students understand the reasons for the writing evaluations given in the text. Then encourage pairs to exchange feedback. The guidelines for evaluation and revision on page 235 can be used whether students work in pairs or independently.

Bear in mind that students may need help in applying their notes and making workable alterations of their first drafts. On a purely mechanical level, for example, some writers may need a guided introduction to the basic proofreading symbols for insertion, deletion, and transposition. See the MANUAL DE COMUNICACIÓN (page 325).

Corrección de pruebas

Emphasize the importance of refining and proofreading written work before submitting it for publication. Proofreading or editing adds to the clarity, correctness, and presentation of an essay or story. Familiarity with the conventions of language and writing—spelling, punctuation, grammar, usage, capitalization, paragraphing, syllabification, accuracy of citations and graphics, and proper manuscript form—is an important part of being an effective writer.

Before they begin this stage, some students may need a guided review of the proofreading symbols used for editing and correcting errors in spelling and mechanics. Go over the list of symbols given in the MANUAL DE COMUNICACIÓN (page 325). Then have partners exchange papers and proofread each other's writing. You may wish to circulate through the class, offering help when needed.

Publicación

In addition to the sharing opportunities mentioned in the text, suggest that students might like to illustrate their biographies with photographs or sketches. They can then post the finished product on the class bulletin board.

Reflexión

Guide students to recognize that time set aside for reflection on the assignment is an investment in the growth of their writing skills. For example, if students had difficulty with the prewriting phase (trying to find a suitable subject for the biography), they might want to get together in small groups to brainstorm topics for the next writing assignment. If they found that freewriting on the computer helped their ideas to flow more freely, they might want to use the computer regularly for writing assignments.

Reteaching

Students having difficulty evaluating and revising may work in groups to read their essays aloud. Encourage writers to focus on telling about their subjects in chronological order.

Closure

Ask students to explain the difference between autobiography and biography.

Assessment Tools

As students work through the writing process, share the following assessment criteria with them so they may use them in self- and peer evaluations.

Assessment Criteria

1　　　2　　　3　　　4　　　5　　　6
(needs　　　　　　　　　　　　(superior)
improvement)

Content

- Introduction captures reader's interest.
- Necessary background is supplied.
- Details are presented in a logical order.
- Vivid language, including sensory images and figures of speech, brings the subject to life.
- A strong conclusion sums up the subject's significance for the writer.

Language Conventions

- Grammar and usage are standard.
- Paragraphs are indented properly.
- Words are spelled correctly.
- Quotation marks are used correctly.

Overall Rating: _____

Enrichment

Media Connection

Work with students to design a photo essay on a "Person of the Year." Begin by dividing the class into small groups that will function as search committees. Have each group draw up a list of three or four candidates for "Person of the Year." Then guide students to reach a consensus on the honoree. They can next work to design a photo essay that will profile this person and his or her achievements through photos and brief captions. After students have completed this activity, arrange for them to exhibit their work in a suitable location.

Taller de oraciones (page 237)

Oraciones sin principio ni fin
(Sentences Without Beginning or End)

This workshop, focusing on run-on sentences, is a follow-up to the previous workshop on punctuation. By acting as editors, students may become aware of run-on sentences that appear in their own writing and learn how to punctuate them correctly.

In the first exercise, students are asked to edit a paragraph of a *semblanza* similar to the one they have written for the TALLER DEL ESCRITOR. Have each pair of students share their solutions to the problems in the paragraph and compile a list of punctuation marks they used to resolve the problems. Point out original solutions, such as the use of a colon, semicolon, or exclamation points, if students suggest them.

Students can arrange the humorous message in the INTÉNTALO TÚ in a number of ways. The message is deliberately ambiguous. Some verb modifiers could belong to more than one sentence. The message could conceivably be addressed to a girl called Socorro. Finally, depending on the punctuation, the message could have been written by Gertrudis or it could be calling on Gertrudis for help. Ask students "¿Quién piensan que envió el mensaje: Gertrudis o la amiga que fue con ella al malecón?"

Suggested reading:

Osorio, José María, ed. "Los dos habladores," in *Mi segundo libro de teatro* (Editorial Everest, España, 1973).

In this humorous play, adapted from a work by Miguel de Cervantes, the author presents a character who talks incessantly. Her dialogue is riddled with run-on sentences and unrelated sentences that are strung together. Following the Spanish seventeenth-century literary premise of curing one evil by using the same evil as a remedy, the play introduces another talker who manages to outtalk the first. In the end, all the characters, male and female, turn out to be equally foolish.

Collection 7: TODOS SOMOS IGUALES

Collection Overview

In each of the three selections in this collection, similarities and contrasts between pairs of people, animals, or ideas play a prominent role. The theme *Todos somos iguales* ("We are all equal") is memorably presented in a prose fable and a lyric poem by José Martí; the same theme is handled with skillful subtlety by Jorge Luis Borges in a brief allegory. Throughout the collection, students will notice that although some characters in the literature may be "greater" by the worldly measures of social status and wealth, they have the same fears, flaws, hopes, and dreams as characters who are "smaller."

The collection opens with José Martí's folk tale "Los dos ruiseñores" ("The Two Nightingales"). Martí's story is a variant of Hans Christian Andersen's fairy tale "The Nightingale." A nightingale that sings for everyone from the emperor of China to the poor fishermen is replaced by a mechanical bird made of jewels and precious metals. When the mechanical bird breaks, the song of the true nightingale restores the dying emperor to health.

Martí's poem "Los dos príncipes" ("The Two Princes") also uses the technique of comparison and contrast to underline the theme of universal needs and values. The lyric presents a king and queen and a poor shepherd couple in an identical situation: Both sets of parents are grieving for a son who has died. Through the poem's title, the use of parallelism, and the choice of details, Martí strongly underlines the theme that we are all equal in certain fundamental ways, without regard to wealth or status.

The final selection is a precise, compact fable by Jorge Luis Borges. "Los dos reyes y los dos laberintos" ("The Two Kings and the Two Labyrinths") will challenge sixth-graders to interpret an allegory. A king tries to trap his enemy in an artfully constructed labyrinth, and for his deceit he is later abandoned in his foe's own labyrinth—the vast wasteland of the desert.

ELEMENTOS DE LITERATURA in this collection introduces students to the literary features of folk tales, fables, and legends. The opening assignments in OPCIONES: PREPARA TU PORTAFOLIO are designed to prepare students step by step for the assignment at the end of the collection: using methods of comparison and contrast to write an evaluation. This assignment synthesizes many of the skills covered in the collection as a whole. Further activities in OPCIONES challenge students to approach themes and ideas through a variety of modes, such as creative writing and science. Finally, in TALLER DE ORACIONES, students have an opportunity to learn how to use prepositional phrases in their own writing.

Introducing the Collection

To encourage students to explore aspects of the collection theme, give them a choice of opening activities. Possibilities include the following:

1. Write this phrase on the chalkboard: NECESIDADES HUMANAS. Then ask students to make a cluster diagram showing some of the ways in which all human beings share the same needs. You might start students off with a few words for their cluster, such as the following: *alimento, agua, aire, amor, belleza.*

2. Introduce students to the concept of the Venn diagram, a powerful analytical tool that they can use to chart similarities and differences. A Venn diagram is composed of two overlapping circles (see page 259). Similarities between two people, ideas, or objects are recorded within the overlapping area, while differences are written to the left and the right. Have students contribute

to the following Venn diagram on lions and tigers:

```
      LEONES              TIGRES
    ┌────────┐         ┌────────┐
   ╱  África  ╲       ╱   Asia   ╲
  │  viven en  │ grandes │ viven en │
  │  la llanura│ felinos │ la selva │
   ╲ sociales ╱ carnívoros ╲solitarios╱
    └────────┘         └────────┘
```

Then encourage students to create a Venn diagram comparing and contrasting what they are like now (likes, dislikes, friends, hobbies, family relationships) with what they were like two or three years ago.

3. It has been said that music is the international language, cutting across all cultural barriers and appealing to universal human feelings and needs. Ask students to discuss different kinds of music. Do they believe that the appeal of music is evidence for the idea *Todos somos iguales?*

Los dos ruiseñores
(The Two Nightingales)

José Martí — page 241

Into the Selection

Summary
The story is set at the imperial court in ancient China. The gallant emperor, admired by his people and fawned on by his mandarins, enjoys many fine possessions, such as a blue and white porcelain palace, gardens of dwarf orange trees, and a beautiful forest. But the chief treasure of his kingdom is a nightingale, whose lovely songs inspire the people.

Strangely, the emperor is ignorant of the nightingale's existence. When he hears of it, he sends his chief mandarin to find the bird. The mandarin, who is no more knowledgeable than the emperor, is led to the nightingale by a humble cook. The bird is persuaded to sing at the palace, where its music delights the emperor and the courtiers.

One day, however, the emperor receives a gift of an artificial nightingale from the emperor of Japan. The mechanical bird captures the spotlight, and the living nightingale disappears. After a year, though, a spring in the nightingale's mechanism snaps, and the bird stops singing. To the fury of the court's music master—a pompous, egotistical fool who has championed the artificial bird—the watchmaker sadly advises the emperor that the mechanical bird should sing no more than once a year.

Five years later, the emperor lies dying. As the mandarins vie in currying favor with his successor, Death comes by night to claim the ailing monarch. Suddenly, however, the sound of sweet music is heard through the window. The live nightingale, having heard of the emperor's condition, has returned to console him with a song of faith and hope. The bird's music is so powerful that it charms away Death, who leaves through the window.

The emperor, having finally learned his lesson, asks how he can repay the nightingale. The bird replies that the emperor's tears have been reward enough. The nightingale declines to live in the palace, saying that it must sing to the poor fishermen as well as the emperor; it will visit the ruler only by night. As the nightingale flies away through the window, the mandarins enter the room, surprised to find their emperor restored to health and vigor.

Antes de leer (page 240)

Punto de partida

Dos clases de ruiseñores
(Two Kinds of Nightingales)
Students may suggest that it is entirely possible for a machine to surpass a human being, at least

in some respects: for example, the speed at which a computer can perform calculations, the accuracy with which robots can work on an assembly line, and the efficiency with which dishwashers can handle huge loads. On the other hand, human beings have emotions, value systems, complex relationships, and free will empowering them to make choices—none of which are generally associated with machines.

Los humanos y las máquinas
(Humans and Machines)

You may wish to divide the class into small groups for this activity. Within each group, assign individual students such roles as Brainstormer, Recorder, Evaluator, and Presenter. Allow enough time for each group to share its results with the class as a whole.

Diálogo con el texto

This activity will be especially valuable for less proficient readers, since Martí's story is quite lengthy and the setting will probably be unfamiliar.

Estrategias para leer

Comparar y contrastar
(Comparing and Contrasting)

Remind students that they use comparison and contrast all the time in everyday life: for example, when they evaluate the taste of different foods, when they comment on the excitement of a sports event, or when they rate a new television program or movie. Comparison and contrast are almost inevitable whenever students make a judgment or give a review.

Elementos de literatura

Sátira (Satire)

Invite students to discuss contexts in which they have encountered satire: for example, newspaper and magazine cartoons, situation comedies on television, skits performed by drama clubs, and impressions or monologues performed by stand-up comedians. Remind the students that irony—which is frequently used in satire—is a contrast between what we assume to be true and what actually turns out to be true. You might have students recall the irony in "Una carta a Dios" by Gregorio López y Fuentes (page 51). Point out that irony may be intended to amuse an audience, or it may have a dark, even bitter tone when a satirist wants to stir up the audience's anger at human folly, vice, or corruption.

Through the Selection

Diario del lector (page 242)

The marginal annotations shown in the text exemplify several reading skills: questioning, making inferences, and drawing conclusions. If you feel that some of your students will benefit, you can extend this activity through another page or two of the text, modeling similar kinds of marginal annotations. You can pause at the end of each section, allowing enough time to monitor and discuss students' notes on an individual basis.

Aduéñate de estas palabras

galán (242)   desterrar (247)
resplandecer (246)   lívido (248)
bullicio (246)   son (248)
pomposo (246)   camposanto (248)

Techniques for Handling the Reading

Before students read this tale, have them preview the setting by looking at the illustrations in the text. You may want to supplement the students' impressions by passing around illustrations of ancient China, especially of the emperor's court. Point out the formality and elaborateness of costumes and hairstyles. Share with students the fact that Chinese emperors were absolute monarchs who were often regarded as divine by their subjects.

Because of this story's length, unfamiliar setting, and disparate contents (a folk tale with touches of whimsical satire), you may want to pair less proficient readers with more fluent ones. Suggest that partners stop at the end of each page to summarize the action and to ask and answer questions.

After students have read the story once, encourage interested readers to experiment with Reader's Theater techniques for some or all of the scenes.

Crea significados (page 251)

Repaso del texto

a. **¿A quién envía el emperador a buscar al ruiseñor?** The emperor sends his chief mandarin to find the nightingale.

b. **¿Quién envía al gran pájaro internacional y cuál es el aspecto de este pájaro?** The emperor of Japan sends the bird, wrapped in a package, to China. The mechanical bird's feathers are made of sapphires, diamonds, and rubies, and its tail is of gold and silver. It sings like a real nightingale when it is wound up.

c. **¿Por qué el maestro de música llama traidor al relojero?** The music master calls the watchmaker a traitor because the watchmaker is honest enough to tell the emperor an unpleasant truth. He says that the artificial nightingale's cylinders are worn and that it should be played only once a year.

d. **¿Por qué el ruiseñor solamente acude por la noche a cantar para el emperador?** The nightingale can come to the emperor only at night because it must sing to the fishermen along the seashore by day.

Primeras impresiones

1. **¿Qué tipo de música preferirías escuchar, la música metódica que produce el ruiseñor mecánico o la música espontánea producida por el ruiseñor viviente? Explica tu respuesta.** Students' answers will vary. Some students may say that they would prefer the spontaneous music produced by the living nightingale, because of the excitement of hearing an actual bird sing in natural surroundings. Other students, however, might say that listening to the artificial nightingale would not be all that different from hearing recorded music on an audiocassette or a compact disc.

Interpretaciones del texto

2. **¿Qué tiene de especial el ruiseñor vivo?** The living nightingale is special because its beautiful song gives such pleasure and inspiration to those who hear it.

3. **¿Por qué es tan importante que el ruiseñor vivo cante tanto a los pescadores como al emperador?** The fact that the nightingale makes no distinctions based on social status or wealth reflects the universal truth that the beauties of nature and music are available for everyone's enjoyment.

4. **¿Por qué el emperador quiere destrozar «en mil pedazos» al pájaro mecánico y qué rasgo de su personalidad revela este impulso?** The emperor wants to smash the mechanical bird when he finally realizes how superior the living nightingale is to the artificial one. This violent, ungracious impulse reveals that the emperor has a tendency to react to events in an excessively emotional way. The living nightingale dissuades the emperor, arguing that the mechanical bird served the emperor well while it could.

5. **Caracteriza al maestro de música; escoge tres palabras para describirlo. ¿Cómo lo *satiriza* el autor en la historia?** Students' words or phrases will vary but might include one or more of the following: *pomposo, necio, egocéntrico, vanidoso, pretencioso, estúpido, egoísta, orgulloso, mezquino*. The music master's vanity and pedantry are satirized through the description of his book in twenty-five volumes and through the account of his rage at the honest watchmaker.

6. **Describe a los mandarines. ¿Cuál es la actitud del narrador hacia ellos?** The mandarins are portrayed as oily courtiers who are not especially intelligent and who focus only on their own social position and advancement. They literally dance attendance on the emperor, but they cannot think for themselves; even the chief mandarin must be led to the nightingale by a humble cook. The narrator evidently has a satirical attitude toward the mandarins.

7. **¿Qué lección aprende el emperador del ruiseñor vivo? ¿Cómo sabemos que ha cambiado gracias al ruiseñor? Trata de encontrar el pasaje donde se revela cómo ha cambiado.** The emperor learns the lesson that it was a mistake to put his

trust in a mechanical object rather than a living being. He also learns a lesson in gratitude and compassion: The nightingale rescues him from death, even though he had earlier rejected the bird. We know that the emperor has changed, from the passage in which he thanks the nightingale profusely and asks how he can repay it.

8. **Encuentra el párrafo que describe a la Muerte cuando se marcha. ¿Por qué crees que el ruiseñor es capaz de convencer a la Muerte para que deje al emperador? Explica tu respuesta.** The paragraph that describes Death as he leaves the emperor's room begins with the words *Y la Muerte seguía mirando al emperador con sus ojos huecos y fríos...* (page 248). The nightingale's song about the cemetery is so beautiful that Death must go and see it. The passage also suggests that the beauty of music is more powerful than death itself.

Conexiones con el texto

9. **¿Te gustaría que el emperador de la historia gobernara tu país? ¿Por qué?** Students' answers will vary. Although the emperor is described at the beginning of the story as generous and brave, he is also portrayed as arbitrary and excessively emotional. The emperor's court is highly stratified and he surrounds himself with flatterers. Some students will say that they would not like to be ruled by such a monarch.

10. **Como muchos cuentos de hadas, esta historia tiene un tema universal que muchos tipos diferentes de personas pueden comprender. ¿Con qué parte de la historia te identificaste más, y por qué?** Students' answers will vary. Some readers will enjoy the satirical portrait of the courtiers, while others will focus on the lyrical descriptions of the nightingale's music. Many readers will especially like the last part of the folk tale, which shows how the emperor learns his lesson.

11. **¿Por qué crees que el autor escogió al ruiseñor como uno de los personajes principales de su historia?** Students' answers will vary. In general, students should point out that the nightingale's ability to sing so sweetly in real life is a critical story element. Another relevant fact about the nightingale for the theme of this tale is the striking contrast between its ordinary, even drab appearance and its marvelous music. This contrast is emphasized when the chief mandarin first sees the bird. The discrepancy between appearance and reality, in turn, underlies the contrast in the tale as a whole between the artificial bird and the living one. Nightingales, of course, are prominent in myth and oral tradition, as well as in literature, in many countries. For more background on their use as symbols, see the discussion in this Teacher's Manual (page 72) of Ana María Fagundo's poem "La canción del árbol" in Collection 6.

Beyond the Selection

Opciones:
Prepara tu portafolio (page 252)

Cuaderno del escritor

1. Compilación de ideas para una evaluación
(Collecting Ideas for an Evaluation)
If you wish, have students work in pairs for this activity. Suggest that students who have difficulty spotting further similarities and differences reread the selection and make a story map.

Investigación/Hablar y escuchar

2. ¿Máquinas frente a humanos?
(Machines Against Humans?)
You may wish to model this activity by holding a brief brainstorming session in which you invite the class as a whole to suggest benefits and drawbacks of computers. Call on volunteers for their suggestions, and create a chart on the chalkboard like the one below:

Ventajas
Computación rápida
Almacenamiento de información
Inconvenientes
Pérdida de puestos de trabajo
Amenaza a la intimidad del individuo

Redacción creativa/Ciencia

3. *Las máquinas inteligentes* (Smart Machines) Students might work in small groups to identify two or three leading characters for a narrative. They can then create a storyboard to outline a plot.

Lengua y literatura (page 253)

Semejanzas y diferencias de significado (Similarities and Differences in Meaning)

In this mini-lesson, students learn how synonyms may be used to avoid repetitive writing. They are asked to look at something they have already written, such as the firsthand biography they wrote for Collection 6. The theme of the lesson ties in with the theme emphasized throughout the collection: comparison and contrast. Students are asked to note both similarities and differences in meaning. As an additional activity, you may ask students to make a chart illustrating similarities and differences of synonyms such as *viejo, anciano, antiguo, mayor.*

Answers

1. Since the story is long, you can tell the students that the synonyms appear in the first two paragraphs. The words to be found vary in difficulty. They also illustrate Martí's skill in choosing words.

   serpiente – culebra
   remolón – perezoso
   trabajo – quehacer
   botella – frasco
   rojo – carmín
   penoso – triste
   rizo – tirabuzón
   bonito – hermoso
   amanecer – aurora

2. The first sentence is wrong because *antigua* is used only in reference to things. In the second sentence, *mayor* is wrong because it is used only for people. In the third sentence, *viejo* is wrong because it is not used to describe children. Other differences between these synonyms are as follows: *Viejo* can have a negative connotation when it refers to people. *Anciano* can be used only for elderly people. In reference to a person who is not extremely old, the proper and polite term is *una persona mayor. Mayor* can also be used to express the relationship of one person's age to another's.

Suggested reading:

Osorio, José María, ed. "La tierra de Jauja," in *Mi segundo libro de teatro* (Editorial Everest, España, 1973).

This delightful play about two rascals who steal a peasant's food includes numerous synonyms for the word *eat*. The synonyms are presented in parallel structures and their effect is comical.

Vocabulario (page 253)

Símbolos chinos (Symbols in Chinese)

Chinese characters are pictorial representations that have become abstract over time. Students are asked to represent words from "Los dos ruiseñores" through drawings. These drawings can be simple and may be composed of several images that together illustrate the meaning of a word. The drawings do not have to resemble Chinese characters. As a final exercise, students may try deciphering other students' drawings.

Elementos de literatura (page 254)

Cuentos populares, fábulas y leyendas (Folk Tales, Fables, and Legends)

Interested students can be encouraged to find more information about the Spanish fabulists mentioned in the text. Tomás de Iriarte y Oropesa (1750–1791) was born in Tenerife, in the Canary Islands. He spent most of his career as a scholar and translator at the Ministry of State in Madrid. A poet, playwright, and satirist, he achieved fame with his *Fábulas literarias* (1782), a collection of scholarly verse essays on topics in literary criticism.

The more traditional animal fable was the province of Iriarte's contemporary and rival, Félix María Samaniego (1745–1801). For his two-volume collection of tales titled *Fábulas en verso castellano* (1781–1784), Samaniego took Aesop, the Latin poet Phaedrus, and the French fabulist Jean de La Fontaine as his models.

For specific examples of fable and legend, you can suggest that students review Lope de Vega's poem "Los ratones" in Collection 5 (page 195), which retells a fable in verse, and that they preview Maricarmen Ohara's "La leyenda del maíz" in Collection 8 (page 283).

Use the brief quiz below to test students' comprehension of the material in ELEMENTOS DE LITERATURA.

1. **¿Qué clase de personajes suele haber en los cuentos de hadas?** (unreal or exaggerated characters such as dragons, giants, or talking animals)
2. **Nombra dos fines u objetivos de los cuentos populares.** (to entertain an audience and to teach a lesson)
3. **¿Qué clase de personajes aparecen en las fábulas?** (talking animals)
4. **¿Son las leyendas siempre ficticias o pueden tener algún fundamento histórico?** (Legends are usually based on a historical person or event.)
5. **¿Qué es la tradición oral?** (Oral tradition is the process of passing stories from one generation to the next by word of mouth.)

Los dos príncipes

(The Two Princes)

José Martí

page 255

Into the Selection

Summary

This brief poem first tells of the death of a prince. The king and queen weep, along with the courtiers. The horses, draped in black, walk mournfully in a slow procession and do not wish to eat. The mourners at the prince's funeral wear crowns of laurel.

In the poem's second part, the speaker offers a contrasting picture: The son of a poor shepherd couple has died. The dejected sheep and a sad dog join the lamentations of the boy's parents. The shepherd himself digs his son's grave and throws in a flower.

Antes de leer (page 255)

Punto de partida

Lo que compartimos (What We Share)
Suggest that if students made a cluster about shared human needs as an introductory activity for this collection, they can use their notes now as a springboard for discussion. Examples of things that people all over the world share are needs for love, nurturing, food, shelter, and health.

Comparte tus ideas

You may wish to have students make a list of ideas that their partners thought of but that they themselves overlooked.

Elementos de literatura

Paralelismo (Parallelism)
Point out that Martí uses parallelism in the poem to juxtapose contrasting details. Ask students to examine closely the first two lines of each part. Draw their attention to the contrast between the king in the palace and the shepherd in the mountains. Point out that the two key nouns *rey* and *pastor* occupy the same position: They are the final words in the second line of each part.

Through the Selection

Adueñate de estas palabras
álamo (256)

Techniques for Handling the Reading

Students should experience no particular difficulty with this short lyric poem. You might have students in groups take turns reading the two parts aloud, or play the recorded version for the class. Be sure that students are able to explain how the poem relates to the collection theme, *Todos somos iguales*.

Crea significados (page 257)

Repaso del texto

a. **¿Por qué está de luto el palacio?** The palace is in mourning because the son of the king and queen has died.
b. **¿Qué llevan los caballos?** The horses wear black plumes and trappings.

c. **¿Dónde está la casa del pastor?** The shepherd's house is in the mountains.

d. **¿Qué arroja el pastor en la tumba de su hijo?** The shepherd tosses a flower into his son's grave.

Primeras impresiones

1. **¿Cómo describirías tus sentimientos después de leer este poema? ¿Te gusta más una persona que otra? ¿Por qué?** Although students' answers will vary, most readers will probably say that the poem made them feel sad and that they sympathized equally with both sets of bereaved parents.

Interpretaciones del texto

2. **¿Cómo reaccionan los animales a la muerte de los niños? ¿Por qué crees que José Martí decidió que actuaran de esa forma?** In the first part, the horses respond to the young prince's death by losing their appetites. In the second part, the sheep and the dog join in mourning the shepherd's son. Martí uses the adjective *cabizbajas* to describe the sheep, and he calls the dog *triste*. The poet has the animals act this way to reinforce the melancholy tone.

3. **¿Qué tema importante revela el título?** The title reinforces the important theme that the two sons are equal; despite their different stations in life, they are both "princes."

4. **¿Qué revela el poema sobre la muerte?** The poem shows that death is the universal lot of human beings, whatever their social status may be.

Preguntas al texto

5. **¿Cómo habría cambiado el poema si estuviera narrado por el rey? Explica tu respuesta.** Students' answers will vary. Many students will suggest that the king would have been more affected by the death of his own son than he would have been by the death of the shepherd's child. Encourage students to support their answers with reasons.

Más allá del texto

6. **¿Por qué, a lo largo de la historia, ciertas culturas requieren un periodo de luto para honrar a los muertos?**

Comparte tus ideas. Answers will vary. Students may point out that a period of mourning can serve various purposes, depending on the culture. In some societies, the institution of mourning seems to exist primarily for the benefit of the dead. In these societies, prayers and funeral offerings focus on helping the dead to make their difficult journey from life to afterlife. In other cultures, a period of mourning helps survivors to deal with their grief. A period of mourning can also serve as an opportunity to give thanks for the life of the deceased.

7. ***The Prince and the Pauper*, de Mark Twain, es la historia de un príncipe y un niño pobre que intercambian sus papeles cuando descubren que su aspecto físico es idéntico. En tu experiencia con películas, series de televisión y libros en los que la gente intercambia identidades, ¿qué clase de cosas descubren los personajes? ¿Cómo cambian de punto de vista después de haberse puesto en el lugar de otra persona?** Students' answers will vary. Students may point out that such plot situations often reveal how great an influence material factors like wealth or social status can have over human beings. In addition, the viewpoints of characters in these situations often change when they discover that wealth and power do not automatically bring happiness. Some of your students may be interested in viewing a film version of Twain's *The Prince and the Pauper*, such as the 1937 production starring Errol Flynn or the more recent version released in 1978 under the title *Crossed Swords*.

Beyond the Selection

Opciones:
Prepara tu portafolio (page 258)

Cuaderno del escritor

1. Compilación de ideas para una evaluación
Categories that students might consider adding to their charts include personification and sound

effects. You might ask them to discuss, for example, why they think Martí does not use rhyme in the poem.

Redacción creativa

2. Amigos por correspondencia (Pen Pals)
Tell students that they might use some of the poem's details as springboards for their letters. For example, riding horses could be one of the royal prince's hobbies. The sheepdog could be a special companion for the shepherd's son. Students might also get some ideas by reviewing the descriptions of court life and of the humble characters in Martí's folk tale "Los dos ruiseñores" (page 241).

Estrategias para leer (page 259)

Uso de métodos de comparación y contraste (Using Methods of Comparison and Contrast)

To maximize students' comprehension of this feature, have them review the poems by Fagundo and Mistral in Collection 6 (pages 213 and 218). One convenient method for review would be to call on volunteers to read each poem aloud.

Note that there is an especially close connection between this feature and the assignment in TALLER DEL ESCRITOR (page 266), where a chart lists other possibilities for comparing and contrasting various works in the anthology.

Los dos reyes y los dos laberintos
(The Two Kings and the Two Labyrinths)

Jorge Luis Borges — page 261

Into the Selection

Summary
The narrator relates the story of a king of Babylonia (the name *Babilonia* or Babylon stands for "confusion") who designs a labyrinth so perplexing that it defies any attempts to escape from its tortuous corridors and stairways. Anyone who dares to enter it perishes. The king of Babylonia welcomes the king of Arabia to his court and sends him into the labyrinth, hoping to see him lost forever. The Arabian monarch wanders through its passageways frightened and confused, but he finally manages to escape after praying for divine aid. Returning to Arabia, he takes revenge by gathering an army and devastating Babylonia. Having taken his rival captive, he leads him to the desert. There he releases him to wander in a labyrinth designed by nature—one with no stairways, doors, or winding corridors.

Antes de leer (page 260)

Punto de partida

Laberintos (Labyrinths)
If students are interested in finding out more about the ancient Greek myths of the artisan Daedalus *(Dédalo),* King Minos of Crete, and the monstrous Minotaur *(el Minotauro),* suggest that they consult a dictionary of mythology under the heading "Minotaur" or "Theseus." Theseus *(Teseo)* was the Athenian hero who succeeded in slaying the Minotaur and—aided by Ariadne, the daughter of Minos—finding his way out of the labyrinth. (Plutarch's life of Theseus is a convenient source for many of these myths.)

You may also want to tell students that throughout history labyrinths have been symbols with many layers of meaning. Intricate mazes were created in gardens as puzzles and delights for the eye. Many labyrinths, though, especially those in ancient myths, were associated with death, danger, sin, magic, secrecy, or complex problems.

Toma nota

Students' speculations may vary. Students may suggest that a labyrinth's purpose might be to trap, to deceive, or to restrain an enemy or a dangerous wild beast. The builder of a labyrinth might be a magician, a cruel king, a mathematician, an artist, or a mad scientist.

Elementos de literatura

Alegoría (Allegory)
You may want to remind students that popular movies like *Star Wars* and *The Lion King* have sometimes been interpreted as allegories. Formal allegories, in which every character, setting, and event has metaphorical or symbolic significance, were especially popular in medieval times. In fact, the appearance of the dying emperor's good and bad deeds toward the end of José Martí's "Los dos ruiseñores" (page 241) echoes medieval allegories like the morality play *Everyman*. Like folk tales and fables, allegories are generally designed to teach moral lessons.

Through the Selection

Aduéñate de estas palabras
congregar (261) estragar (261)
proferir (261) vedar (262)

Techniques for Handling the Reading
You may wish to have a proficient reader give an oral reading of this selection, while other students follow along in their texts. The powerful narrative is deceptively simple, and some of your students may be puzzled by issues such as the characters' motives or the metaphorical meaning of the story as a whole. Allow sufficient time for the students to reread Borges's allegory once or twice before they proceed to the questions in CREA SIGNIFICADOS.

Crea significados (page 264)

Repaso del texto

a. **¿Por qué afirma el narrador que el primer laberinto era un escándalo?** The narrator claims that the first maze is "scandalous" because confusion and marvels are the province of God, not of human beings.

b. **¿Cómo escapó el rey de los árabes del laberinto?** The king of Arabia escapes the labyrinth by imploring divine aid.

c. **¿A quién se le amarró encima de un camello veloz?** The king of Babylonia is tied on top of the camel.

d. **¿Qué le dice el rey de los árabes al rey de Babilonia antes de abandonarlo en el desierto?** Before abandoning him in the desert, the Arabian king tells the king of Babylonia that he has brought him to a labyrinth where there are no stairways, doors, winding corridors, or walls.

Primeras impresiones

1. **¿Cuál de los dos laberintos piensas que fue construido con mayor inteligencia? ¿Por qué?** Students' answers will vary. On the one hand, the king of Babylonia's labyrinth is very cleverly constructed. The desert turns out to be the more powerful labyrinth, however, because it is the setting for the evil king's death. Some students may suggest that the desert was constructed by a master architect—nature, or a deity—who cannot be outdone by mere humans.

Interpretaciones del texto

2. **¿Por qué crees que el rey de Babilonia construyó un laberinto y qué nos dice de él esta decisión? Explica tu respuesta.** The king of Babylonia builds the labyrinth to intimidate his subjects. His decision reveals that he is proud, cruel, and mocking.

3. **¿En qué se parece el segundo rey al primero? ¿En qué son diferentes? Ofrece ejemplos del texto que apoyen tu respuesta.** The second king resembles the first in that he is proud and mocking. He is different from the first in that he professes a belief in God.

4. **¿En qué se parece el segundo laberinto al primero? ¿En qué difieren?** Both labyrinths are places of confusion and mortal danger. They are different, however, in that the second one is a natural setting—the desert—rather than an artificial construction.

Preguntas al texto

5. **Aunque la historia da un mensaje sobre la humildad, también revela algo sobre la venganza. ¿Qué piensas que revela sobre la venganza?** Students' answers will vary. Some students will say that the king of Arabia's vengeance was justified, while other students will criticize it as excessive and self-defeating.

Beyond the Selection

Opciones:
Prepara tu portafolio (page 265)

Cuaderno del escritor

1. Compilación de ideas para una evaluación
Additional common elements that students may note include the following: the themes of pride versus humility and appearance versus reality; remote or exotic settings in place and time; use of personification in "Los dos ruiseñores" and "Los dos príncipes"; the existence in all three selections of a serious moral lesson.

Dramatización

2. Los dos reyes en escena
(The Two Kings Onstage)
Remind students that their dialogue should move the plot forward and should be appropriate to the personalities of the speakers.

Taller del escritor (page 266)

La persuasión/Evaluación (Evaluation)

Presenting the Workshop

See the MANUAL DE COMUNICACIÓN (page 324) for an overview of the writing process. You may wish to devote all or part of a class session to reviewing the major aspects of each stage of the process.

Before students begin the assignment, suggest that they also read the material on evaluation in ESTRATEGIAS PARA LEER (page 305). Then encourage them to suggest and comment on some springboards for evaluation essays. For example, you might have students examine and discuss newspaper or magazine reviews of interesting books, films, or concerts.

Next, be sure that students understand that evaluation is a form of *persuasive* writing. Authors of an evaluation seek to persuade their readers that their judgment of a topic or work is reasonable and convincing. Guide students to recognize the crucial role of criteria, or standards, in a persuasive evaluation. Also help them to recognize that comparison and contrast are powerful tools in evaluating a subject's strengths and weaknesses.

Antes de escribir

Point out that students do not need to restrict themselves to works in this anthology. They could, for example, focus the essay on two favorite poems, songs, or movies on the same theme. Or they could read the book or short story from which one of their favorite movies was adapted and then compare the film with the original source.

The important goal in the prewriting phase is to identify a topic that offers a promising basis for comparison and contrast *and* for the application of specific, reasonable criteria. Recommend that students review the sections titled ELEMENTOS DE LITERATURA in this anthology as they draw up their lists of criteria for evaluating a poem, story, or essay.

After students have identified a pair of works to compare and contrast, suggest that they use a chart to list significant details: similarities, differences, strengths, and weaknesses. Below the chart, they can make notes pinpointing what they like and don't like in the two works they have chosen.

Toward the end of the prewriting stage, students should try drafting a thesis statement for the essay. Their goal in this statement should be to summarize their evaluation in one or two sentences. Ask students to use the model statement about "La canción del árbol" and "El ruego del libro" as a springboard for other thesis statements about pairs of works. Point out that the model thesis statement in the text indicates that the essay will discuss both similarities and differences. Also draw students' attention to the specific mention in the thesis statement of several elements of poetry: personification, theme, rhyme, and imagery. Encourage students to make their thesis statements as specific as they can.

El borrador

When you discuss the block method and the point-by-point method, stress that no matter which form of organization students choose, they should be consistent. With the block method, for example, students should list points for each work in the same order. With the point-by-point method, they should treat the works in the same order under each point.

Stress the importance of transitional words and phrases in evaluative writing. Transitions help readers to recognize the relationship of ideas and details. You may want to have students practice identifying transitions by asking them to reread several paragraphs of a story or essay in the anthology and making a list of all the transitional words and phrases they find.

Evaluación y revisión

When students have finished a first draft, ask them to examine carefully the pair of models in the text (pages 269–270). Students may work independently, or you may wish to devote some time in a class session to analyzing and discussing this material. If you choose to have students work in class, call on volunteers to read the model drafts aloud. Then call on volunteers to comment on each draft. Make sure that students understand the reasons for the writing evaluations given in the text. Then encourage partners to exchange feedback. The guidelines for evaluation and revision on page 269 can be used whether students work in pairs or independently.

Bear in mind that students may need help in using their notes to make workable alterations of their first drafts. On a purely mechanical level, for example, some writers may need a guided introduction to the basic proofreading symbols for insertion, deletion, and transposition. See the MANUAL DE COMUNICACIÓN (page 325).

Corrección de pruebas

Emphasize that proofreading or editing adds to the clarity, correctness, and effective presentation of an essay. Familiarity with the conventions of language and writing—spelling, punctuation, grammar, usage, capitalization, paragraphing, syllabification, accuracy of citations and graphics, and proper manuscript form—is an important part of being an effective writer.

Before they begin this stage, some students may need a guided review of the proofreading symbols used for editing and correcting errors in spelling and mechanics. Go over the list of symbols given in the MANUAL DE COMUNICACIÓN (page 325). Then have partners exchange papers and proofread each other's writing. You may wish to circulate through the class, offering help when needed.

Publicación

In addition to the sharing opportunities mentioned in the text, suggest that students might like to publish their evaluations on a computer newsgroup or World Wide Web site, inviting responses from others who are familiar with the same literary works.

Reflexión

Guide students to recognize that time set aside for reflection on an assignment is an investment in the growth of their writing skills. For example, recognizing that one aspect of the project was especially challenging means that students can seek special assistance for their next effort.

Reteaching

Students having difficulty can be encouraged to return to their prewriting charts that show details. Have students expand or refine their lists of similarities and differences. Also encourage them to list specific quotations or details from each work that support an overall evaluation.

Closure

Ask students to explain the difference between an evaluation of a pair of subjects and an observational essay.

Assessment Tools

As students work through the writing process, share the following assessment criteria with them, so that the students can use them in self- and peer evaluations.

Assessment Criteria

1   2   3   4   5   6
(needs   (superior)
improvement)

Content

- Introduction captures readers' interest.
- Works being compared and evaluated are clearly identified, and main idea is stated.

- Details are presented clearly and coherently in accordance with either the block method or the point-by-point method.
- Details persuasively support the main idea in the essay.
- An effective conclusion restates the main idea.

Language Conventions

- Grammar and usage are standard.
- Paragraphs are indented properly.
- Words are spelled correctly.
- Quotation marks are used correctly.

Overall Rating: _____

Enrichment

Arts and Media Connection

Work with students to develop a class arts festival on the theme *Todos somos iguales*. A student festival can consist of a program of live dramatic and musical performances, movie screenings, and poetry readings, as well as exhibits of photographs and original artwork, such as drawings and collages.

Taller de oraciones (page 271)

El arte de dar información
(The Art of Giving Information)

This workshop focuses on ways to create longer, more intricate sentences to provide more detail and information. It reinforces the lesson on prepositional phrases in Collection 3 and examines how prepositional phrases can be used as verb modifiers. The workshop guides students to consider these four questions while they write: *where*, *when*, *how*, and *with whom*. Prepositional phrases are useful tools that can help students convey this type of information.

The INTÉNTALO TÚ provides the opportunity for a community activity in which answering the questions *where*, *when*, *how* and *with whom* is essential. It also reinforces evaluation skills. For this activity, you may want to have students look at restaurant reviews or tourist guides. You might ask them to do the following:

- identify *complementos circunstanciales* in their reading of guides and reviews and note what questions they answer
- use the materials to model their own review
- submit their review to the school newspaper
- prepare a guide along with other students and place it in the school library

Collection 8
HUELLAS DE GRANDES ESPÍRITUS

Collection Overview

The final collection in this anthology, titled *Huellas de grandes espíritus* ("Footprints of Great Spirits"), offers students four exceptionally imaginative pieces of literature. The theme of the collection concerns belief in what is not readily apparent or tangible. As they read these selections—a pair of short stories, a legend, and a lyric poem—your students will discover that "great spirits" can have a lasting impact on those who believe in them. Students may be challenged to redefine their notions of what a "great spirit" might be.

Ana María Matute's short story "El árbol de oro" ("The Tree of Gold") will readily appeal to students on a surface level, since the narrator is a child whose experiences at school include a teacher who plays favorites and a schoolyard bully. On a more profound level, though, the story is a deeply moving, mystical tale of belief that will challenge students to make their own interpretations. The narrator of the story relates that Ivo, an unusual child who has been entrusted with the key to the school library, claims to see a brilliant tree of gold through a crack in the wall. When the narrator finally gets possession of the key, he is disappointed to glimpse only a barren stretch of dirt through the crack. He feels that Ivo has swindled him. However, several years later, after Ivo has died, the narrator has a revelation about the tree of gold. This story shows why Ana María Matute is one of Spain's most acclaimed contemporary writers of fiction.

In "La leyenda del maíz" ("The Legend of Corn"), Maricarmen Ohara tells a Bolivian tale explaining the origins of corn. A young man and a young woman from two warring nations fall in love and elope. The woman's father declares war on the husband's people, and in the course of the battle the woman is killed. A corn plant springs from the ground where she fell. Historically, corn has been the most important food in the diet of many indigenous peoples, and this legend presents an imaginative reconstruction of the origins of its seminal role.

Susana Mendoza's "Cuentos de junio" ("Stories of June") is a modern myth that will appeal to many students. Three young sisters meet a glorious jaguar who resembles the sun, giving off a warm glow as the morning advances and burning with fire when he becomes angry. The jaguar eventually leaps to the rim of a high cliff and disappears in the clouds. The girls' grandfather believes that the jaguar is the sun, and even the most skeptical of the sisters is able to suspend her disbelief.

The final selection in the collection is intended for enrichment. The speaker in "El pájaro libre" ("The Free Bird") by Juan Ramón Jiménez imagines a bird's song in the distance. The song conjures up a vision of the brightness of the orchards and the sea, even as the speaker remains indoors. Many readers will recognize Jiménez, who won the Nobel Prize for literature in 1956, as the author of the children's classic *Platero y yo*.

A cultural feature in this collection focuses on the multifaceted figure of the jaguar in folklore, while ELEMENTOS DE LITERATURA rounds out students' acquaintance with literary genres by providing an introduction to the elements of the novel.

The opening assignments in OPCIONES: PREPARA TU PORTAFOLIO are designed to prepare students for the assignment in TALLER DEL ESCRITOR to write a speculation about causes or effects. This assignment synthesizes many of the skills that are covered in the collection as a whole. Further activities in OPCIONES challenge students to explore themes and ideas through a variety of modes, such as art, drama, and research. Finally, in TALLER DE ORACIONES, a lesson on sentence variety helps students to make stylistic choices in their writing.

Introducing the Collection

To encourage students to explore some aspects of the collection theme, give them a choice of opening activities. Possibilities include the following:

1. Who are some of the "great spirits"? Have small groups of students make a photographic collage of people who they think have had a lasting impact on their times. These "great spirits" could include political leaders, musicians or other artists, athletes, philosophers, and scientists. When students have finished, arrange for them to display their work and explain their choices.
2. Invite students to research a specific ancient or contemporary culture whose religious beliefs include "great spirits." Offer some examples such as the following: American Indian beliefs in animal spirits, ancient Egyptian religion, medieval and contemporary Christian belief in angels, Hindu belief in 330 million divinities, the ancestor cults of ancient Rome or of modern Indonesia and Madagascar. What powers do such spirits have? How are they worshiped or honored? Have students share their findings in oral reports.

El árbol de oro
(The Tree of Gold)

Ana María Matute — page 275

Into the Selection

Summary

This story is set in a rural Spanish village some decades ago. The narrator attends the village school one autumn and discovers that a mysterious, thin boy named Ivo commands the attention of teacher and students alike. Miss Leocadia, the teacher, favors the boy by assigning him the coveted task of fetching books from the library, which is in a locked room in a tower. One day, Ivo confides in the narrator, saying that on his visits to the tower he puts his eye up to a crack in the wall through which he observes a magnificent tree of gold.

Fascinated and envious, the narrator finally gets an opportunity to see Ivo's secret for himself. When Ivo falls ill, Miss Leocadia allows another student to get the books from the tower. Having bribed this pupil to surrender the key to the tower, the narrator eagerly presses his eye to the crack in the wall. To his dismay, however, all he sees is the dried earth of the plain stretching out toward the horizon. Feeling that Ivo has swindled him, he forgets all about the key and the tree of gold.

Two years later, the narrator returns to the mountain village. As he passes the cemetery at sunset, he has a vision of a large and beautiful tree of gold against the night sky. Searching at the foot of the tree, he finds a black iron cross that marks the grave of Ivo Márquez, aged ten. The narrator states that he felt not sadness but a strange and very great happiness.

Antes de leer (page 274)

Punto de partida

«*Todo es según el color del cristal con que se mira.*» ("Everything Depends on the Color of the Glass Through Which You Look.")
You might suggest that students brainstorm a list of benefits they can derive from meeting people with different backgrounds, interests, or hobbies.

Toma nota

Instead of writing for this activity, some students might be encouraged to draw a quick sketch, play a piece of music recorded on an audiocassette, or comment orally on a photograph.

Diálogo con el texto

Since this story is relatively challenging, encourage students to jot down notes as they read. During their first reading, for example, they can focus on the author's striking imagery. Tell students not to worry at this stage if they have the impression that the story raises as many questions as it answers.

Elementos de literatura

Punto de vista

You may wish to have students review the discussion of point of view in ELEMENTOS DE LITERATURA in Collection 3 (see page 110). Make sure that students understand why the first-person point of view is limited: The narrator can relate only what he or she directly witnesses or experiences.

Through the Selection

Diario del lector (page 276)

The sample comments in the margin exemplify various reading strategies, including questioning, making inferences, and drawing conclusions. If you feel that some of your students will benefit, you can extend this activity through another page of the text, modeling similar kinds of marginal annotations. You can pause at the end of each section, allowing enough time to monitor and discuss students' notes on an individual basis.

Adueñate de estas palabras

codiciada (276)
embustero (277)
zozobra (277)
desasosegar (277)
hucha (278)
estafar (278)
sosegada (278)

Techniques for Handling the Reading

Although this story has a clear plot line, it presents students with a number of mysteries and unanswered questions. For example, the story never really explains Ivo's magnetic appeal to the teacher and the other students. However, students probably know peers like Ivo who have a strong sense of individuality.

Likewise, the author never explains why the books are locked in a tower or why, when Ivo becomes ill, the teacher reverses her rule and allows other pupils to fetch the books. Advise students that some of their questions about cause and effect in the story can serve as springboards for discussion. The essential qualities to bring to the story are an open mind and the willingness to use one's imagination.

Since imagery and symbolism are so important in Matute's tale, you may wish to have students review the discussions of these elements in Collection 4 (page 161) and Collection 6 (page 222). To prompt students' consideration of imagery, urge them to note how the author uses images in the story's first paragraph to establish a melancholy mood. Then have students contrast the images in the final paragraph, which produce a very different atmosphere for the story's conclusion.

The symbolism in this story is especially intriguing. You can challenge students to discuss possible symbolic meanings for the characters (Miss Leocadia, Ivo, the narrator, and Mateo Heredia), as well as for the tower, the key, the money that changes hands, the books, and the tree of gold.

Finally, after students have read the story and discussed the questions in CREA SIGNIFICADOS, you can call on volunteers to speculate on the story's connections with the collection theme. Do students think that Ivo is a great spirit, and if so, why? What other connections with "great spirits" might the story suggest?

Crea significados (page 279)

Repaso del texto

a. **¿Cuál fue la tarea que le encomendaron a Ivo?** The books for the reading lessons at school are kept locked in a library in a tower. Ivo is entrusted with the task of fetching the books and returning them to the tower after the daily classes.

b. **¿Qué piensa Ivo que le ocurriría si se subiera a una rama del árbol?** He thinks he might be turned into gold.

c. **¿Qué observa el narrador cuando mira por la rendija?** The narrator sees only the dusty soil of the plain stretching to the horizon.

d. **¿Qué observa el narrador al final de la historia?** The narrator sees a tree turned into gold against the setting sun. At the foot of the tree, a cross marks the grave of Ivo, who has died at the age of ten.

EL ÁRBOL DE ORO **97**

Primeras impresiones

1. **Completa la siguiente oración: Pienso que el árbol de oro era _____.** Students' answers will vary. Some readers may suggest that the tree was merely a hallucination in the mind of a sick child. Many students, however, may say that the tree was either real or symbolically true for Ivo and that it could have represented an ideal of beauty, a dream of happiness, a treasured secret, or religious faith.

Interpretaciones del texto

2. **¿Crees que el *punto de vista* del narrador es digno de confianza? Es decir, ¿crees todo lo que te cuenta? Si no es así, ¿qué es lo que te produce dudas, y por qué?** Students' answers will vary. Most readers will agree that the narrator seems reliable. Ask students who have doubts to point to specific passages of the story and to support their opinions with reasons.

3. **¿Por qué crees que Ivo le dice al narrador de esta historia: «Me es completamente igual que te lo creas o no . . .»?** Students' answers will vary. In general, they should point out that Ivo's remark is consistent with his characterization in the story as a self-confident child who has no particular need for the approval of his peers or for popularity at school. In addition, the tree of gold seems to exist in the eye of the beholder—it is visible to those who believe in it.

4. **¿Por qué supones que Ivo recibe un trato especial?** Ivo receives special privileges not because he is intelligent or comic, according to the narrator, but because of his air of mystery and his ability to command the attention of the teacher, Miss Leocadia.

5. **¿Por qué crees que la voz narrativa dice al final: «Y no daba tristeza alguna, sino, tal vez, una extraña y muy grande alegría»?** Students' answers will vary. Perhaps the narrator's happiness can be explained by the feeling that Ivo had not swindled him after all and that the narrator can now share the child's special vision of beauty.

Conexiones con el texto

6. **¿Cómo responderías si alguien te dijera que ha visto un árbol de oro como el que Ivo asegura ver?** Students' responses will vary from the dismissive to the curious. Ask them to explain their reactions.

Preguntas al texto

7. **De la forma en que está escrita la historia, nadie podría demostrar si existe o no un árbol de oro. Si quisieras una prueba definitiva de la existencia del árbol, ¿qué clase de evidencia exigirías?** Again, students' answers will vary. They might suggest, for example, that they would want to see the evidence of a photograph, or a leaf from one of the branches, or corroborating evidence from other eyewitnesses.

Beyond the Selection

Opciones:
Prepara tu portafolio (page 280)

Cuaderno del escritor

1. Compilación de ideas para una especulación sobre causas o efectos (Collecting Ideas for a Speculation About Causes or Effects)
Tell students that promising topics for their essays might include a natural phenomenon or process, a current national or local controversy, and the effects of advances in technology.

Redacción

2. Ivo en la torre (Ivo in the Tower)
Remind students that they should use first-person pronouns when they write from Ivo's point of view. Also tell them to be sure that their portrayal of Ivo as narrator is consistent with his characterization in the story.

Dramatización

3. El teatro del lector (Reader's Theater)
Tell students that their stage directions could refer to how the lines of dialogue are delivered or to gestures or movements on stage.

Lengua y literatura (page 281)

Las palabras tienen más de un significado
(Words Have More Than One Meaning)

Using a humorous example, this mini-lesson shows students that words can have more than one meaning. Discuss the scenario with the students and ask the following questions:

- ¿Qué significados tienen las palabras *órgano* y *pie*?
- ¿Cómo sabes lo que quieren decir en cada situación?

Point out the meanings the dictionary gives for the word *pie* and the way students can use the dictionary to check meanings and usage. You may refer them to the sample dictionary entry in the MANUAL DE COMUNICACIÓN (page 327). You may want to let the students come up with as many meanings as possible for the other words before checking the dictionary. Illustrating the meanings of the words in the INTÉNTALO TÚ should prove entertaining to students.

The second part of the mini-lesson examines how words can have different meanings in different languages. Have students discuss the differences in meaning between the English and Spanish words in the pairs. These pairs can also be the basis of jokes or comic illustrations.

Vocabulario (page 281)

¡Albricias es alegría en árabe!
("Albricias" Means "Joy" in Arabic!)
This exercise will help students get a feel for the beauty of Spanish words that come from Arabic. This exercise is one of several that build on the ESCENA CULTURAL feature on the origin of Spanish words in Collection 4.

The exercise points out Arabic influences with which students may be familiar. Let students who have tasted Middle Eastern foods describe them to the other students. They may be familiar with *alcapurrias* or *kibbeh,* which are readily available at Middle Eastern restaurants. *Alcapurrias* are fried dough filled with ground meat. The dough is made by grating yucca and letting the flesh dry. *Horchata de ajonjolí* is a milky summer drink made with crushed sesame seeds, almonds, or rice. *Almojábanas* are rice and cheese balls; originally, they were covered in a sugar syrup and eaten for dessert. Other foods include *alcaparras* (capers).

The exercise calls attention to the name of a tree mentioned in Matute's story: *arzadú*. Students learn that Arabic words adopted into the Spanish language can often apply to agriculture. They are asked to write their own description of a garden, using the words in the ALCANCÍA, many of which they may already know.

Other words that are appropriate for the exercise include:

escarlata	alubia
alcancía	algodón
azucena	azúcar
albahaca	ojalá
añil	alberca
alborozo	

You may want to use a book on gardens and/or pictures of the Alhambra and Arabic gardens in Southern Spain.

La leyenda del maíz
(The Legend of Corn)

Maricarmen Ohara — page 283

Into the Selection

Summary

The uneasy peace of two warlike peoples, the Charcas and the Chayantas, is broken when Huayru, a Chayanta youth, elopes with the beautiful Maiza Chojclu, the daughter of the Charcas' chief. Maiza's infuriated father declares war, and Huayru must fight against his new wife's people. Soon after Maiza Chojclu prays to the gods for a miracle, a fierce battle begins, and Maiza is mortally wounded by an enemy arrow. Stunned by the sad event, the combatants lay down their arms. Huayru tearfully buries his bride and falls asleep over the grave. When he awakens in the morning, he sees a miracle: the sprouting of the first corn plant.

Antes de leer (page 282)

Punto de partida

Conflictos: causas y efectos
(Disagreements: Causes and Effects)
Before they begin this selection, have students review the discussion of legends in ELEMENTOS DE LITERATURA, Collection 7 (page 254). Stress that legends are often based on historical people or events, for example, the wars between two peoples. Ask students to give some examples of wars that have been the subject of legends. Suggestions might include the ancient Trojan War, the Civil War in the United States, and the Mexican war of independence from Spain.

Toma nota

You may wish to have students work in small groups for this activity. Possible causes might include religious conflicts, ethnic strife, and economic clashes. Alternative solutions might include compromises such as the partitioning of territory and economic treaties.

Estrategias para leer

Evaluación (Evaluation)
Stress that evaluation combines personal taste and subjective responses with more objective standards on which many people might reasonably agree.

Through the Selection

Adueñate de estas palabras

belicoso (283)   pasmado (284)
convocar (283)   oprimido (284)
alternativa (284)   sepultado (284)

Techniques for Handling the Reading

This straightforward narrative should not pose any stumbling blocks for most readers in your class. Tell students that like most legends, this tale from Bolivia combines realistic elements with fantastic or supernatural ones. You can also remind students that legends are often told to explain the origins of natural phenomena. Make sure that students use the footnotes and glossary entries for unfamiliar words.

Literatura y cultura
(Literature and Culture) (page 285)

El símbolo del maíz (The Symbol of Corn)
The importance of corn in religious and cultural symbolism is closely related to its critical role in the historical development of civilizations. According to anthropologists, corn was probably first cultivated in the Tehuacán Valley of southern Mexico about 5,000 years ago. The discovery that dried corn could be stored enabled people to settle in permanent locations. An equally important discovery was the *nixtamal* process, by which the indigenous people of Central America released the proper balance of nutrients in corn by boiling the kernels in a mixture of water and white lime.

Crea significados (page 286)

Repaso del texto
Students' lists of events will vary but should include the following basic framework: (1) The Charcas and Chayantas were perennial rivals; (2) one day on the border of the two peoples' territories, Huayru, the son of the Chayantas' chief, glimpsed the beautiful Maiza Chojclu, the daughter of the chief of the Charcas, and fell in love with her; (3) the two young people decided to elope; (4) the angry father of Maiza Chojclu declared war on the Chayantas, and Huayru was forced to fight against his wife's people; (5) Maiza Chojclu prayed to the gods to stop the war; (6) an enemy arrow mortally wounded her and she died in her husband's arms; (7) the war was called off, with the girl as its only victim; (8) Huayru, having shed many tears on his wife's grave, awoke in the morning to see a miracle: the sprouting of the first corn plant.

Primeras impresiones

1. **¿Cuál es tu *evaluación* inmediata de esta leyenda? ¿Es interesante? ¿Se la recomendarías a un amigo?** Students' evaluations will vary. Ask them to explain the criteria on which they based their judgments.

Interpretaciones del texto

2. **¿Por qué la muerte de Maiza Chojclu hizo que terminara la batalla?** All the warriors are so stunned by the sad event that they lay down their weapons.
3. **¿Qué simboliza la aparición de la planta de maíz?** The corn plant seems to symbolize Maiza Chojclu. It has the same light green color as the girl's clothes. Like the girl, the plant is healthy and slender. The plant seems to be supported by the arrow that took away the girl's life. The grains of corn resemble Maiza Chojclu's teeth, and they are as sweet as she was in life.
4. **¿Consideras que Maiza es un «gran espíritu»? ¿Por qué?** Students' answers will vary. Most readers will agree that her sacrifice could be regarded as a precious gift or as a miracle by the people who told this legend.

Preguntas al texto

5. **¿Qué podría haber servido de inspiración a los antiguos pobladores de Bolivia para crear este mito sobre el maíz? ¿Por qué habrían escogido el maíz en vez de otra cosecha?** Students' answers will vary. One purpose of telling the myth might have been to explain how two previously hostile peoples had become friends or allies. Another purpose might have been to explain the origins of an important crop.
6. **¿Qué crees que ocurriría entre los charcas y los chayantas después de la muerte de Maiza? ¿Seguirían luchando?** Students' answers will vary. Encourage students to support their responses with reasons.

Más allá del texto

7. **Basándote en la historia o en tu experiencia personal, ¿qué otros "«grandes espíritus» han hecho prevalecer la paz por encima de las disputas o la guerra?** Students' answers may vary. They may mention "great spirits" such as Mohandas Gandhi, Martin Luther King, Jr., and Cesar Chavez, all renowned peacemakers. In addition, many students will be able to draw on their personal experience for examples of peacemaking.

Beyond the Selection

Opciones:
Prepara tu portafolio (page 287)

Cuaderno del escritor

1. Compilación de ideas para una especulación sobre causas o efectos
Students might work in small groups for this activity.

Investigación/Arte

2. Las leyendas del maíz (Legends About Corn)
If students are unfamiliar with the setup of a diorama, you might show them pictures of dioramas located in museums of natural history or in zoos. The various branches of the Smithsonian Institution in Washington, D.C., use dioramas to bring historical scenes to life. Suggest that students use anthologies of North and South American Indian myths and legends as sources for this activity.

Hablar y escuchar

3. El nombre de los árboles
(The Naming of Trees)
Advanced students may be interested in researching the scientific names of trees and plants. These names often refer to a significant aspect of a tree or plant's appearance, or to the naturalist who discovered or first described the species.

Escena cultural (page 288)

El jaguar en el mito y el folclor
(The Jaguar in Myth and Folklore)

Actividades para empezar
You can supplement this activity by asking volunteers to bring in pictures of jaguars from magazines or natural-history reference books.

Actividades de cierre
1. Help students find reference sources for this activity. The school librarian may be able to suggest useful materials.

2. Suggest that students look for springboards among the connections noted in the cultural feature in the text: for example, the links between the jaguar and war, religion, and death. Recommend that students prewrite by making an informal outline for the essay.
3. According to Allen F. Roberts (see below, **For Further Reading**), leopards may be the most frequently portrayed animals in African art. Suggest that students begin this activity by researching the size, habitat, and hunting behavior of these big cats.

For Further Reading

These are titles you may wish to consult as background reading.

Belli, Gioconda. "Journey to the Lost City of the Jaguar." *Nature Conservancy* May/June 1994: 11–14.

Coe, Michael D. *The Maya* (Thames and Hudson, New York, 1993).

Lumpkin, Susan. *Big Cats* (Facts on File, New York, 1993).

Macdonald, David, ed. *The Encyclopedia of Mammals* (Facts on File, New York, 1984).

Montejo, Victor. *The Bird Who Cleans the World and Other Mayan Fables* (Curbstone Press, Willimantic, 1991).

Montgomery, Sy. *Spell of the Tiger: Man-Eaters of Sundarbans* (Houghton Mifflin, Boston, 1995).

Rabinowitz, Alan. *Jaguar* (Doubleday, New York, 1986).

Roberts, Allen F. *Animals in African Art: From the Familiar to the Marvelous* (The Museum for African Art, New York, 1995).

Saunders, Nicholas J. *People of the Jaguar: The Living Spirit of Ancient America* (Souvenir Press, London, 1989).

Schueler, Donald G. *The Temple of the Jaguar: Travels in the Yucatan* (Sierra Club Books, San Francisco, 1993).

Sunquist, Fiona. "Jaguar," in *Kingdom of Cats* (National Wildlife Federation, Washington, D.C., 1991).

Townsend, Richard F. *The Aztecs* (Thames and Hudson, London, 1992).

Wessing, Robert. *The Soul of Ambiguity: The Tiger in Southeast Asia* (Center for Southeast Asian Studies, Northern Illinois University, Illinois, 1986).

Wolfe, Art, and Barbara Sleeper. *Wild Cats of the World* (Crown Publishers, New York, 1995).

Cuentos de junio
(Stories of June)

Susana Mendoza — page 295

Into the Selection

Summary

Early one morning, a mother and her three young daughters walk to the mountains to gather mushrooms. Puzzled by flashes of light in the forest, the youngest girl, Chagua, investigates a deep ravine, where she spies a huge jaguar shimmering with light amid thousands of dazzling reflections. Chagua runs to warn her mother and sisters of the danger. Despite their disbelief, her sisters accompany the girl to the ravine, where indeed they encounter the jaguar.

Despite the animal's imposing appearance, he seems rather meek. The girls notice that he is covered with thousands of golden scales, and that his color changes from red to yellow as the morning advances toward noon. When the sisters question him, he adamantly denies that he is lost and moves off, somewhat irritated. The girls follow the jaguar, crossing valleys and ridges until they come to a high cliff. There the jaguar jumps from the rim and is lost in the clouds.

The three sisters hurry back to the spot where they have left their basket. Their mother smiles incredulously when they tell their story. After the family returns home, however, the grandfather listens to the tale attentively. After some thought, he declares that the jaguar was really the sun. The girls speculate, each in her own way, about this theory. When two roars in the West coincide with twilight and darkness, even the skeptical Licha, the eldest of the three girls, becomes convinced that Grandfather is right.

Antes de leer (page 294)

Punto de partida

¿Qué pasaría si el sol...?
(What Would Happen If the Sun...?)
Before students begin work on their cause-or-effect chart, you may wish to remind them that in each of the selections they have read so far in this collection, they have encountered a blend of realistic and fantastic or supernatural elements. The upcoming story is written in the same vein.

Elementos de literatura

La literatura fantástica (Fantasy)
Encourage students to name examples of fantasy from their reading. Why do they think this form of fiction is so popular and enduring? You can tell them that fantastic tales are often passed on orally—they are easy to remember, entertaining, and appealing to the imagination.

Through the Selection

Adueñate de estas palabras

encino (296)
eucalipto (296)
rocío (296)
destello (296)
deslumbrar (296)
cañada (296)
jadeante (298)
husmear (298)
hálito (298)
escama (299)
conforme (299)
estío (299)
impertinencia (300)
erizar (300)
reverberar (300)
colérico (300)
berrinchudo (300)
risco (300)
escollo (300)
poniente (302)
crepúsculo (302)

Techniques for Handling the Reading

The straightforward plot line of this story ought to make it accessible to most of your students. A recording of this selection, available on audiocassette, features creative renditions of the three sisters, the jaguar, and the grandfather. Most students will enjoy listening to this entertaining tale.

You may want to point out that readers should consult the footnotes and glossary for meanings of unfamiliar words. If students are puzzled by the existence of a *tigre* in the Western Hemisphere, call their attention to footnote 9. You may also want to suggest that students review the material about folk tales in ELEMENTOS DE LITERATURA for Collection 7 (see page 254).

Crea significados (page 303)

Repaso del texto

Students' frames for their comic strips will vary. Sample frames might run as follows: (1) the girls and their mother gathering mushrooms; (2) Chagua peering down at the jaguar in the ravine; (3) the three sisters questioning the jaguar; (4) the jaguar disappearing at the rim of the cliff; (5) Grandfather talking with the girls; (6) Licha pondering Grandfather's theory as twilight falls.

Primeras impresiones

1. **Completa las oraciones:**
   - **Más tarde, esa misma noche, el tigre _____.**
   - **Al día siguiente, el tigre _____.**
   Students' answers will vary. They may suggest that the jaguar roars again toward dawn, and that the next day the jaguar reappears, first in the ravine and then on the mountainside.

Interpretaciones del texto

2. **Mendoza describe el sol como si fuera un tigre. ¿Qué características tienen en común el tigre y el sol?** Like the sun, the jaguar glitters as if it were a source of light. Both change hues from red to gold as the day advances, and both give off heat.

3. **¿Qué clase de personalidad tiene el tigre? Describe en tres palabras su carácter.** Students' characterizing words will vary but may include the following:
   flamante
   digno
   majestuoso
   irritable
   benévolo

4. **¿Piensas que el tigre se ha perdido verdaderamente, o conoce bien la cañada? ¿Por qué?** Students' answers will vary. Stu-

dents may suggest that the jaguar was in the ravine only temporarily, at a time of day when the rays of the sun penetrated and illuminated the gully.

5. **¿Por qué crees que el abuelo sabe quién es el tigre?** Students' answers will vary. The grandfather is portrayed as a wise elder who knows the secrets of nature and can pass on traditional wisdom and values.

Conexiones con el texto

6. **¿Qué personaje de la historia se comporta más como tú? ¿Por qué?** Students' answers will vary. Ask students to support their choices with reasons and examples.

Preguntas al texto

7. **¿Crees que esta historia podría suceder en un ambiente diferente, como una ciudad o el lugar donde vives? ¿Qué elementos de la historia cambiarían?** Most students will respond that this story could be set in their city or home town, but the plot might be influenced by the change in setting. Some students may suggest that the story could not take place in a modern setting where scientific theories about the weather would take precedence over belief in anything fantastic.

8. **Prepara un cuadro de realidad y fantasía como el que aparece abajo. En una columna, anota los sucesos de la historia que podrían haber ocurrido. En la otra, anota los sucesos que crees que no podrían ocurrir en la vida real.** Students' answers will vary. Entries in the fantasy column might include the sisters' conversation with the jaguar, the jaguar's disappearance at the rim of the cliff, the grandfather's claim that the jaguar is the sun, and the golden scale that Chagua pulls from the jaguar when she touches him. Realistic elements might include the girls' gathering of mushrooms in the forest, the descriptions of the changing weather, and the description of twilight and nightfall.

Beyond the Selection

Opciones:
Prepara tu portafolio (page 304)

Cuaderno del escritor

1. Compilación de ideas para una especulación sobre causas o efectos
After pairs develop the possible effects in their speculations, suggest that two pairs join to exchange and comment on each other's ideas.

Redacción

2. Elogio del sol (Praise of the Sun)
Recommend that students research Central and South American myths. Students can find information in encyclopedia articles that deal, for example, with Mayan, Aztec, and Incan civilizations.

Dramatización

3. Leyendas del sol (Legends About the Sun)
Again, students will find that encyclopedia articles on myths about the sun are helpful springboards for this activity.

Investigación

4. Solamente los hechos (Just the Facts)
Recommend that students use an introductory science textbook for this activity. They can supplement their research by consulting almanacs and astronomy reference works.

Arte

5. Un poema sobre el sol
(A Poem About the Sun)
As students begin this activity, encourage them to list as many sensory images from the story as they can.

Estrategias para leer (page 305)

Evaluación de un libro
(Writing a Book Report)

You may wish to have students review the material on evaluation in the TALLER DEL ESCRITOR for Collection 7 (see page 266). In addition, encourage students to examine book or movie reviews in newspapers and magazines.

Elementos de literatura (page 306)

La novela (The Novel)

After students have read this feature, encourage them to suggest some examples of each type of novel mentioned in the text: science fiction, historical novels, and detective novels or mysteries. Students should be encouraged to offer brief summaries, as well as evaluations and comments about each work. Give the same encouragement to anyone in the class who is familiar with the titles shown on the book jackets on page 306.

You may use the True-False quiz below to assess students' mastery of the information in this feature.

1. **La novela pertenece al género de ficción.** (T)
2. **El fin principal de la novela es persuadir al lector para que cambie de opinión acerca de un asunto polémico.** (F)
3. **La trama de una novela suele girar en torno a un conflicto y tiene un clímax.** (T)
4. **Normalmente, la novela se desarrolla en una sola escena.** (F)
5. **La novela suele tener una extensión de entre 100 y 500 páginas.** (T)

A leer por tu cuenta
El pájaro libre
(The Free Bird)

Juan Ramón Jiménez page 308

Summary

As he sits in a shadowy room with a closed piano, the speaker of the poem entreats a bird in the distance to sing. The bird's music conjures up visions of a river, a ship, a beautiful orchard with orange trees, and a shady pine grove. With the last breeze, the sunset brings calm and silent wonder to the speaker's soul.

Adueñate de estas palabras

zumbar (309)

Techniques for Handling the Reading

Call on volunteers to read each section of the poem aloud. You might also play the audiocassette recording of the poem to the class, which should help students appreciate the lyricism of the author's words. Then invite students to hold a brainstorming session about how the poem relates to the collection theme, *Huellas de grandes espíritus*. In what sense could the bird in the poem be called a "great spirit"? In what sense might the poem's speaker also be a great spirit?

Taller del escritor (page 310)

La exposición/
Especulación sobre causas o efectos
(Speculation About Causes or Effects)

Presenting the Workshop

For an overview of the writing process, see the MANUAL DE COMUNICACIÓN (page 324). You may wish to devote all or part of a class session to reviewing the major aspects of each stage of the process.

Before students get started, encourage them to suggest and comment on some springboards for writing a speculation about causes or effects. For example, you might ask students to examine newspaper editorials or science articles in magazines. Both types of writing should furnish abundant examples of cause-and-effect relationships.

Antes de escribir

You may point out that "What if?" questions for a speculation about causes or effects may appear to overlap with "What if?" prewriting questions for a short story (see page 126). However, there are some important differences between the two types of writing. Short stories are a kind of fiction, while cause-and-effect essays are nonfiction. The purpose of most short stories is to entertain, while the purpose of most cause-and-effect writing is to inform, to persuade, or both. Stress that because of the persuasive aspect of the assignment in this workshop, students need to gather evidence in Step 5 of prewriting.

El borrador

Although many students will find that making an outline is helpful at this stage, stress that the important goal now is for writers to get their thoughts down on paper (or on the computer). Students will have plenty of time later to correct any errors in spelling, grammar, or mechanics.

Evaluación y revisión

When students have finished their first drafts, ask them to examine carefully the pair of models in the text (pages 313–314). Students may work independently, or you may wish to devote some time in a class session to analyzing and discussing this material. If you choose to have students work in class, call on volunteers to read the model drafts aloud. Then call on volunteers to comment on each draft. Make sure that students understand the reasons for the writing evaluations given in the text. Point out the way the writer of Draft 2 varies the sentence structure by writing the third sentence of the paragraph as a question. Encourage peer reviewers to exchange feedback. The guidelines for evaluation and revision on page 313 can be used whether students work in pairs or independently.

Students may need help in applying their notes and making workable alterations of their first drafts. On a purely mechanical level, for example, less proficient writers may need a guided introduction to the basic proofreading symbols for insertion, deletion, and transposition. See the MANUAL DE COMUNICACIÓN (page 325).

Corrección de pruebas

Emphasize the importance of polishing and proofreading written work before submitting it for publication. Before students begin this stage, they may need a guided review of the proofreading symbols used for editing and correcting errors in spelling and mechanics. Go over the list of symbols given in the MANUAL DE COMUNICACIÓN (page 325). Then have partners exchange papers and proofread each other's writing. You may wish to circulate through the class, offering help when needed.

Publicación

In addition to the sharing opportunities described in the text, you may want to encourage writers to present their speculations on causes or effects to a class of younger students.

Reflexión

Encourage students to get together in small groups to share their reflection statements. Remind writers that reflecting on the assignment can generate valuable feedback and tips for future writing projects.

Reteaching

Students having difficulty can be encouraged to work in pairs to sort out their evidence and supporting details. Tell pairs to focus on limiting details so that everything included in the essay clearly supports the writer's main idea. Then have pairs concentrate on presenting details in either chronological order or order of importance.

Closure

Ask students to explain the difference between a speculation about causes or effects and a report of information.

Assessment Tools

As students work through the writing process, share the following assessment criteria with them, so they may use them in self- and peer evaluations.

Assessment Criteria

1   2   3   4   5   6
(needs   (superior)
improvement)

Content

- Introduction identifies the topic clearly and states whether the essay will focus on causes or effects.
- Any necessary background information is supplied.
- Body of essay presents evidence for causes or effects.
- Supporting details are organized in an order that is clear and easy to follow.
- Conclusion summarizes the essay's main points.

Language Conventions
- Grammar and usage are standard.
- Paragraphs are indented properly.
- Words are spelled correctly.
- Quotation marks are used correctly.

Overall Rating: _____

Enrichment

Art Connection
Work with students to develop an exhibition of photographs, drawings, and paintings of people, animals, or objects that the students consider "great spirits." Have small groups of students research subjects for the exhibition, and encourage each group to develop a brief caption for each visual that explains why the person, animal, or object shown may be considered a "great spirit." If they wish, students can model their exhibitions and captions on those seen in a museum. When students have completed this activity, arrange for them to display their exhibition.

Taller de oraciones (page 315)

La oración es flexible
(Sentences Are Flexible)

In Spanish, syntax is very flexible, and different parts of a sentence can be arranged in various ways for emphasis and style. In this workshop, students explore the different effects produced by changes in syntax.

The workshop begins with a traditional children's song that deviates from the standard order of subject, predicate, noun, and adjective. If a student knows the song, encourage him or her to sing it for the class. The song in its entirety reads:

Estaba la blanca paloma
sentada en un verde limón.
Con el pico cortaba la rama.
Con la rama cortaba la flor.
Ay, ay, ay.
¿Cuándo veré a mi amor?
Me arrodillo a los pies de mi amante.
Me levanto constante.
Dame una mano,
dame la otra.
Dame un besito
sobre tu boca.

The exercise explores the different ways of arranging the parts of the first sentence. In the sentence, the position of the subject, the adjectives, and the verb modifier can change. Students are asked to write new sentences in order to examine the effect of each arrangement of words. The first *comienzo* is poetic; the second is standard; the third can go either way.

Students are then asked to examine the position of adjectives. When adjectives are placed in front of nouns, the effect can be lyrical. Students first examine the position of adjectives in the selection "El pájaro libre" (page 308) and are asked to write their own poem imitating that of Jiménez for the INTÉNTALO TÚ.

In AL REVISAR TU TRABAJO, students are asked to place verb modifiers at the beginning of their sentences. The exercise provides them with specific cause-or-effect words to get them started. This stylistic device will give their cause-or-effect essays variety of sentence structure and the more formal tone that is appropriate to this type of writing. You may want to point out that when a verb modifier is moved to the beginning of the sentence, a comma follows the modifier, as in the example. You can also discuss the position of the verb modifiers in verses 2, 4, and 7.

The GUÍA DEL LENGUAJE has sections on adjectives and *complementos circunstanciales,* along with exercises.

FOR FURTHER READING

Lecturas suplementarias

You may wish to preview these selections before recommending them for supplementary reading.

Colección 1
Desafíos

Rodolfo G. Otero (Argentina, 1949). *La travesía.* Novela. Editorial Noguer, Barcelona, 1989.

Para los cinco hermanos protagonistas de esta narración, lo que prometía ser un simple viaje de vacaciones se convierte en una peligrosa travesía a través del desierto, sin comida ni agua. Gracias a la ayuda de Nicanor Reyes, un gaucho que los ayuda en su trayecto, sobreviven. La experiencia sólo dura una semana pero los cinco hermanos se sienten como si hubieran envejecido un año.

Rodolfo Guillermo Otero, que es hijo de aviador y maestra, heredó de la madre su facilidad para comunicarse con los niños y del padre su capacidad para dejar volar la imaginación. Licenciado en Derecho, ejerció unos años como abogado pero, en 1977, abandonó la profesión y se dedicó a la radio y la televisión. Junto con *El verano del potro, La travesía* obtuvo en Argentina un premio de guiones de cine juvenil. Asimismo, *La travesía* recibió una mención al Premio Lazarillo en España. En la actualidad Otero forma parte del comité directivo del Movimiento Argentino de Educación por el Arte.

Manuel de Jesús Galván (República Dominicana, 1834–1911). *Enriquillo* (1882). Las Américas Publishing, Nueva York, 1984.

La obra trata de acontecimientos históricos que ocurrieron durante el siglo XVI en Santo Domingo y se centra en el personaje de Enriquillo, un cacique que al principio es fiel a los españoles pero más tarde se rebela contra ellos. La novela se basa en los acontecimientos relatados por Bartolomé de Las Casas y otros cronistas. Esta colección contiene los dos primeros capítulos de la novela que narran el encuentro entre el jefe indio Gueroa e Higuemota su prima, que está casada con un noble español. Gueroa huye de quienes mataron a su familia y le pide a Higuemota que le entregue su hijo para ayudarlo a luchar por la libertad de su pueblo.

Manuel de Jesús Galván dedicó gran parte de su vida a la política. Fue secretario del presidente Santana, años más tarde embajador en Estados Unidos y varias veces ministro en su país. Quizás el conocimiento histórico y político de su patria, unido a su interés por la literatura, fue lo que inspiró a escribir la novela histórica *Enriquillo,* sin duda una de las obras más destacadas del romanticismo hispanoamericano y a la que el autor debe su prestigio como escritor.

Colección 2
Si tú supieras...

Antonio Rodríguez Almodóvar (España, 1941). «Corazón de hierro». Cuento. Pertenece al libro *El bosque de los sueños I.* Ediciones Siruela, Madrid, 1993.

«Corazón de hierro», al igual que el resto de los «sueños» que componen los dos volúmenes de la obra, combina elementos de la fábula y de la vida cotidiana. Esta combinación hace que la realidad se confunda con los sueños de los personajes y los hace cuestionar la realidad de sus sueños. En el cuento un anciano le lee a un muchacho, Juan Zacarías, la historia «La ciudad de oro». Cuando el anciano acaba y se marcha, Zacarías queda fascinado y lo sigue, internándose en lugares y situaciones insospechadas que harán al lector dudar de su verosimilitud.

Antonio Rodríguez Almodóvar ha investigado el cuento tradicional y por su trabajo de recopilación y restauración del folclor oral en *Cuentos al amor de la lumbre* (1983–1984) le otorgaron el Premio Nacional de Literatura Infantil y Juvenil. También obtuvo el Premio Internacional de

Literatura Juvenil Infanta Elena por su novela *Un lugar parecido al paraíso* (1991), y es responsable de la colección *Cuentos de la media lunita* (1986–1992).

Carmen Martín Gaite (España, 1925). *Caperucita en Manhattan.* Novela. Ediciones Siruela, Madrid, 1990.

Basándose en el clásico cuento de Perrault, Carmen Martín Gaite nos cuenta una versión muy singular. La Caperucita de Carmen Martín Gaite vive en Brooklyn, N.Y., se llama Sara, tiene diez años y quiere llevarle una tarta de fresa a su abuelita, una cantante que vive en Manhattan. Tampoco falta el lobo, Mr. Woolf, que es un pastelero multimillonario, y Miss Lunatic, una mendiga que vive escondida en la Estatua de la Libertad.

A lo largo de su carrera literaria, Carmen Martín Gaite ha ganado varios premios (Café de Gijón, Nadal, Anagrama de Ensayo y Premio de la Crítica). Entre su obra creativa más importante se encuentran las novelas *Ritmo lento* (1963), *El cuarto de atrás* (1978), *Nubosidad variable* (1992) y *La reina de las nieves* (1994); las colecciones de cuentos infantiles *El pastel del diablo* (1985) y *El castillo de las tres murallas* (1981) y los libros de investigación histórica *Usos amorosos del siglo XVIII en España* (1972) y *Macanaz, otro paciente de la Inquisición* (1969).

Augusto Monterroso (Guatemala, 1921). «La mosca que soñaba que era un águila». Cuento. Pertenece al libro *La oveja negra y demás fábulas* (1969). Editorial Alfaguara Juvenil, Madrid, 1988.

El autor logra en este relato breve, como todos los suyos, hacernos reflexionar más allá de la lectura. En este caso el personaje, una mosca que en su sueño nocturno se convierte en águila, representa, por un lado, el deseo de querer que sus sueños se cumplan y, por otro, el temor de abandonar la realidad.

Aunque nació en Honduras y vive en México desde 1956, Augusto Monterroso siempre se ha considerado a sí mismo guatemalteco. Políticamente comprometido desde muy joven, tuvo que abandonar su país y se exilió en México donde ha realizado la mayoría de su obra literaria. La narrativa de Monterroso se caracteriza por su finísimo sentido del humor y la brevedad de sus textos. Tiene publicados libros de ensayo y ficción entre los que figuran: *Obras completas (y otros cuentos)* (1959), *Movimiento perpetuo* (1972), *Lo demás es silencio* (1978), *La palabra mágica* (1983) y el libro de memorias *Los buscadores de oro* (1993).

Colección 3
Enfrentarse a los riesgos

Jairo Aníbal Niño (Colombia, 1941). *De las alas caracolí.* Relato. Editorial Oveja Negra, Bogotá, 1985.

Utilizando el mar como escenario, este relato de Jairo Aníbal Niño trata de unos niños que en el proceso de rescatar un objeto muy preciado por ellos, viven grandes aventuras. Algunos de los fantásticos personajes y lugares que conocen son un árbol bajo cuyas ramas siempre llueve, casas que contienen otras viviendas en su interior, la casa isla, los lirivalsos (unos seres diminutos, con cara de payasos, diez alas y cuatro manos) y Yaruk, un ser de extraordinaria fuerza.

Aunque Jairo Aníbal Niño es más conocido como dramaturgo, también es poeta y autor de varios libros de cuentos. El más conocido, *Zoro*, recibió el premio Enka de literatura infantil en 1977. Otros títulos son *Punto final*, *Puro pueblo* y *Toda la vida*.

Como autor teatral se destaca *El monte calvo* que recibió el premio Festival Mundial de Teatro de Nancy (Francia) y *Las bodas de lata o el baile de los arzobispos* por la que fue galardonado en el Festival de Teatro Presidente de la República.

Arturo Trejo Villaforte (México, 1953). «Una aventura inolvidable». Cuento. Pertenece al libro *Atrapados en la escuela*. Editorial Selector, México, 1994.

Inspirado por las lecturas de libros de viajes, un niño de 12 años decide capitanear una expedición con un grupo de compañeros. Un día 12 de octubre, fecha en que Cristóbal Colón llegó a América, y en una balsa que bautizan «La Niña», como una de las carabelas de Colón, emprenden un viaje nocturno en el que enfrentan muchas dificultades. Al final de la travesía no obtienen la «gloria» del famoso navegante pero sí la satisfacción personal de su aventura.

Arturo Trejo Villafuerte pertenece a una generación joven de escritores mexicanos que, al igual que sus contemporáneos, como Paco Ignacio Taibo II y José Agustín, ha sabido llegar a un público juvenil utilizando en sus narraciones situaciones familiares y describiéndolas con un lenguaje actual. Es periodista y traductor al español de Dylan Thomas, W. B. Yeats y e. e. cummings, entre otros. Fundador del Taller de Poesía Sintética, es asimismo autor de los libros *Mester de hotelería* (1979), *A quien pueda interesar* (1982) y la colección *Doce modos* (1976).

Colección 4
Un más allá

Juan Valera (España, 1824–1905). «El pájaro verde». Cuento. Editorial Escuela Española, Madrid, 1986.

Este cuento, al igual que *La muñequita, La buena fama* o *El pescadorcito Urashima*, está situado en un mundo fantástico y poblado de elementos mágicos, príncipes y hechiceros. La historia trata de una hermosa princesa a la que su padre quiere casar, pero todos los príncipes pretendientes que piden su mano son desdeñosamente rechazados por la bella muchacha. Una mañana mientras se peina, un pájaro verde entra por la ventana y le arrebata la cinta de sus cabellos. A partir de entonces las visitas del misterioso pájaro se repiten y la indiferencia de la princesa se transforma en ansiedad por volver a verlo.

Juan Valera estudió Filosofía en la Universidad de Málaga (España) y más tarde se licenció en Derecho. Sus primeras publicaciones fueron poemas en revistas literarias. Desempeñó cargos públicos en diferentes países y de una de estas experiencias surge la novela *Genio y figura* (1895). Fue fundador del periódico *El Contemporáneo* y en 1861 fue elegido miembro de la Real Academia de la Lengua Española. Su obra literaria no se limita a la poesía y la novela, Juan Valera es también autor de estudios históricos y políticos, ensayos, crítica literaria y teatro. Entre sus textos más importantes se destacan sus novelas *Pepita Jiménez* (1874), *El comendador Mendoza* (1877), *Doña Luz* (1879) y *Juanita la Larga* (1895).

Tulio Febres Cordero (Venezuela, 1860–1938). «La leyenda del díctamo». Pertenece al libro *Mitos y tradiciones*. Editorial Biblioteca Popular, Venezolana.

El título alude a una yerba que, al parecer, crece en lo alto de los páramos andinos y que, según los indígenas, tiene la virtud de prolongar la vida. Este relato nos cuenta la misteriosa historia de una reina indígena que contrae una extraña enfermedad que la va debilitando día a día. Poseedora de un anillo de gran valor, se lo confía a su doncella favorita, Mistajá, para que suba al Páramo de los Sacrificios y lo ofrezca a cambio de su bienestar físico; Mistajá lo entierra en el centro de la cima y de ahí brota la yerba que le devolverá la salud a su reina.

Tulio Febres fue miembro de la Academia Venezolana de la Lengua y profesor de la Universidad de los Andes pero se le recordará como historiador y escritor costumbrista. Es autor de los libros *Mitos y tradiciones* y *Tradiciones y leyendas*, volumen en donde se encuentra el relato *El perro nevado*, que es a la literatura venezolana lo que el burro de *Platero y yo* es a la española. Es también autor de *Memorias de un muchacho* (1924).

Ramón del Valle Inclán (España, 1886–1936). «El miedo». Cuento. Pertenece al libro *Jardín umbrío* (1903). Editorial Espasa-Calpe, Madrid, 1994.

«El miedo» es una historia de duendes y almas en pena que está inspirada en una de tantas leyendas que se contaban en Galicia. Aunque la voz del narrador es la de un hombre casi anciano que nos cuenta lo que le sucedió cuando era un joven cadete y acudió a una capilla para confesarse, los personajes son esqueletos que parecen rebelarse en sus tumbas.

Ramón del Valle Inclán es uno de los escritores más importantes de la literatura española. Pocos se han esmerado tanto en el uso del lenguaje como Valle Inclán. Sus obras más importantes son *Sonatas* (1902–1905), *Luces de* bohemia (1920 y 1924), *Divinas palabras* (1920), *Tirano Banderas* (1926) y la serie de novelas *El ruedo ibérico* (1927).

Colección 5
La convivencia

El Inca Garcilaso de la Vega (Perú, 1539–1616). «Historia de Pedro Serrano». Fragmento de *Comentarios reales*. Editorial Biblioteca Ayacucho, Caracas, 1985.

Anticipándose varios siglos al personaje del escritor inglés Daniel Defoe, este *Robinson Crusoe* peruano es sin duda el primer libro de aventuras de este tipo. La breve «Historia de Pedro Serrano» cuenta la aventura de un español que logra nadar a una isla desierta después de que su barco naufraga. En ella se las ingenia para sobrevivir a solas durante tres años. Luego, cuando llega otro hombre a la isla, ambos se ven obligados a convivir juntos con la naturaleza.

Comentarios reales, que se publicó en Lisboa en 1609, y la *Historia general del Perú* (1616) relatan la historia del imperio inca, la conquista española y las posteriores guerras civiles del virreinato. Ambas obras tienen tintes autobiográficos y, a menudo, se ha puesto en duda su valor histórico. Sin embargo, eso no rebaja la calidad del Inca Garcilaso como prosista, ya que es considerado como uno de los más importantes del siglo XVI.

Monserrat del Amo (Madrid, 1927). *El abrazo del Nilo*. Narrativa. Editorial Bruño, Madrid, 1990.

En *El abrazo del Nilo*, Montserrat del Amo nos hace compartir la experiencia de sus protagonistas, unos jóvenes que recorren el Nilo en una canoa. El libro es además una aventura cultural, ya que la autora nos habla de los nubios, del Valle de los Reyes y de Nefertiti, insertándolos en el relato a la vez que nos ofrece una lección sobre la convivencia y el respeto mutuo entre dos pueblos diferentes.

Montserrat del Amo se doctoró en Literatura Hispánica y fue durante varios años profesora de Literatura. Autora de cuentos, novelas, poemas y obras de teatro, tiene publicados más de cuarenta libros. Ha recibido numerosos premios literarios, entre otros, el Lazarillo de 1960, el Doncel de 1969 y el Nacional de Literatura Infantil y Juvenil de España de 1970. En 1991 obtuvo el premio CCEI al mejor libro del año por *La casa pintada*. Otros títulos suyos importantes son: *Zuecos y naranjos* (1972), *Soñado mar* (1981), *El fuego y el oro* (1984) y *La encrucijada* (1986).

Jorge Ibargüengoitia (México 1928–1983). «Cuento de la niña condecorada». Pertenece al libro *Piezas y cuentos para niños*. Editorial Joaquín Mortiz, México, 1989.

En las tres breves piezas teatrales y los siete cuentos que componen este volumen hay personajes tradicionales como ranas, magos, ratones y, por supuesto, niños. Lo que es menos tradicional es la forma con que Ibargüengoitia los presenta. En el cuento seleccionado, la protagonista, Mandolina, es una niña admirada por los adultos pero resentida por los niños. Con muy pocas palabras el autor nos ofrece una moraleja que no es convencional: lo admirado no siempre es lo deseado y, a veces, nos aleja de la armonía con los demás.

Jorge Ibargüengoitia inició su carrera literaria como autor teatral con *Susana y los jóvenes* (1954). Sin embargo su fama mayor la consiguió como novelista con narraciones que se caracterizaban por su humor e ironía. *Los relámpagos de agosto* (1964), *Estas ruinas que ves* (1974), *Las muertas* (1977) y *Los conspiradores* (1981) son algunos de los títulos de sus novelas. También fue autor de un libro de relatos breves *La ley de Herodes y otros cuentos* (1967) y uno de ensayos, *Viajes a la América ignota* (1962). En 1983, junto con Manuel Scorza y otros escritores que regresaban de un congreso de escritores en Madrid, murió en un accidente de avión.

Colección 6
El paisaje de la amistad

Elena Fortún (España, 1886–1954). *Celia y sus amigos* (1939). Novela. Editorial Aguilar, Madrid, 1982.

Celia y sus amigos es el quinto tomo de una saga que la autora comenzó en 1928. En este volumen Celia pasa de la niñez a la adolescencia y nos cuenta su viaje con Antonio y Casilda, su amistad con Raymond, un muchacho francés, su encuentro con un grupo de niños chinos y la sesión de cine que organiza con sus amigos en la casa de sus tíos. En el último capítulo, "la Celia niña" se despide del lector para dar paso a su hermano Cuchifritín, que aparecerá en el volumen siguiente (*Cuchifritín el hermano de Celia*) como personaje principal.

Elena Fortún es el seudónimo de Asunción Aragoneses Urquijo. Siempre relacionada con la literatura infantil colaboró en numerosas publicaciones, como la revista *Blanco y Negro* en cuyo suplemento dominical, *Gente menuda,* salió por primera vez el personaje de Celia. Esta saga familiar, que comenzó en 1928, continuaría casi hasta su muerte y es considerada hoy en día como un clásico dentro de la literatura infantil española. En 1994 se llevó a las pantallas del cine. En 1987 un manuscrito inédito fue encontrado que corresponde al periodo de la Guerra Civil Española. Éste, *Celia en la revolución,* tiene un gran valor documental.

Ángela C. Ionescu (Rumania, 1937). *Los amigos.* Relatos. Editorial Bruño, Madrid, 1991.

Utilizando un lenguaje poético y un tono de misterio, el libro contiene tres pequeños relatos que se relacionan por medio de los personajes y por el sentido de la amistad que la autora defiende. En ella nos cuenta la historia de un grupo de amigos y su relación con Marta, que les sirve de lazo de unión a la vez que les da ánimo y los ayuda a ver el mundo de una forma diferente.

A pesar de que nació en Rumania, a Ángela C. Ionescu se le considera una autora española. Doctora en Filosofía y Letras, es profesora de Literatura Infantil en la UNED (Universidad Española a Distancia). Lleva publicando desde comienzos de los años sesenta y pertenece al grupo de escritoras que, junto a Ana María Matute, Carmen Kurtz y Montserrat del Amo, renovaron la literatura infantil española. Ha recibido, entre otros, el premio Lazarillo, el Amade, el Doncel de cuentos infantiles y el internacional Ciudad de Trento por su obra *El país de las cosas perdidas* (1971). Otros libros suyos son *Detrás de las nubes* (1963), *Arriba en el monte* (1967), *La flor de la sal* (1987) y *Déjame solo* (1990).

María Elena Walsh (Argentina, 1930). «Los amigos». Poema. Pertenece al libro *Tutú Marambá.* Editorial Luis Fariña, Buenos Aires, 1966.

Aunque el título del libro, *Tutú Marambá,* hace referencia al duende malvado de un mito brasileño, María Elena Walsh ha querido modificar la leyenda ofreciéndonos un poemario en el que todos los personajes, los animales y los humanos son bondadosos y tienen un alto sentido de la amistad. El poema seleccionado es un breve canto a los amigos con los que compartimos tanto las diversiones como las preocupaciones a lo largo de nuestras vidas.

María Elena Walsh inició su trayectoria como escritora con el libro *Otoño imperdonable* (1947). Otras publicaciones suyas son *Apenas viaje* (1948), *Baladas con Ángel* (1951), *Casi milagro* (1958) y *Hecho a mano* (1965). Su inspiración se nutre con frecuencia de la poesía popular y son bien apreciados sus cuentos y poemas para niños.

Colección 7
Todos somos iguales

José Manuel Marroquín (Colombia 1827–1908). «El tigre y el conejo». Fábula. Pertenece al volumen I de *Historia y antología de la literatura infantil iberoamericana.* Editorial Everest, León (España), 1987.

El tono humorístico de la fábula seleccionada, como todas las del autor, la hace divertida y didáctica a la vez. «El tigre y el conejo» nos muestra a dos animales de desigual fuerza que se encuentran en una cueva. El más débil, impulsado por el miedo, recurre a su ingenio para lograr espantar al tigre. El final ofrece una moraleja doble. Por una parte suguiere la posibilidad de que el heroísmo es algo accidental y, por otra, señala que en determinadas situaciones hasta dos animales tan dispares pueden sentir el mismo temor.

José Manuel Marroquín, al igual que su contemporáneo Carrasquilla (también incluido en la Colección 8), compartió su interés y dedicación por la educación y el mundo de la juventud. Fue pedagogo y llegó a ser presidente de la República de Colombia. Sus fábulas permanecen más vigentes que las de otros autores quizás debido a su humor.

Arturo Souto (España, 1930). «Coyote 13». Poema. Pertenece al libro *La plaga del crisantemo* (1960). Incluido en el volumen *Los mejores cuentos mexicanos,* editado por Gustavo Sáinz. Editorial Océano-Éxito, Barcelona, 1984.

«Coyote 13» es la historia de un vaquero solitario que cuida en las llanuras a sus rebaños. Su mundo, que es "tan chico que le cabría en el sombrero", se reduce a esos llanos y su vida se centra en el empeño de matar a los coyotes que atacan a su ganado. El protagonista logra hacerlo con todos excepto con el número trece, el más viejo, que siempre se le escapa. Su incapacidad de matarlo se convierte en un reto a su orgullo y honor, pero cuando finalmente lo tiene al alcance de un tiro, percibe el miedo en la mirada de la bestia y decide no matarlo porque descubre que tienen algo en común. Como él, el coyote está viejo y solo. Gracias a esa experiencia se salva a sí mismo de la indiferencia que lo dominaba, y la presencia del coyote le garantiza compañía y un deseo de vivir.

Aunque Arturo Souto nació en Madrid, su obra es considerada literatura mexicana ya que a los doce años se trasladó con su familia a México, país donde todavía reside. Es profesor y funcionario de instituciones culturales y tiene varias publicaciones de crítica literaria como *Grandes textos creativos de la literatura española* (1967), *Apuntes sobre la teoría literaria de Azorín y la Generación del 98* (1955) o *El Romanticismo* (1955). A pesar de que sólo escribió un libro de relatos, *La plaga del crisantemo* (1960), es considerado un clásico moderno y el cuento seleccionado para esta colección, *Coyote 13,* es uno de los que aparecen con más frecuencia en las antologías.

León Felipe (España, 1884–1968). «Como tú...». Poema. Pertenece a *Versos y oraciones del caminante* (1920). Editorial Visor, Madrid, 1983.

En este poema el autor se dirige a una piedra y establece una comparación entre su propia vida y la del guijarro. Utilizando dicho símil se nos revela la personalidad humilde de la voz del verso y su carácter peregrino, a la vez que nos aproxima a nuestra igualdad con la naturaleza.

León Felipe tuvo en su juventud profesiones tan dispares como las de actor de teatro y farmacéutico. Exiliado a Estados Unidos a causa de la Guerra Civil Española, ejerció como profesor de Literatura Española. Asimismo, se dedicó a la enseñanza en México, país al que se mudó más tarde y en el que residió hasta su muerte. La poesía de León Felipe, inspirada en gran medida por el poeta estadounidense Walt Whitman y por los versículos bíblicos, nunca se ajustó a ningún convencionalismo. Sus libros más importantes son *Español del éxodo y del llanto* (1939), *Ganarás la luz* (1943), *Llamadme publicano* (1950) y *El ciervo* (1958).

Colección 8
Huellas de grandes espíritus

Pablo Neruda (Chile 1904–1973). «Amor América». Poema. Pertenece al *Canto general* (1950). Incluido en la edición *Pablo Neruda para niños*. Ediciones de la Torre, Madrid, 1988.

Este es el primer poema de la gran epopeya americana de Neruda titulada *Canto general,* que con sus casi 15 mil versos es el más extenso escrito en Hispanomérica. El canto "Amor América" es un lamento de la destrucción de las civilizaciones precolombinas a manos de los conquistadores. Pablo Neruda concibió la idea del *Canto general* en los viajes que efectuó por toda Iberoamérica. *Alturas de Machu Picchu,* un largo poema que también pertenece a la misma obra, lo escribió tras visitar en Perú la ciudad perdida de los incas.

Pablo Neruda publicó sus primeros poemas en 1918 y 1919 en revistas literarias. En 1924 se publicó *Veinte poemas de amor y una canción desesperada*. Otro de sus libros más importantes es *Residencia en la tierra* que apareció en dos volúmenes, uno en 1933 y el segundo en 1935. Neruda recibió el Premio Nobel en 1971.

Ricardo Carrasquilla (Colombia, 1827–1886). «El abrazo». Romance. Incluido en el volumen *Romancero colombiano: Homenaje a Simón Bolívar* (1883). Editorial Banco de la República, Bogotá, 1980.

Este romance forma parte de los que componen el *Romancero colombiano,* volumen que varios poetas de ese país dedicaron a la memoria de Simón Bolívar. Ricardo Carrasquilla no evoca ninguna acción guerrera del general pero nos transmite el fervor y el entusiasmo que el pueblo siente por él por medio de personajes como una anciana que no quiere morir sin haber recibido un abrazo del Libertador.

Ricardo Carrasquilla es una importante figura en la historia de la literatura infantil de Colombia. Es autor de una gran selección de fábulas morales. Dedicó parte de su vida al magisterio y fue fundador del Liceo de la Infancia, colegio en el que se educaría otra gran figura de la literatura colombiana, José Asunción Silva. Otras obras suyas son: *Ofrendas del ingenio, Coplas* y *Las fiestas de Bogotá.*

Eduardo Caballero Calderón (Colombia, 1910). «La varita mágica». Cuento. Pertenece al volumen II de *Historia en cuentos.* Carlos Valencia Editores, Bogotá, 1989.

En la serie de cuatro volúmenes que componen esta colección, Caballero Calderón se propuso ofrecer a los niños una visión de la historia en la que mezcla personajes reales con otros inventados. Un buen ejemplo es «La varita mágica», la historia de Bochica, un dios indígena que reestablece el bienestar de su pueblo con un «quesque» (varita) de oro. Este relato está contado por un niño indígena al fraile Bartolomé de Las Casas.

Eduardo Caballero Calderón fue embajador de su país, periodista, ensayista y narrador. Sus obras se caracterizan por sus valores humanos y su gran interés en la vida campesina. Así lo muestran novelas suyas como *Siervo sin tierra* (1954), *El Cristo de espaldas* (1952), *Manuel Pocho* (1962) y *Caín* (1959).

Rubén Darío (Nicaragua, 1867–1916). «Caupolicán». Poema. Pertenece a *Azul...*(1888). Incluido en el volumen *Rubén Darío para niños.* Ediciones de la Torre, Madrid, 1988.

Inmortalizado por Alonso de Ercilla en su poema épico *La Araucana,* Caupolicán era el cacique de los araucanos durante el enfrentamiento de esta tribu indígena contra los conquistadores españoles. Rubén Darío ha escogido para su poema el momento en que Caupolicán supera la prueba de resistencia y de fuerza de voluntad que lo convertirá en jefe de su pueblo. El poeta destaca el poder físico del héroe que encarna las cualidades y la belleza de su gente.

A Rubén Darío se le valora como uno de los poetas de mayor importancia del mundo hispánico. Su obra revolucionó toda la literatura escrita en español en su época y su influencia es considerada por la crítica literaria como una de las más decisivas de este siglo. Sus textos más importantes son *Prosas profanas* (1896) *Cantos de vida y esperanza* (1905) y *El canto errante* (1907).

TRANSPARENCIES

The *Audiovisual Resources* for *Elements of Literature* © 1997 contains fine art transparencies. A number of these transparencies are recommended for use with selections in the *Encuentros* program.

Collection 1 *Desafíos*

6.1.3
"Mary"
Gregory Hildebrandt
Link: "Trabajo de campo"

6.4.1
"Elephants"
M. John English
Link: ESCENA CULTURAL on Animal Communication

Collection 3 *Enfrentarse a los riesgos*

6.3.1
"Reflections: Tribute to Our Iron Skywalkers"
Arnold Jacobs
Link: collection theme

6.5.2
"Cumpleaños"
Carmen Lomas Garza
Link: "Chanclas"

Collection 4 *Un más allá*

6.7.1
"Mt. Vesuvius"
Joseph Mallord William Turner
Link: collection theme

6.8.2
"A Magnificent Steed as Black as Night"
Edward Julius Detmond
Link: collection theme

6.8.3
"Éowyn and the Nazgûl"
Brothers Hildebrandt
Link: collection theme

6.3.3
Amazing Stories cover
Frank R. Paul
Link: "Todo el verano en un día"

Collection 5 *La convivencia*

6.1.2
"Cloak of Heritage"
Kevin Warren Smith
Link: collection theme

Collection 6 *El paisaje de la amistad*

6.2.1
"Sing to the Stars"
Sandra Speidel
Link: *Yo sé por qué canta el pájaro enjaulado*

Collection 7 *Todos somos iguales*

6.8.2
"A Magnificent Steed as Black as Night"
Edward Julius Detmond
Link: "Los dos ruiseñores"

Collection 8 *Huellas de grandes espíritus*

6.6.1
"An Apartment Corner"
Claude Monet
Link: "El árbol de oro"

6.1.1
"Afternoon Shadows"
Robert Vickrey
Link: "Cuentos de junio"

Nombre _____ Clase _____ Fecha _____

de *Cuando era puertorriqueña* • *Esmeralda Santiago* p. 3

Examen de lectura
Puntuación _____

Vocabulario

Escribe en la línea antes de cada oración el sinónimo correspondiente a la(s) palabra(s) subrayada(s). (3 puntos por pregunta)

Palabras para escoger				
cima	susurro	grieta	debatir	penumbra
trancazo	cautelosamente	fangoso	estrépito	siniestro

_____ 1. Lo vi huyendo bajo la <u>media luz</u> de la tarde.

_____ 2. Después de una tarde entera de lluvia, el camino estaba <u>lleno de barro</u>.

_____ 3. En las <u>puntas</u> de montañas de gran altura es difícil respirar.

_____ 4. Su mirada <u>extraña</u> provocó que sufriera pesadillas durante la noche.

_____ 5. <u>Cuidadosamente</u> se levantó y se asomó a la ventana.

_____ 6. Los cantos de los insectos desaparecieron cuando se refugiaron en <u>los agujeros</u> de las paredes.

_____ 7. Ni la estática de la radio, ni los <u>azotes</u> del viento pudieron evitar que se durmiera.

_____ 8. Cuando escuchaban la caída de algún árbol <u>discutían</u> qué árbol era y en qué dirección había caído.

_____ 9. Un <u>ruido muy fuerte</u> se oyó en la cocina: se había caído toda la vajilla.

_____ 10. El <u>sonido</u> del río producía una sensación de paz.

Lectura a fondo

En el espacio en blanco escribe la letra que corresponde a la **mejor** respuesta. (5 puntos por pregunta)

_____ 11. Cuando empieza el relato de Esmeralda Santiago, su familia
   a. se va a cambiar de casa.
   b. se prepara para protegerse de un huracán.
   c. celebra que ha pasado un huracán.
   d. repara los destrozos de un huracán.

_____ 12. ¿Cuál de las oraciones siguientes indica que el texto es una autobiografía?
   a. Los hombres montaron un juego de dominó.
   b. El cielo bajó hasta la cima de las montañas.
   c. Busqué a Delsa, Norma, Héctor...Por primera vez no tuve que correrles detrás.
   d. La niebla se colgaba sobre el patio, alrededor de ramas y pedazos esparcidos.

_____ 13. Esmeralda Santiago contrasta
   a. la fuerza del huracán con la paz del ojo del huracán.
   b. las familias puertorriqueñas con las familias de los Estados Unidos.
   c. la riqueza del campo y el destrozo que causa el huracán.
   d. los papeles de los niños y las niñas.

_____ 14. El huracán es un recuerdo bonito para Esmeralda Santiago porque
   a. era la única oportunidad que tenía de estar con sus familiares.
   b. debido al destrozo del huracán su familia emigró a los Estados Unidos.
   c. recuerda con cariño la cooperación de las familias durante el huracán.
   d. los huracanes son algo típico de Puerto Rico.

_____ 15. Al final del fragmento la narradora afirma: «...las figuras de nuestros padres y hermanos moviéndose cautelosamente en un mundo sin extremos ni imágenes, y esa franja de sol viajando a través del patio sin tocarlos ni una vez». ¿Por qué hay una franja de sol si había un huracán?
   a. En ese momento el huracán ya se había terminado.
   b. En ese momento estaba pasando el ojo del huracán.
   c. Estaba amaneciendo.
   d. Esmeralda Santiago está soñando.

Respuesta a fondo

16. El estado de ánimo dentro de la casa durante el huracán es de armonía. Basándote en el texto, explica por qué. (10 puntos)

_____

_____

17. En la tabla anota lo que se hizo (en relación a los elementos que se enumeran en la columna de la izquierda) antes de la llegada del huracán. (10 puntos)

al nene	
a los niños	
la casa de los vecinos	
la comida	

Composición

18. Describe cómo actuó la gente durante el huracán. Por su comportamiento, ¿crees que el huracán es un acontecimiento extraordinario, o algo a lo que ya están acostumbrados? (25 puntos)

Nombre _____ Clase _____ Fecha _____

Trabajo de campo • *Rose Del Castillo Guilbault*   p. 13

Examen de lectura   Puntuación _____

Vocabulario

Escribe en la línea antes de cada oración el sinónimo que corresponde a la(s) palabra(s) subrayada(s). (2 puntos por pregunta)

Palabras para escoger			
capataz	nitidez	plazo	desalentar
costear	ser incapaz	mediar	ceñir

_____ 1. Mis padres me dijeron que no me podían <u>pagar</u> los gastos del viaje.

_____ 2. Mi papá <u>habló por nosotras</u> con el jefe para que nos dieran el trabajo.

_____ 3. Me <u>até</u> el pañuelo a la cintura.

_____ 4. El <u>último día para entregar</u> el trabajo es el quince de diciembre.

_____ 5. El <u>encargado del campo</u> les enseñó cómo recoger los ajos.

_____ 6. Recuerdo con <u>claridad</u> mi primer trabajo en el campo.

_____ 7. Las noticias del mal tiempo me <u>desanimaron</u>.

_____ 8. Mi perro no <u>tiene la habilidad</u> de reconocer a alguien por el olor.

Lectura a fondo

En el espacio en blanco escribe la letra que corresponde a la **mejor** respuesta. (5 puntos por pregunta)

_____ 9. La narradora empezó a trabajar en el campo porque
   a. era el trabajo que hacía su padre.
   b. le gustaba hacer ese trabajo.
   c. ese era el único trabajo que sabía hacer.
   d. estaba aburrida.

_____ 10. El trabajo que hizo en el campo consistía en
   a. cosechar papas.
   b. recoger uvas.
   c. recoger ajos.
   d. recoger algodón.

_____ 11. ¿Por qué le preocupa al jefe del padre que trabajen la niña y la madre?
   a. La madre de Rose se cansa con facilidad.
   b. Es ilegal que trabajen los niños.
   c. Rose y la madre no tienen experiencia.
   d. Quieren el dinero para irse a México.

_____ 12. La niña y la madre deciden trabajar en el campo porque
   a. quieren irse de vacaciones.
   b. el padre se lo pide.
   c. quieren ser igual que los hombres.
   d. le hacen falta más trabajadores al jefe.

_____ 13. El último día, cuando la niña siente que ya no puede volver a los surcos
   a. no vuelve al trabajo.
   b. vuelve al trabajo y lo termina sola.
   c. ella, la madre y el padre terminan el trabajo juntos.
   d. sólo vuelven al trabajo la madre y el padre.

Respuesta a fondo

14. ¿Qué siente la niña al pensar en su experiencia de trabajo? ¿Prefiere olvidarla o le parece buena a pesar del enorme esfuerzo? Justifica tu respuesta en las líneas que siguen. (12 puntos)

_____
_____
_____

15. En el siguiente diagrama de constelación anota los obstáculos que la madre y la hija tuvieron que pasar para conseguir el dinero. (12 puntos)

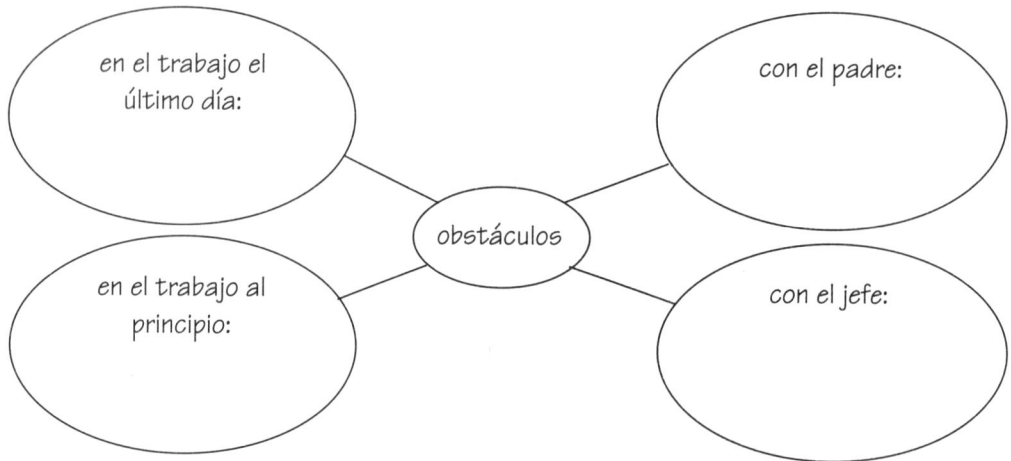

Composición

16. Al principio del texto la narradora explica que aunque trabajar en los campos no tiene nada de romántico, «sí es una experiencia rica en lecciones importantes para la vida, lecciones acerca del trabajo, los valores familiares y lo que significa crecer como mexicano en los Estados Unidos». Explica lo que aprendió la narradora acerca del trabajo y los valores familiares. (35 puntos)

Nombre _____ Clase _____ Fecha _____

de *Negrita* • *Onelio Jorge Cardoso* p. 22

Examen de lectura   Puntuación _____

Vocabulario

Escribe en la línea antes de cada oración el sinónimo correspondiente a la(s) palabra(s) subrayada(s). (3 puntos por pregunta)

Palabras para escoger			
remanso	montero	retozar	follaje
atajar	apesadumbrado	gajo	colindante

_____ 1. El rumor del agua que caía en la corriente detenida del río se mezclaba con el sonido del viento.

_____ 2. Las hojas de los árboles no los dejaban ver el cielo.

_____ 3. Estuvimos recogiendo ramas para la fogata toda la mañana.

_____ 4. Pedro, que vivía en la finca de al lado, venía cargando un saco.

_____ 5. Mi amigo estaba triste porque había roto un jarrón antiguo de su mamá.

_____ 6. La perrita llegó saltando a la casa del dueño.

_____ 7. Es su costumbre interrumpir a la gente cuando habla.

_____ 8. El cazador volvió a la finca con dos patos y un concjo.

Lectura a fondo

Escribe en el espacio en blanco la letra que corresponde a la **mejor** respuesta. (5 puntos por pregunta)

_____ 9. El montero iba a ahogar a Negrita porque
   a. el dueño de la finca se lo ordenó.
   b. al montero no le gustaban los perros.
   c. al dueño de la finca no le gustaban los perros.
   d. Ninguna de las respuestas es correcta.

_____ 10. ¿Cuál de las siguientes respuestas contrasta con la descripción del río?
   a. la alegría de los niños
   b. la pena del montero
   c. la pena de los niños
   d. el peligro del bosque

_____ 11. Antes de llevarla al río, ¿qué había hecho el montero para salvar a Negrita?
   a. La había escondido.
   b. La había dejado escapar.
   c. La había dejado con unos vecinos.
   d. La había regalado.

_____ 12. ¿Qué sucedió cuando soltaron a Negrita en el río?
   a. Se escapó.
   b. Se ahogó.
   c. Nadó hacia el niño más pequeño.
   d. Nadó hacia el montero.

Respuesta a fondo

13. ¿Qué crees que habrían hecho los niños si su padre hubiera permitido que ahogaran a Negrita? Justifica tu respuesta en las líneas que siguen. (14 puntos)

_____

_____

14. En la constelación anota cuatro elementos que se asocian al río. (12 puntos)

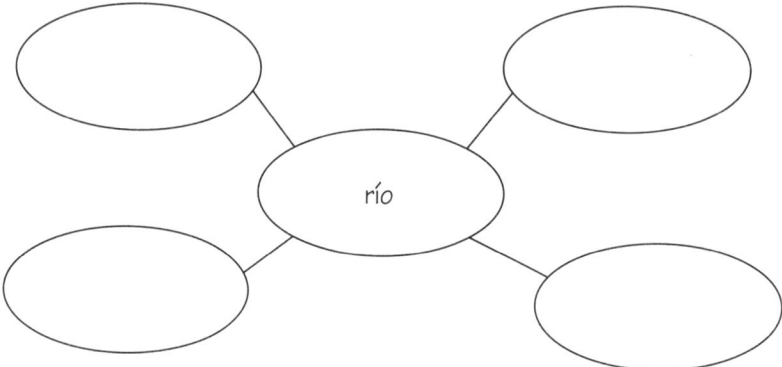

Composición

15. El compañerismo entre los animales y las personas siempre ha sido un tema popular dentro de la literatura. A través del resto de la novela, Negrita y Bruno pasan por grandes aventuras en las que se ayudan mutuamente. Describe en dos párrafos los beneficios que aportan los animales a las personas. (30 puntos)

Nombre _____ Clase _____ Fecha _____

Una carta a Dios • *Gregorio López y Fuentes* p. 51

Examen de lectura   Puntuación _____

Vocabulario

Escribe en las líneas numeradas debajo del texto el sinónimo correspondiente a la(s) palabra(s) subrayada(s). (3 puntos por pregunta)

Palabras para escoger			
mortificar	determinación	afligir	fortificar

La (**1**) resolución hecha por el ministro, en la que se establecía que se (**2**) asegurarían todas las ventanas de las casas tenía (**3**) entristecida a toda la población. La idea de que por un largo tiempo la luz no entraría por sus ventanas los dejaba (**4**) sin consuelo.

1. _____
2. _____
3. _____
4. _____

Lectura fondo

Escribe en el espacio en blanco la letra que corresponde a la **mejor** respuesta. (5 puntos por pregunta)

_____ **5.** La tierra necesitaba «una lluvia, o al menos un fuerte aguacero» para que
   a. no se secara el trigo.
   b. acabaran de crecer el maíz y el frijol.
   c. el campo se limpiara de insectos.
   d. hubiera agua para beber.

_____ **6.** ¿Cuál fue la consecuencia del granizo?
   a. Los hijos de Lencho se pusieron a trabajar en el correo.
   b. Lencho perdió la esperanza.
   c. La destrucción del maíz y el frijol.
   d. Todas las anteriores.

_____ **7.** Lencho necesitaba los cien pesos para
   a. mandar a sus hijos pequeños a la escuela.
   b. abrir una frutería.
   c. volver a sembrar y vivir durante el año.
   d. pagar lo que debía.

____ **8.** El dinero que recibió Lencho
  a. se lo había dado el cartero solo.
  b. se lo habían dado el cartero, el jefe de la oficina y varios amigos.
  c. se lo mandó Dios.
  d. se lo mandaron sus hermanos.

____ **9.** Lencho, al recibir poco más de cincuenta pesos,
  a. pensó que Dios se equivocó.
  b. pensó que en la oficina de correos se quedaron con el resto.
  c. se puso loco de alegría.
  d. pensó que debía aceptar lo que le mandaron.

Respuesta a fondo

10. El hecho de que Lencho no recibió la cantidad de dinero que había pedido, ¿afectó de alguna manera su fe? (16 puntos)

11. Completa con la información correspondiente el siguiente esquema de causa y efecto. (12 puntos)

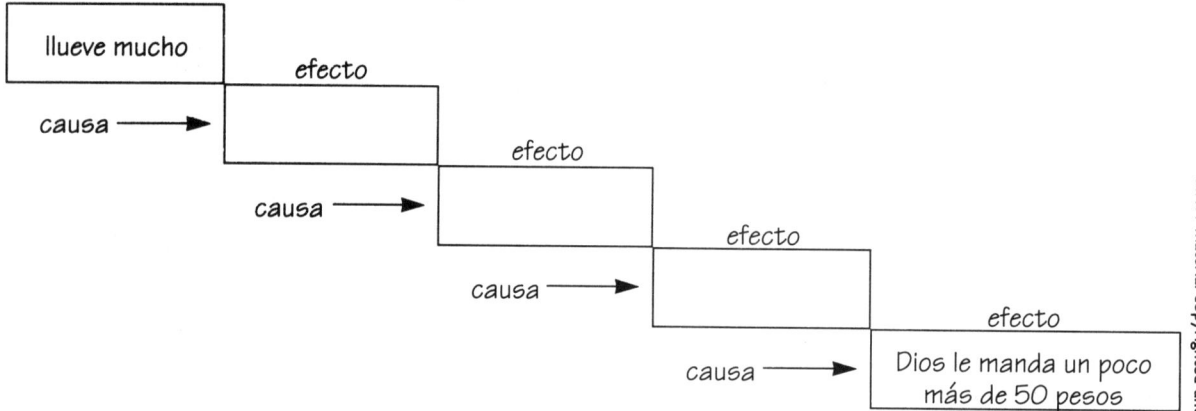

Composición

12. ¿Qué harías tú si recibieras una carta como la de Lencho? (35 puntos)

Nombre _____ Clase _____ Fecha _____

El adivinador de máscaras • *Antonio Robles*   p.61

Examen de lectura   Puntuación _____

Vocabulario

Escribe en la línea antes de cada oración el sinónimo correspondiente a la(s) palabra(s) subrayada(s). (3 puntos por pregunta)

Palabras para escoger		
fracasar	caprichoso	incógnita
estrafalario	posterior	impertinencia

_____ **1.** Ellos tienen dos jardines; uno delante de la casa y otro en la parte <u>trasera</u>.

_____ **2.** Desde que me teñí el pelo de azul mi hermana me dice que me estoy volviendo muy <u>raro</u>.

_____ **3.** Tupé cometió el <u>atrevimiento</u> de enojarse con los Reyes Magos por el regalo que le habían traído.

_____ **4.** Me di cuenta de que Pepe era <u>mimado</u>, cuando le dió un berrinche porque no le compraron el gorro que quería.

_____ **5.** Después de ver las notas, Manolín le dijo a Tupé: «para ti no existen <u>secretos</u>».

_____ **6.** <u>Fallar</u> en su trabajo como escritor le hizo pensar que no servía para nada.

Lectura a fondo

En el espacio en blanco escribe la letra que corresponde a la **mejor** respuesta. (6 puntos por pregunta)

_____ **7.** ¿Cuál era la reacción de las personas que Tupé reconocía bajo las máscaras?
     a. Se llenaban de ira.
     b. Se mantenían indiferentes.
     c. Se ponían contentos.
     d. Se ponían a charlar con el niño.

_____ **8.** Tupé dice que las máscaras, como en las matemáticas, eran una X porque
   a. los hombres se conducen siempre de la misma manera.
   b. son como un número desconocido que hay que averiguar.
   c. uno puede explicar cualquier cosa con las matemáticas.
   d. es imposible predecir la conducta de la gente.

_____ **9.** Tupé se entera de la verdadera identidad de la última máscara
   a. porque se lo dice su amigo Manolín.
   b. porque lo reconocen los adultos.
   c. por una noticia en el periódico.
   d. porque la persona se quita la máscara.

_____ **10.** Lo que verdaderamente pasó con la última máscara, es que
   a. era un hombre muy graciosamente vestido de mono.
   b. no era una máscara.
   c. era una persona que no era del pueblo.
   d. todas las respuestas anteriores

Respuesta a fondo

11. ¿Por qué crees que Tupé no había tomado en cuenta la estampa del hombre? (15 puntos)

_____

_____

12. En los cuadros escribe la secuencia que lleva a Tupé a reconocer a las personas detrás de las máscaras en los días de Carnaval. (18 puntos)

en la calle, cuando vienen las máscaras	de regreso a casa	finalmente

Composición

13. Escribe una composición en la que explicas en qué aspectos se parece la conducta humana a la de un animal. ¿Quiere decir esto que el hombre y los animales se encuentran en un plano de igualdad? Explica tu postura basándote en el cuento. (25 puntos)

Nombre _____ Clase _____ Fecha _____

La casa de las tres viudas, de *Memorias* • *Pablo Neruda*   p. 71

Examen de lectura   Puntuación _____

Vocabulario

En el espacio antes de cada oración el sinónimo correspondiente a la(s) palabra(s) subrayada(s).
(3 puntos por pregunta)

Palabras para escoger				
colosal	emerger	esquivar	acosar	agredir
sobriamente	pavor	súbitamente	vedado	melancólico

_____ 1. Al llegar la noche, comenzó a sentir un miedo horrible.

_____ 2. Estaba seguro de que lo perseguía un fantasma por las noches.

_____ 3. Estaba prohibido entrar al bosque.

_____ 4. En Chile las montañas son enormes.

_____ 5. Cuando pensaba en su tierra, se ponía triste.

_____ 6. Un dragón azul salió del centro del lago.

_____ 7. La casa estaba decorada con moderación, sin demasiados adornos ni colores.

_____ 8. El oso atacó al cazador.

_____ 9. Llegué al pórtico después de pasar entre los troncos cortados y el aserrín.

_____ 10. Ibamos caminando tranquilamente y de repente se desató una tormenta.

Lectura a fondo

En el espacio en blanco escribe la letra que corresponde a la **mejor** respuesta. (5 puntos por pregunta)

_____ 11. ¿Cuál de las siguientes expresiones es un ejemplo de personificación?
   a. «Me gustó la aventura de irme solo, adivinando los caminos».
   b. «Las tres damas apagadas se encendieron».
   c. «Entró una empleada indígena y susurró algo al oído de la señora mayor».
   d. «El Pacífico allí se desencadena y ataca con intermitencia las rocas y los matorrales...».

_____ 12. ¿Qué le permitió a Neruda llegar hasta la casa de las tres viudas?
   a. su buen sentido de orientación
   b. un viajero le indicó el camino
   c. las luces de la casa
   d. los perros que ladraban

_____ 13. En la casa de las tres viudas, Neruda
   a. se sorprende por la elegancia del lugar.
   b. se sorprende por los vestidos de las viudas.
   c. se maravilla por el conocimiento de Chile que tienen las viudas.
   d. compone sus primeros versos.

Respuesta a fondo

14. ¿Qué simboliza para Neruda la casa de las tres viudas en medio de aquel entorno solitario e inhóspito? Justifica tu respuesta en las líneas que siguen. (10 puntos)

_____

_____

15. Completa el siguiente esquema anotando las impresiones de Neruda en los momentos que se indican. (20 puntos)

cuando toca y nadie le contesta	cuando entra al salón	cuando están en el comedor	al amanecer

Composición

16. Algunos lugares de la naturaleza, como las montañas y el mar en la autobiografía de Neruda, están frecuentemente ligados a sentimientos importantes y profundos; escribe una composición en la que explicas por qué un lugar de la naturaleza es importante para ti. Básate en tu experiencia y tu imaginación. (25 puntos)

Nombre _____ Clase _____ Fecha _____

El pescador y la Madre del Agua • *Santo Neiva* p. 93

Examen de lectura Puntuación _____

Vocabulario

Escribe en los espacios en blanco las palabras del cuadro que mejor completen el texto.
(3 puntos por pregunta)

Palabras para escoger				
imperar	sepultar	proa	deslizar	regir
internar	paraje	centellear	varar	desentonar

Nuestro barco se quedó (1)_____ en las rocas costeras hace una semana. Tuvimos que salir por la (2)_____, y después nos (3)_____ por las resbalosas piedras hacia la playa. Éramos ocho, y un ambiente de inquietud (4)_____ entre nosotros; nuestra principal duda era si éramos los únicos humanos en ese lugar. Un grupo de cuatro personas, en el cual yo estaba incluida, se (5)_____ en la selva más allá de la playa para investigar. Mi punto de vista era el que (6)_____ en esa expedición. En la selva nos llegaba poca luz, unos cuantos rayos (7)_____ cuando el viento movía la vegetación. De repente un (8)_____ sin maleza se presentó ante nosotros; pudimos ver varias piedras alineadas perfectamente, este sitio (9)_____ enormemente con la selva en la que habíamos estado caminando. Nos acercamos y cavamos bajo una piedra: había un cuerpo (10)_____ en la tierra.

Lectura a fondo

En el espacio en blanco escribe la letra que corresponde a la **mejor** respuesta. (5 puntos por pregunta)

_____ 11. ¿Qué era lo que atraía a los marineros hacia el lugar donde finalmente desaparecían?
   a. unas luces extrañas
   b. la belleza de la Madre del Agua
   c. la voz de la Madre del Agua
   d. los lamentos de la Madre del Agua

_____ 12. ¿Por qué sale la Madre del Agua a hablar con el pescador?
   a. Quería hacerlo desaparecer, pues le molestaba su insistencia.
   b. Le quería hacer compañía.
   c. Le había impresionado la insistencia con la que el pescador intentaba pescar.
   d. todas las anteriores

_____ 13. ¿Por qué se comía la Madre del Agua a los pescadores?
   a. porque no quería que siguieran sacando peces del río
   b. porque era una asesina
   c. porque antes había sido serpiente
   d. porque así se lo habían ordenado

_____ 14. ¿Qué es lo primero que le propone la Madre del Agua al joven pescador para dejar de comerse a los pescadores?
   a. que los días de luna llena le traigan pescado
   b. que los días de luna llena le entreguen a un pescador
   c. que los días de luna llena le traigan toda la harina de maíz que la aldea pueda preparar
   d. que los días de luna llena nadie vaya a pescar

_____ 15. ¿Por qué cambió la Madre del Agua el acuerdo que había pactado con el joven pescador?
   a. porque el pescador no cumplió su compromiso
   b. porque ella era inconstante
   c. porque no le llevaban suficiente comida
   d. porque se sentía sola

Respuesta a fondo

16. ¿Qué significa para ti el triunfo de la Madre de Agua sobre el pescador? (10 puntos)

_____

_____

17. En la constelación anota lo que, finalmente, la Madre del Agua le pidió al pueblo y al pescador. (10 puntos)

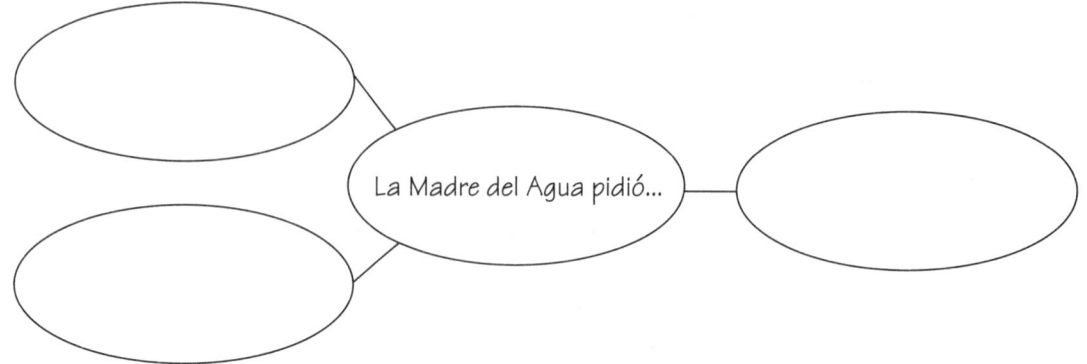

Composición

18. Inventa una leyenda que explique la presencia de algún fenómeno natural. Si quieres, puedes escoger alguno de los siguientes fenómenos: los temblores, la lluvia, las estaciones del año. (25 puntos)

Nombre _____ Clase _____ Fecha _____

La bamba • *Gary Soto* p. 103
Chanclas • *Sandra Cisneros* p. 113

Examen de lectura   Puntuación _____

Vocabulario

Escribe en los espacios en blanco las palabras del cuadro que mejor completen el texto.
(5 puntos)

Palabras para escoger				
ceder	ademán	empinar	presumir	atorar

Juan (1)_____ hoy su silla a la nueva compañera para (2)_____ de que es muy educado, pero en el momento en que (3)_____ la cabeza pedantemente, se (4)_____ con una pata de la silla; todos nos reímos, y él con un (5)_____ muy serio nos dijo que no le causábamos ninguna gracia.

Lectura a fondo

En el espacio en blanco escribe la letra que corresponde a la **mejor** respuesta. (5 puntos por pregunta)

La bamba

_____ 6. ¿Por qué levantó Manuel la mano para participar en el festival de la escuela?
   a. Sus padres lo presionaron.
   b. Su profesor lo invitó.
   c. Quería impresionar a los demás.
   d. Quería ganar un premio.

_____ 7. ¿Por qué tuvo que repetir Manuel varias veces las palabras, «Para bailar la bamba...»?
   a. porque así lo había decidido
   b. porque al profesor se le olvidó quitar el disco
   c. porque el disco estaba rayado
   d. porque se le olvidó la otra parte de la canción

_____ 8. ¿Por qué tenía miedo Manuel de participar en el festival?
   a. por lo que le pasó a su hermano
   b. por lo que le pasó a su amigo que tocaba la trompeta
   c. por lo que le pasó durante la Semana de Ciencias.
   d. porque no había ensayado

Chanclas

_____ 9. ¿Por qué no quería salir a bailar Esperanza?
   a. porque los zapatos le quedaban grandes
   b. porque llevaba los zapatos de su hermana
   c. porque llevaba sus zapatos viejos
   d. porque no le gustaba bailar con su tío

_____ 10. ¿Con quién bailó Esperanza toda la noche?
   a. con su hermano
   b. con su tío
   c. con el muchacho mayor
   d. con su papá

Respuesta a fondo

11. ¿Cuál es el valor más importante que destacan los cuentos? No hay una sola respuesta correcta, por lo tanto justifica tu eleccíon en las siguientes líneas. (10 puntos)

_____

_____

12. En el siguiente diagrama de Venn anota las diferencias y las semejanzas entre Manuel y Esperanza. (10 puntos)

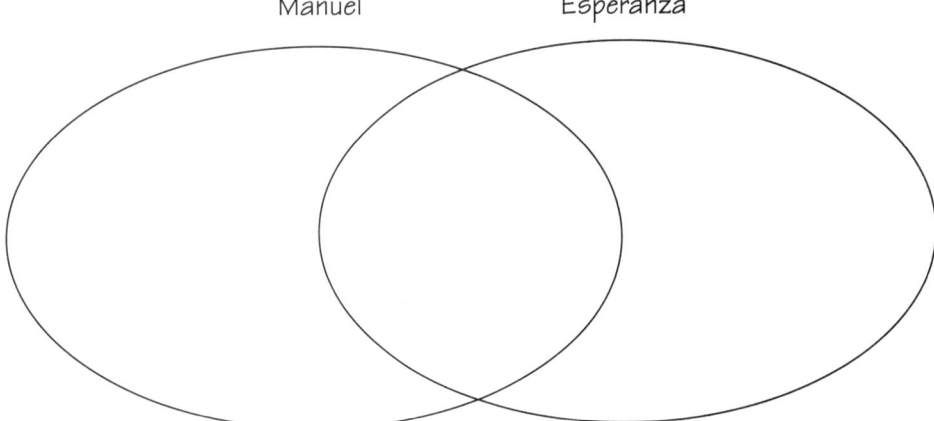

Composición

13. En «La bamba» y «Chanclas» los personajes principales vencen de alguna manera su indecisión y salen adelante. Explica cómo la voluntad puede ser la base para alcanzar las metas que uno se propone. Piensa en tu experiencia y en los textos. (30 puntos)

Nombre _____ Clase _____ Fecha _____

El cuendú • *Horacio Quiroga*

p. 135

Examen de lectura

Puntuación _____

Vocabulario

Escribe en los espacios en blanco las palabras del cuadro que mejor completen el sentido de la oración. (5 puntos por pregunta)

Palabras para escoger		
erizar	reanudar	púa
adherido	sombrío	huraño

1. Es un animal muy curioso, con _____ que levanta cuando se siente intimidado.

2. El cuendú vive en las partes más _____ del bosque.

3. Cuando vuelve a la tranquilidad _____ su pasito cojo.

4. Aunque era un animal _____, el cuendú se me acercaba cuando tenía hambre.

5. El cuendú se _____ y no nos dejaba sacarlo de la bolsa.

6. Si el cuendú no está asustado lleva las púas _____ al cuerpo.

Lectura a fondo

En el espacio en blanco escribe la letra que corresponde a la **mejor** respuesta. (5 puntos por pregunta)

_____ 7. El narrador no estaba seguro de que el cuendú sobreviviría porque
   a. era un animal muy viejo.
   b. era un animal tímido.
   c. animales como ése no sobreviven en cautiverio.
   d. no había suficiente comida.

_____ 8. ¿Cuál de las siguientes expresiones es una opinión?
   a. Mantiene pegadas al cuerpo sus larguísimas púas.
   b. Es un animal nocturno.
   c. Tiene una actitud de penitencia.
   d. Lo entregué al director del museo.

_____ 9. El cuendú se alimentaba de
   a. insectos y plantas.
   b. cáscaras de naranja y maíz.
   c. pequeños roedores.
   d. desperdicios.

_____ 10. ¿Para qué instaló el narrador una glorieta y puso al cuendú en compañía de dos halcones y una urraca?
   a. para aprovechar mejor el espacio
   b. para que el cuendú no estuviera solo
   c. para observar cómo se relacionaba el cuendú con otros animales
   d. para enseñar al cuendú a vivir en libertad

_____ 11. Finalmente, el narrador deja al cuendú
   a. en el bosque.
   b. en un laboratorio.
   c. en un zoológico.
   d. en una reserva ecológica.

Respuesta a fondo

12. Describe en tus propias palabras el carácter del cuendú. (10 puntos)

_____

_____

13. En el siguiente cuadro anota la información que describe al cuendú. (10 puntos)

cola	
púas	
ojos	
forma de caminar	

Composición

14. Inventa un animal fantástico que tenga, como el cuendú, características contradictorias. Explica la utilidad que tienen. Puedes basarte en algún animal mítico que te resulte conocido a través de tus lecturas, o que sea objeto de alguna leyenda popular. (25 puntos)

Nombre _____ Clase _____ Fecha _____

Todo el verano en un día • *Ray Bradbury*

p. 145

Examen de lectura

Puntuación _____

Vocabulario

En el espacio antes de cada oración escribe el sinónimo correspondiente a la(s) palabra(s) subrayada(s). (3 puntos por pregunta)

Palabras para escoger				
estaca	repercusión	audición	predecir	desconcertado
marejada	amainar	tumultuosamente	abalorio	amortiguado

_____ 1. Las tormentas eran muy fuertes, como esas <u>olas enormes</u> que inundan las islas.

_____ 2. El pueblo estaba <u>preocupado</u> por la falta de agua desde hacía tres días.

_____ 3. <u>Los ecos</u> de los truenos se oían entre los montes.

_____ 4. La selva en Venus crecía <u>sin orden ni medida</u> ante los ojos de los niños.

_____ 5. Un <u>débil</u> sonido de sirenas llegaba hasta mis oídos por la ventana.

_____ 6. Su regalo era un collar con <u>cuentas</u> de colores.

_____ 7. Margot aseguraba que los científicos habían <u>anunciado</u> la salida del sol para ese día.

_____ 8. Con la ayuda de <u>palos afilados</u> pudo montar su tienda de campaña.

_____ 9. Los niños se asomaban a las ventanas para ver cómo <u>disminuía la fuerza de la lluvia</u>.

_____ 10. Perdió de golpe el <u>sentido del oído</u>.

Lectura a fondo

En el espacio en blanco escribe la letra que corresponde a la **mejor** respuesta. (5 puntos por pregunta)

_____ 11. Los niños odiaban a Margot porque
   a. ella sí recordaba cómo era el sol.
   b. era muy probable que se regresara a la Tierra.
   c. era una niña diferente.
   d. todas las respuestas anteriores

ENCUENTROS CURSO DE INTRODUCCIÓN 137

_____ 12. Margot escribió en su poema: «Creo que el sol es una flor,/ que florece solamente una hora» porque en Venus el sol salía
   a. una hora diariamente.
   b. una hora cada siete días.
   c. una hora cada siete años.
   d. una hora cada siglo.

_____ 13. Cuando el autor del cuento dice que los niños siempre se despertaban «con el tamborileo rítmico, la caída interminable de collares de limpios abalorios sobre el techo» está hablando metafóricamente de
   a. la lluvia.
   b. los sueños de los niños.
   c. un collar de Margot.
   d. las voces de sus padres.

_____ 14. Según el cuento, ¿cuál es la descripción más precisa de Venus?
   a. Está cubierto de ríos.
   b. Está cubierto de una gran selva.
   c. Tiene una combinación de desiertos y selvas.
   d. No había noche ni día.

_____ 15. El silencio que acompañó la salida del sol se debía a que
   a. la maestra pidió a los niños que no hicieran ruido.
   b. un niño del salón descompuso el aparato de sonido.
   c. la lluvia se detuvo.
   d. los niños se querían portar bien para salir afuera.

Respuesta a fondo

16. En tu opinión ¿cuál sería la actitud de Margot después de que los niños vieron el sol y la liberaron? No hay una sola respuesta correcta, por lo tanto justifica tu elección en las líneas que siguen. (10 puntos)
    a. indiferencia
    b. venganza
    c. rencor
    d. alegría

17. En el diagrama de constelación anota cómo veían los demás niños a Margot. (10 puntos)

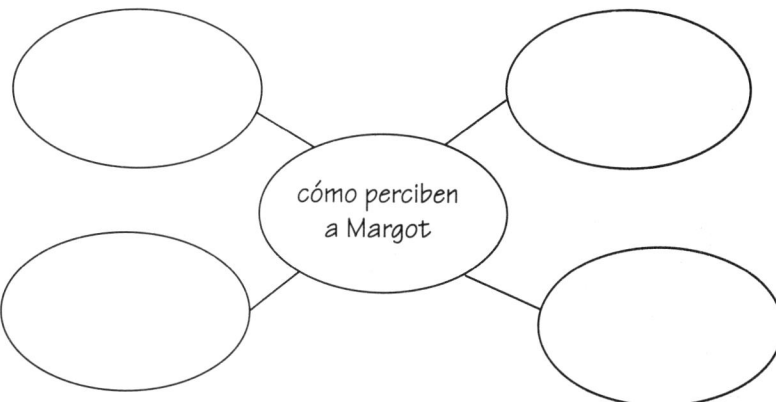

Composición

18. En el cuento, Venus y la lluvia pueden representar la Tierra y los motivos que tiene el hombre para disfrutar o no de las condiciones en las que vive. Selecciona un lugar de la ciudad o pueblo en el que vives que contribuya a la felicidad o infelicidad de la gente. Describe el lugar y explica cómo se relaciona con el estado de ánimo de la gente. (25 puntos)

Nombre _____ Clase _____ Fecha _____

El trópico • *Rubén Darío* — p. 157
La isla Sangalakki • *Norbert Wu* — p. 164

Examen de lectura   Puntuación _____

Vocabulario

Empareja las palabras con su sinónimo o definición. (3 puntos por pregunta)

_____ 1. parásito   a. muchacho
_____ 2. estela   b. simultáneamente
_____ 3. semejar   c. que es activo de día
_____ 4. mozo   d. rastro
_____ 5. carmín   e. que no deja pasar la luz
_____ 6. ecosistema   f. rojo
_____ 7. unísono   g. comunidad de organismos que
_____ 8. diurno   se relacionan entre sí en
_____ 9. acechar   un mismo ambiente
_____ 10. opaco   h. parecer
                            i. observar
                            j. organismo que vive a costa de otro

Lectura a fondo

En el espacio en blanco escribe la letra que corresponde a la **mejor** respuesta. (5 puntos por pregunta)

El trópico

_____ 11. El poema habla de
   a. una montaña.
   b. un pueblo.
   c. el campo.
   d. un lago.

_____ 12. ¿A qué sentido se refiere el verso «escarabajos de oro y carmín»?
   a. tacto
   b. oído
   c. vista
   d. olfato

La isla Sangalakki

_____ 13. ¿Con qué compara el arrecife el autor del artículo?
   a. con una carretera
   b. con una ciudad
   c. con un país
   d. con una familia

_____ 14. ¿Para qué van a la isla Sangalakki las tortugas verdes?
   a. Las tortugas encuentran comida en la isla.
   b. Las tortugas mueren en la isla.
   c. Las tortugas ponen huevos en la isla.
   d. Las tortugas viven en la isla.

_____ 15. En la isla Sangalakki se ha protegido la vida de las tortugas verdes
   a. comprando al gobierno la concesión de los huevos.
   b. prohibiendo la caza.
   c. poniendo los huevos en un criadero artificial.
   d. trayendo tortugas de otras islas.

Respuesta a fondo

16. ¿Qué es lo que caracteriza la vida en el arrecife? No hay una sola respuesta correcta, por lo tanto justifica tu elección en las líneas que siguen. (10 puntos)
   a. la interdependencia
   b. el peligro
   c. la belleza

_____

_____

17. Anota en el cuadro la información adecuada. (10 puntos)

Tortugas verdes

lo que las protege	lo que las amenaza

Composición

18. Escribe una composición explicando cómo los miembros de tu comunidad se necesitan unos a otros. (25 puntos)

_____ 10. ¿De qué manera le dio el consejo Patronio?
   a. Le contó una historia.
   b. Lo llevó a conocer a unos labradores.
   c. Le presentó a un hombre muy sabio.
   d. Lo llevó al teatro.

_____ 11. El consejo de Patronio al conde es que
   a. conviene montar en burro.
   b. sea más democrático.
   c. siga su propia conciencia.
   d. la gente es ignorante.

Los ratones

_____ 12. Los ratones representan a
   a. todos los animales que victimiza el gato.
   b. los griegos.
   c. los demás ratones.
   d. los seres humanos.

_____ 13. Subraya los versos que riman en este fragmento de «Los ratones».
   ...y, encrespando el grueso lomo
   dijo al senado romano,
   después de hablar culto un rato:
   ¿quién de todos ha de ser
   el que se atreva a poner
   ese cascabel al gato?

Respuesta a fondo

14. ¿Qué moraleja se podría sacar del poema «Los ratones»? Justifica tu respuesta en las siguientes líneas. (14 puntos)

Nombre _____ Clase _____ Fecha _____

Los dos labradores • *José María Osorio Rodríguez*   p. 185
Los ratones • *Lope de Vega*   p. 195

Examen de lectura   Puntuación _____

Vocabulario
Escribe en el espacio antes de cada oración el sinónimo correspondiente a la(s) palabra(s) subrayada(s). (3 puntos por pregunta)

Palabras para escoger			
culto	desasosegado	encrespar	ronzal
dictar	prudencia	cascabel	pollino

_____ 1. Mi primer encuentro con un <u>burro</u> fue bastante desagradable porqu[e] me pegó una patada.

_____ 2. Mi conciencia y entendimiento me <u>dirán</u> como aconsejaros.

_____ 3. El escritor, que era muy <u>sabio</u>, habló de otros países y culturas.

_____ 4. El disfraz ganador era tan horrible que se me <u>pusieron de punta</u> l[os] pelos al verlo.

_____ 5. Después de mucho discutir concluyeron que ponerle <u>una campa[nilla al]</u> gato era lo mejor.

_____ 6. El investigador estaba <u>intranquilo</u>: tenía que resolver un caso y [no] había comenzado.

_____ 7. Los dos labradores tiraron del burro por <u>la cuerda</u>.

_____ 8. Comencé a conducir con <u>cuidado</u> cuando supe que la carrete[ra era] peligrosa.

Lectura a fondo
En el espacio en blanco escribe la letra que corresponde a la **mejor** respuesta. (5 puntos [por] pregunta)

Los dos labradores

_____ 9. ¿Qué era lo que preocupaba a Lucanor cuando le pidió consejo a Patr[onio?]
   a. No sabía si actuaba con justicia.
   b. No lograba la aprobación de su pueblo.
   c. No lograba que lo obedecieran.
   d. No lograba que lo hicieran rey.

15. ¿Qué ventajas tienen los cuentos o las fábulas en lugar de decir algo directamente? Justifica tu respuesta basándote en «Los dos labradores»? (12 puntos)

_____

_____

Composición

16. Al igual que las moralejas de las fábulas, los refranes contienen una lección. Explica uno de los siguientes refranes, u otro que te guste, refiriéndote a tu propia experiencia. (25 puntos)

>De tal palo, tal astilla.
>No hay mal que por bien no venga.
>Más vale tarde que nunca.
>En boca cerrada, no entran moscas.
>Más vale prevenir que curar.

Nombre _____ Clase _____ Fecha _____

La canción del árbol • *Ana María Fagundo* — p. 213
El ruego del libro • *Gabriela Mistral* — p. 218

Examen de lectura   Puntuación _____

Vocabulario

Escribe en los espacios en blanco del texto las palabras del cuadro (en su forma adecuada) que mejor completen las oraciones. (5 puntos por pregunta)

Palabras para escoger				
aliento	marchitar	amapola	recobrar	liviano

La enfermedad lo ha dejado (1)_____ como una hoja de papel. Casi no tiene

(2)_____, y no puede salir a su jardín de (3)_____, que sin sus cuidados

ha comenzado a (4)_____. Ahora estamos arreglándole el jardín con la esperanza de

que (5)_____ la salud.

Lectura a fondo

Escribe en el espacio en blanco la letra que corresponde a la **mejor** respuesta. (5 puntos por pregunta)

La canción del árbol

_____ 6. Este poema trata de
   a. la amistad.
   b. la migración de los pájaros.
   c. la primavera.
   d. el odio.

_____ 7. ¿Cómo expresa el árbol sus sentimientos?
   a. Escribe un poema.
   b. Cambia su aspecto físico.
   c. Sus ramas le cantan sus penas al viento.
   d. Habla con las amapolas.

El ruego del libro

_____ 8. ¿Qué significado tiene el título del poema?
   a. que la niña le pide algo al libro
   b. que el libro le pide algo a la niña
   c. que alguien reclama un libro
   d. que la niña no le hace caso al libro

_____ 9. El libro piensa que leer es
   a. profundo.
   b. fácil.
   c. divertido.
   d. inteligente.

_____ 10. El libro dice que es
   a. duro como una piedra.
   b. azul como el mar.
   c. fino como una pluma.
   d. delicado como una flor.

Respuesta a fondo

La canción del árbol

11. ¿Cómo crees que se siente el árbol? Justifica tu respuesta refiriéndote a las descripciones del poema. (10 puntos)

_____

_____

El ruego del libro

12. Anota en el siguiente diagrama de constelación cuatro temas de lectura que menciona el libro. (10 puntos)

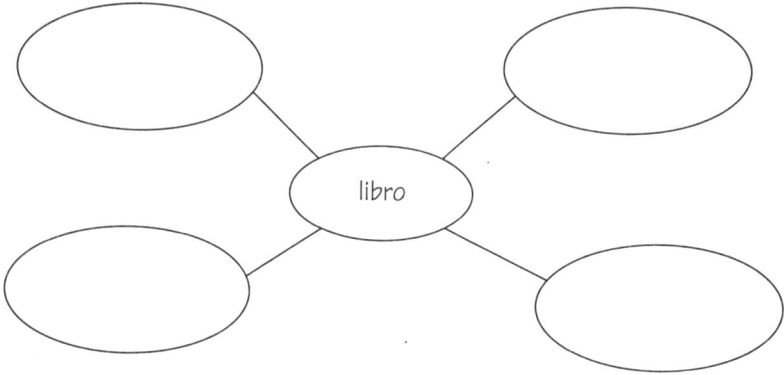

Composición

13. ¿Qué le contestarías al libro del poema? Escríbele una respuesta a su ruego. (30 puntos)

Nombre _____ Clase _____ Fecha _____

de *Yo sé por qué canta el pájaro enjaulado* • Maya Angelou

p. 224

Examen de lectura

Puntuación _____

Vocabulario

Escribe en la línea antes de cada oración el sinónimo correspondiente a la(s) palabra(s) subrayada(s). (3 puntos por pregunta)

Palabras para escoger				
proponerse	afable	afrentosa	integridad	maña
alabar	vestigio	substraer	infalible	facciones

_____ 1. Maya <u>decidió</u> llevar una vida cristiana para agradecerle a Dios el maravilloso hermano que tenía.

_____ 2. Todos <u>admiraban</u> a Bailey por su belleza.

_____ 3. Cuando mi hermano se vengaba, yo borraba de mi cara cualquier <u>rastro</u> de alegría.

_____ 4. Una de las habilidades de Bailey era la de <u>robar</u> los pepinillos del barril sin que el tío se diera cuenta.

_____ 5. Sus buenas acciones demuestran que es una persona con <u>un carácter sin falta</u>.

_____ 6. Mi mamá admiraba el carácter <u>agradable</u> de mi amigo Pedro.

_____ 7. Los <u>rasgos</u> de su cara parecen dibujados por un artista.

_____ 8. Siempre castigaban a Bailey por su conducta <u>atrevida</u>.

_____ 9. El té de la abuela es uno de esos <u>que nunca falla</u>; una hora después de tomarlo te sientes como nuevo.

_____ 10. Juan tiene mucha <u>habilidad</u> para salirse con facilidad de situaciones peligrosas.

Lectura a fondo

En el espacio en blanco escribe la letra que corresponde a la **mejor** respuesta. (5 puntos por pregunta)

_____ 11. El guiño de Bailey a Maya, después de que ella ha sido agredida por su apariencia física, indica que
- a. él tambien pensaba que Maya era muy fea.
- b. pensaba que él era el más guapo.
- c. la quería sin que le importara su apariencia.
- d. le iba a prestar su juguete favorito para consolarla.

_____ 12. ¿Por qué Bailey no tenía que temer grandes castigos?
- a. Nunca se portaba mal, así que nunca lo castigaban.
- b. Los grandes castigos sólo eran para Maya.
- c. Bailey era el orgullo de la familia, y por eso casi no lo castigaban.
- d. Si alguien intentaba castigarlo, Maya lo impedía.

_____ 13. En un día de verano, camino a la escuela, Bailey olía como un «ángel avinagrado», ¿por qué?
- a. Había estado enfermo, y le dieron un baño de vinagre para curarlo.
- b. Maya se enojó con él y le tiró el frasco de pepinillos en la ropa.
- c. Traía en los bolsillos los pepinillos que el tío le había regalado.
- d. Traía en los bolsillos los pepinillos que había robado de la tienda.

_____ 14. Maya recuerda a Bailey como
- a. una sombra en su infancia.
- b. una presencia sin importancia en su vida.
- c. la persona más admirable de su mundo.
- d. la persona que le hizo descubrir la literatura.

Respuesta a fondo

15. En tu opinión, ¿por qué Maya no sonreía frente a los adultos? Justifica tu respuesta en las líneas que siguen. (10 puntos)

_____

_____

16. En la constelación a continuación, anota las cualidades de Bailey descritas por Maya? (20 puntos)

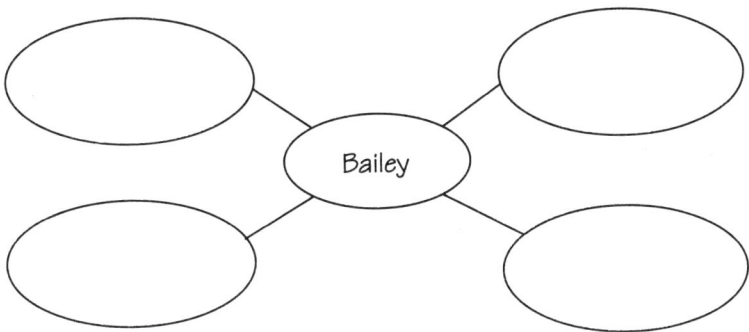

Composición

17. Haz una descripción de Maya Angelou basándote en el texto. ¿Con quién te identificas más, con Maya o con Bailey? ¿Por qué? (20 puntos)

Nombre _____ Clase _____ Fecha _____

Los dos ruiseñores • *José Martí*

p. 241

Examen de lectura

Puntuación _____

Vocabulario

Empareja las palabras con su sinónimo. (5 puntos por pregunta)

_____ 1. galán
_____ 2. resplandecer
_____ 3. bullicio
_____ 4. pomposo
_____ 5. desterrar
_____ 6. lívido
_____ 7. son
_____ 8. camposanto

a. ruido
b. cementerio
c. muy pálido
d. exagerado
e. hermoso
f. sonido agradable
g. echar
h. brillar

Lectura a fondo

En el espacio en blanco escribe la letra que corresponde a la **mejor** respuesta. (5 puntos por pregunta)

_____ 9. ¿Cuál era la actividad nocturna favorita del emperador?
   a. Se ponía sus mejores ropas para que todos lo notaran y, después, se iba a ver a su pueblo.
   b. Escondía su barba para que nadie lo reconociera y se iba a un sótano a apostar con unos criminales.
   c. Escondía su barba para que nadie lo reconociera y se iba a ayudar a su pueblo.
   d. Se ponía sus mejores ropas y salía de paseo con la Corte.

_____ 10. ¿Por qué le dice el ruiseñor al emperador que no se puede quedar a vivir en el palacio?
   a. No puede ser infiel a los pescadores que lo esperan en sus casas a la orilla del mar.
   b. No se lleva bien con el maestro de música.
   c. No quiere hacer enfadar al emperador del Japón.
   d. Teme que le vuelvan a remplazar con otro pájaro artificial.

_____ 11. La Muerte no se lleva al emperador porque
   a. su salud mejora.
   b. el emperador todavía es jóven.
   c. regresa el ruiseñor.
   d. entran al cuarto los mandarines.

ENCUENTROS CURSO DE INTRODUCCIÓN 153

_____ 12. ¿Cómo encontraron los mandarines al ruiseñor?
   a. El viejo que cuidaba el portón les dijo dónde estaba.
   b. Los mandarines ya sabían donde estaba pero querían esconderlo.
   c. El adivino de la corte les indicó dónde estaba.
   d. Una cocinera del palacio les dijo que ella lo escuchaba en el bosque cuando le llevaba comida a su madre.

Respuesta a fondo

13. En la constelación escribe las virtudes del ruiseñor natural. (20 puntos)

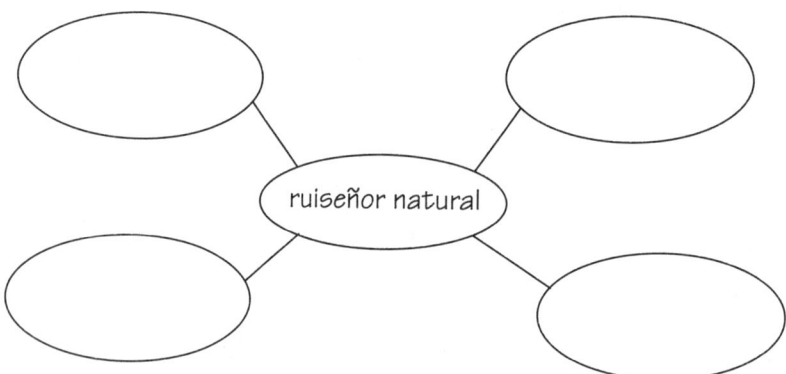

Composición

14. «Mejor mil veces es este pájaro artificial; porque con el pájaro vivo, nunca se sabe cómo va a ser el canto, y con éste, se está seguro de lo que va a ser; con éste todo está en orden»; ésta es la opinión del maestro de música, pero a final de cuentas el pájaro vivo fue mejor. Escribe sobre alguna experiencia en la que hayas concluido que lo desconocido e impredecible es mejor que lo conocido y predecible. (20 puntos)

Nombre _____ Clase _____ Fecha _____

Los dos príncipes • *José Martí* — p. 255
Los dos reyes y los dos laberintos • *Jorge Luis Borges* — p. 261

Examen de lectura   Puntuación _____

Vocabulario

Escribe en los espacios en blanco las palabras del cuadro que mejor completen el texto.
(5 puntos por pregunta)

Palabras para escoger				
álamo	proferir	congregar	estragado	vedado

Los habitantes de la ciudad se (1)_____ alrededor del (2)_____ en el centro de la ciudad, el último árbol que quedaba en esa zona. Acercarse a él estaba (3)_____, así que se mantenían alejados. La gente, al ver aquel árbol (4)_____ por el tiempo y la contaminación, (5)_____ lamentos llenos de desesperanza.

Lectura a fondo

En el espacio en blanco escribe la letra que corresponde a la **mejor** respuesta. (5 puntos por pregunta)

Los dos príncipes

_____ 6. ¿Por qué los caballos del rey no quieren comer, y las ovejas del pastor vienen todas cabizbajas al portón?
   a. Los hijos de sus amos han muerto.
   b. Los animales tienen una enfermedad que los hace actuar de esa manera.
   c. Sus amos no los tratan bien.
   d. Los caballos y las ovejas han perdido a sus crías.

_____ 7. El poema es un ejemplo de paralelismo porque
   a. trata, en parte, sobre las matemáticas.
   b. la rima se repite.
   c. las dos partes del poema tienen el mismo tema y desarrollo.
   d. el rey y el pastor nunca llegan a conocerse.

_____ 8. El tema del poema es que
   a. el dolor es lo mismo para un rico que para un pobre.
   b. los ricos se vuelven más ricos y los pobres más pobres.
   c. la muerte acaba con la belleza de la juventud.
   d. las riquezas de nada sirven en momentos de tristeza.

Los dos reyes y los dos laberintos

_____ 9. ¿Por qué no quería entrar nadie al laberinto del rey de Babilonia?
   a. Un minotauro que vivía adentro mataba a todas las personas que entraban.
   b. Era tan fácil salir que la gente se aburría de estar adentro.
   c. Era un laberinto tan confuso que todo el que entraba se perdía.
   d. Entrar al laberinto era retar a Dios.

_____ 10. ¿Qué hizo el rey de Arabia al regresar a su país?
   a. Juntó a sus arquitectos y les pidió que construyeran el laberinto más complicado del mundo.
   b. Juntó a su gente, fue a destruir Babilonia y tomó preso al rey.
   c. Les contó a sus capitanes la historia del rey de Babilonia y su maravilloso laberinto.
   d. Invitó al rey de Babilonia a visitar su laberinto.

Respuesta a fondo

11. ¿En qué se parecen un desierto y un laberinto? Explica tu respuesta. (10 puntos)

_____

_____

12. En un diagrama de Venn escribe las diferencias y semejanzas entre los entierros de los dos príncipes. (10 puntos)

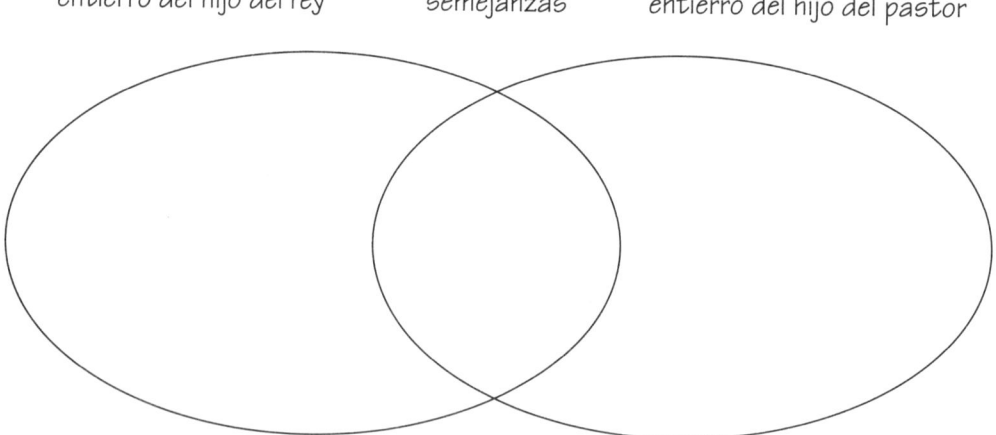

Composición

13. Escribe una fábula en la que incluyas alguno de los temas de las historias que leíste, por ejemplo: muerte, venganza, igualdad o fe. Recuerda que las fábulas tienen una moraleja. (30 puntos)

Nombre _____ Clase _____ Fecha _____

El árbol de oro • *Ana María Matute*

p. 275

Examen de lectura

Puntuación _____

Vocabulario

En el espacio antes de cada oración escribe el sinónimo correspondiente a la(s) palabra(s) subrayada(s). (5 puntos por pregunta)

Palabras para escoger		
embustero	zozobra	desasosegar
codiciar	hucha	estafado

_____ 1. Lo que más <u>deseábamos</u> de Ivo era la llave de la torrecita.

_____ 2. Con <u>preocupación</u> le dije a Ivo que era un mentiroso.

_____ 3. Vacié mi <u>alcancía</u> para pagarle a Mateo lo de la entrada a la torrecita.

_____ 4. Ayer jugamos a ver quién era el más <u>mentiroso</u>: mi hermana ganó diciendo que ella siempre dice la verdad.

_____ 5. Leer un cuento de misterio antes de dormir la <u>puso intranquila</u>, así que no pudo dormir.

_____ 6. Me sentí <u>engañado</u> al no ver ningún árbol en la torrecita.

Lectura a fondo

En el espacio en blanco escribe la letra que corresponde a la **mejor** respuesta. (6 puntos por pregunta)

_____ 7. ¿Qué es lo que más admiraban los niños en Ivo?
  a. su apariencia física
  b. que la maestra lo protegía
  c. las cosas que contaba
  d. su inteligencia

_____ 8. Ivo es un niño
  a. envidioso.
  b. misterioso.
  c. enfermo.
  d. mentiroso.

ENCUENTROS CURSO DE INTRODUCCIÓN 157

_____ 9. ¿Qué hace el narrador para conseguir entrar en la torrecita?
   a. Le da todo su dinero a la maestra.
   b. Le da todo su dinero a Mateo.
   c. Convence a Ivo de que le preste la llave.
   d. Entra a escondidas.

_____ 10. ¿Qué fue lo que vio el narrador por la rendija?
   a. el brillo plateado de los álamos
   b. el árbol de oro
   c. la seca tierra de la llanura
   d. un río luminoso

_____ 11. ¿Qué sucedió dos años después cuando el narrador volvió al pueblo?
   a. Vio el árbol de oro y la tumba de Ivo a sus pies.
   b. Encontró a Ivo y fueron a ver el árbol de oro.
   c. La maestra le explicó el origen del árbol de oro.
   d. Preguntó por Ivo y ya nadie lo recordaba.

Respuesta a fondo

12. ¿Qué representa el árbol de oro? Justifica tu respuesta en las líneas que siguen. (10 puntos)

_____

_____

13. El cuento nos permite asociar el árbol de oro a cosas positivas; anota en la constelación los elementos positivos con los que se puede asociar al árbol de oro. (10 puntos)

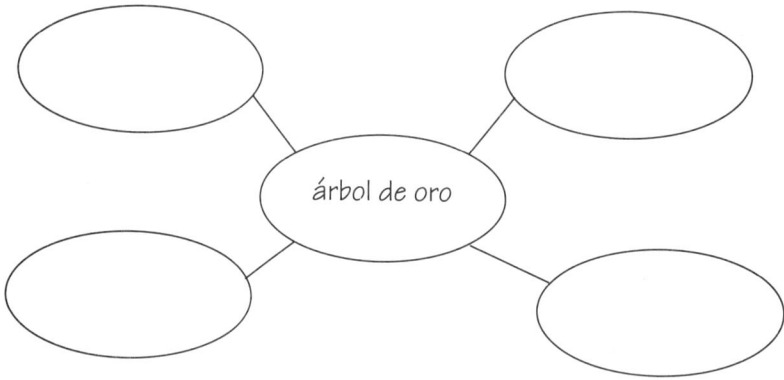

Composición

14. Escribe un final distinto para el cuento. (20 puntos)

Nombre _____ Clase _____ Fecha _____

La leyenda del maíz • *Maricarmen Ohara* p. 283

Examen de lectura   Puntuación _____

Vocabulario

Escribe en los espacios en blanco de las oraciones las palabras del cuadro que mejor completen el sentido de las oraciones. (5 puntos por pregunta)

Palabras para escoger		
oprimido	belicoso	sepultar
pasmado	convocar	alternativa

1. Los charcas y los chayantas eran pueblos _____, siempre estaban dispuestos a pelear.

2. Huayru no tenía otra _____ más que pelear.

3. Huayru amaneció con el corazón _____ por la tristeza.

4. Después del accidente se _____ una reunión para resolver el problema.

5. La belleza de ese gato callejero me dejó _____; terminé llevándomelo a casa.

6. _____ nuestro tesoro en la parte de atrás del jardín.

Lectura a fondo

En el espacio en blanco escribe la letra que corresponde a la **mejor** respuesta. (5 puntos por pregunta)

_____ 7. ¿Cuáles eran las armas por las que eran famosos los pueblos Charca y Chayanta?
   a. flechas y hondas
   b. espadas y arcos
   c. hondas y espadas
   d. flechas y espadas

_____ 8. ¿Dónde se conocieron Huayru y Maiza Chojclu?
   a. en la casa de Huayru
   b. junto a un río
   c. en la casa de Maiza Chojclu
   d. en el monte

_____ 9. ¿Por qué los hijos de los caciques ocultaban que estaban enamorados?
   a. Aún eran muy jóvenes.
   b. Sus pueblos eran enemigos.
   c. Querían darles la sorpresa a sus padres.
   d. Pensaban irse lejos de allí.

_____ **10.** En muchas culturas de Latino América el maíz se llama
   a. choclo.
   b. huayru.
   c. maiza.
   d. chayanta.

Respuesta a fondo

11. Según esta leyenda, ¿qué significado tiene el nacimiento del maíz? No hay una sola respuesta correcta, por lo tanto justifica tu elección en las líneas que siguen. (10 puntos)
   a. El amor es vida.
   b. El odio entre los pueblos no tiene sentido.
   c. Los dioses se preocupan por el bien de los hombres.

_____

_____

12. ¿En qué se parece la planta de maíz a la princesa charca? (20 puntos)

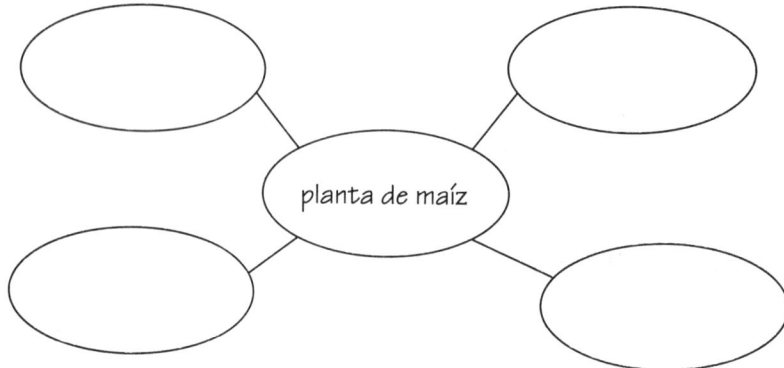

Composición

13. ¿Crees que el conflicto entre los charcas y los chayantas se pudo haber resuelto de otra manera? Explica tu respuesta. (20 puntos)

Nombre _____ Clase _____ Fecha _____

Cuentos de junio • *Susana Mendoza* p. 295

Examen de lectura   Puntuación _____

Vocabulario

Escribe en los espacios en blanco las palabras del cuadro que mejor completen el sentido de las oraciones. (3 puntos por pregunta)

Palabras para escoger				
destello	escollo	rocío	hálito	cañada
impertinencia	jadeante	husmear	colérico	poniente

1. Las ramas estaban cubiertas del _____ de la mañana.
2. Chagua llegó _____ después de correr tanto.
3. Cuando el tigre bostezaba, su _____ humedecía las piedras.
4. El sol _____ se reflejaba sobre el mar.
5. Estuve _____ por la cocina y descubrí el pastel que me prepararon.
6. Cometió la _____ de decirle que el vestido le parecía feo.
7. El maestro se puso _____ cuando todos lo desobedecimos al mismo tiempo.
8. Desde mi ventana, veía el _____ de la luz del faro.
9. La barca se quedó atascada entre los _____ de la bahía.
10. En la _____ al sur del pueblo corre el río.

Lectura a fondo

En el espacio en blanco escribe la letra que corresponde a la **mejor** respuesta. (5 puntos por pregunta)

_____ 11. ¿Para qué habían ido la madre y sus hijas al monte?
   a. para recoger leña
   b. para recoger carbón
   c. para recoger hongos
   d. para recoger fruta

_____ 12. El tigre está cubierto de
   a. musgos y líquenes.
   b. hojas de helecho.
   c. escamas.
   d. rayas.

_____ 13. ¿Cómo desapareció el tigre?
   a. Se metió debajo del agua.
   b. Dio un enorme salto hacia las nubes.
   c. Se perdió en el bosque.
   d. Desapareció en un agujero.

Respuesta a fondo

14. ¿Por qué se presenta al tigre como un animal que no es salvaje, sino más bien inofensivo y amistoso? Justifica tu respuesta en las líneas que siguen. (15 puntos)

_____

_____

15. Anota en la constelación las cosas que suceden en la naturaleza que nos indican que el tigre es el sol. (15 puntos)

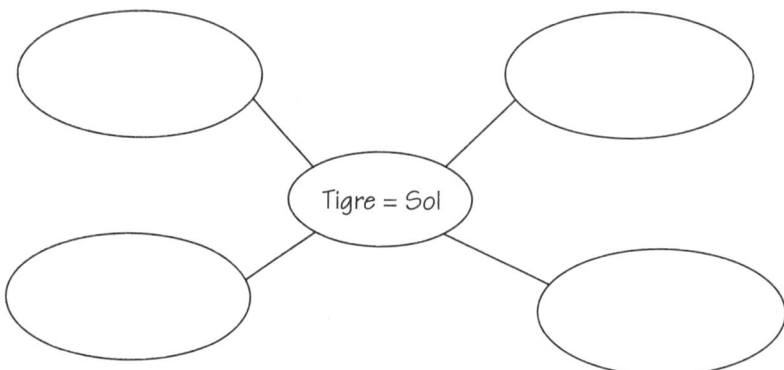

Composición

16. En el cuento, el abuelo representa la sabiduría. ¿Crees que en nuestra sociedad se valora a la gente mayor? Explica tu respuesta. (25 puntos)

ANSWER KEY TO TESTS

Hoja de respuestas
de *Cuando era puertorriqueña*
Esmeralda Santiago
Edición del estudiante (página 3)

Vocabulario
1. penumbra
2. fangoso
3. cima
4. siniestro
5. cautelosamente
6. grieta
7. trancazo
8. debatir
9. estrépito
10. susurro

Lectura a fondo
11. b
12. c
13. a
14. c
15. b

Respuesta a fondo
16. Se percibe la armonía entre la familia y los vecinos por el calor y la paz que se siente en sus juegos y la manera en que todos contribuyen a la comida.
17.

al nene	protegerlo para que no le diera el aire
a los niños	llevarlos a casa de la vecina
la casa de los vecinos	tapar ventanas y puertas
la comida	todos contribuyeron con algo

Composición
18. Una respuesta apropiada será aquella en la cual el estudiante indique que el huracán es algo para lo que se requiere mucha preparación y que perturba el ritmo de la vida diaria; pero también parece ser que los adultos han hecho estos preparativos en otras ocasiones, por lo cual el huracán es un acontecimiento que parece ocurrir por lo menos una vez al año.

Hoja de respuestas
Trabajo de campo
Rose del Castillo Guilbault
Edición del estudiante (página 13)

Vocabulario
1. costear
2. mediar
3. ceñir
4. plazo
5. capataz
6. nitidez
7. desalentar
8. ser incapaz

Lectura a fondo
9. c
10. c
11. c
12. a
13. c

Respuesta a fondo
14. Todas las respuestas son correctas, pero se podría afirmar que Rose considera que la experiencia le enriqueció la vida.
15. en el trabajo, el último día: la niña estaba tan cansada que no quería trabajar más
con el padre: al padre no le parecía bien que su esposa trabajara
en el trabajo, al principio: a la niña se le caían los ajos del saco
con el jefe: el jefe creía que las mujeres no podrían aguantar lo suficiente como para terminar el trabajo

Composición
16. Las respuestas pueden variar. Una respuesta adecuada puede hablar de lo duro que es el trabajo en el campo y, por lo tanto, de la importancia que tiene la solidaridad familiar para salir adelante.

Hoja de respuestas
de *Negrita*
Onelio Jorge Cardoso
Edición del estudiante (página 22)

Vocabulario
1. remanso
2. follaje
3. gajo
4. colindante
5. apesadumbrado
6. retozar
7. atajar
8. montero

Lectura a fondo
9. a
10. b
11. a
12. c

Respuestas a fondo
13. Los niños seguramente se pondrían tristes, se enojarían con el montero y, probablemente, con su padre por haber permitido que ahogaran a Negrita.
14. el sol, los árboles y los peces, entre otras posibilidades

Composición
15. El estudiante deberá apoyar su respuesta con ejemplos concretos de su experiencia.

Hoja de respuestas
Una carta a Dios
Gregorio López y Fuentes
Edición del estudiante (página 51)

Vocabulario
1. determinación
2. fortificar
3. mortificar o afligir
4. mortificar o afligir

Lectura a fondo
5. b
6. c
7. c
8. b
9. b

Respuesta a fondo
10. En ningún momento duda de que Dios le haya mandado el dinero. Tampoco duda de que Dios le haya mandado una cantidad menor de la que pidió. Este hecho demuestra aún más la fe inquebrantable de Lencho.
11. Se perdió la cosecha; escribe una carta a Dios; en el correo leen su carta.

Composición
12. El estudiante deberá indicar las razones que lo llevarían a responder de manera determinada a la carta de Lencho.

Hoja de respuestas
El adivinador de máscaras
Antonio Robles
Edición del estudiante (página 61)

Vocabulario
1. posterior
2. estrafalario
3. impertinencia
4. caprichoso
5. incógnita
6. fracasar

Lectura a fondo
7. a
8. b
9. c
10. b

Respuestas a fondo
11. Lo que pasa al final del cuento es sorpresivo, pues detrás de las máscaras siempre podía identificar a la persona, cosa que no sucede con la última máscara. No se había fijado en que los animales se pueden parecer a los humanos al igual que los humanos se parecen a los animales.

12.

en la calle, cuando vienen las máscaras	de regreso a casa	finalmente
Tupé mira a los ojos detrás de la máscara y se graba las miradas.	Tupé busca, en su libro de estampas, la misma mirada bajo la imagen de un animal.	Va a su cuaderno de notas e identifica al animal con una persona del pueblo.

Composición

13. Una respuesta apropiada será aquella en la que se muestre que el estudiante presenta, efectivamente, aspectos en los que animales y hombres son parecidos y diferentes basándose en el cuento.

Hoja de respuestas
**La casa de las tres viudas, de *Memorias*
Pablo Neruda
Edición del estudiante (página 71)**

Vocabulario
1. pavor
2. acosar
3. vedado
4. colosal
5. melancólico
6. emerger
7. sobriamente
8. agredir
9. esquivar
10. súbitamente

Lectura a fondo
11. d
12. b
13. a

Respuesta a fondo
14. Podría decirse que Neruda admira la casa de las tres viudas porque en ella está presente el gusto por la literatura, que de alguna manera es parte de la tradición del pasado.

15.

cuando toca y nadie le contesta	cuando entra al salón	en el comedor	al amanecer
se llena de pavor	cree estar soñando	se sorprende con la elegancia	piensa que todo puede haber sido un sueño

Composición
16. Las contestaciones se apoyarán en la experiencia del estudiante. También se deberá valorar la imaginación con la cual el estudiante describe el lugar.

Hoja de respuestas
**El pescador y la Madre del Agua
Santo Neiva
Edición del estudiante (página 93)**

Vocabulario
1. varar
2. proa
3. deslizar
4. imperar
5. internar

6. regir
7. centellear
8. paraje
9. desentonar
10. sepultar

Lectura a fondo
11. c
12. c
13. c
14. c
15. d

Respuestas a fondo
16. Parece simbolizar el triunfo de la naturaleza sobre el hombre.
17. Que enterraran sus armas; Que el pescador cubriera la orilla del río con la sábana que había tejido el pueblo; Que el pescador entrara con ella al río.

Composición
18. Una buena contestación seguramente integrará un elemento mágico o fantástico y la conducta de algunas personas o elementos personificados, como causa de un fenómeno natural.

Hoja de respuestas
La bamba, Gary Soto
Chanclas, Sandra Cisneros
Edición del estudiante (páginas 103 y 113)

Vocabulario
1. ceder
2. presumir
3. empinar
4. atorar
5. ademán

Lectura a fondo
6. c
7. c
8. c
9. c
10. b

Respuesta a fondo
11. En ambos cuentos la familia es un elemento esencial en la superación de los personajes principales; en los cuentos se destaca la importancia que tiene el reconocimiento de los demás para la vida en sociedad.
12. Manuel: canta, está en la escuela.
    Esperanza: baila, le avergüenzan sus zapatos viejos, está en una reunión familiar.
    Manuel y Esperanza: tienen miedo de lo que piensen los demás.

Composición
13. Una respuesta puede describir la perseverancia de una persona en alguna actividad (por ejemplo, la tenacidad para aprender una lengua que no es la propia) y los resultados positivos que se derivan de dicho esfuerzo.

Hoja de respuestas
El cuendú
Horacio Quiroga
Edición del estudiante (página 135)

Vocabulario
1. púa
2. sombrío
3. reanudar
4. huraño
5. erizar
6. adherido

Lectura a fondo
7. c
8. c
9. b
10. b
11. c

Respuestas a fondo
12. El cuendú es un animal tímido y huraño, pero también tiene algo de amistoso y dócil.

13.

cola	que sirve para agarrar
púas	lanza sus púas si lo atacan
ojos	grandes y saltones
forma de caminar	camina cojeando

Composición

14. Las respuestas pueden variar. Se deberá valorar la imaginación del estudiante.

Hoja de respuestas
Todo el verano en un día
Ray Bradbury
Edición del estudiante (página 145)

Vocabulario
1. marejada
2. desconcertado
3. repercusión
4. tumultuosamente
5. amortiguado
6. abalorio
7. predecir
8. estaca
9. amainar
10. audición

Lectura a fondo
11. d
12. c
13. a
14. b
15. c

Respuestas a fondo
16. Las respuestas pueden variar.
    a. Indiferencia. No le importaba no haber visto el sol, porque sabía que pronto iba a regresar a la Tierra.
    b. Venganza. Lo que le hicieron fue horrible, y herir a sus compañeros era la única manera de sentirse un poco mejor.
    c. Rencor. Los odiaba profundamente, pero no podía demostrar a los otros niños cuánto la habían lastimado.
    d. Alegría. Ahora tenía algo en común con sus compañeros y podía recordar con ellos lo maravilloso que era el sol.
17. Cómo perciben a Margot: aislada, silenciosa, frágil, con piel muy blanca, etc.

Composición

18. Una respuesta apropiada será aquella en la cual el estudiante demuestre comprensión de la pregunta y explique, por medio de un ejemplo, cómo el entorno en que vive una persona puede afectar su estado de ánimo.

Hoja de respuestas
El trópico, Rubén Darío
La isla Sangalakki, Norbert Wu
Edición del estudiante (páginas 157 y 164)

Vocabulario
1. j
2. d
3. h
4. a
5. f
6. g
7. b
8. c
9. i
10. e

Lectura a fondo
11. c
12. c
13. b
14. c
15. a

Respuestas a fondo
16. Todas las respuestas son correctas; sin embargo, en el texto se pone más énfasis en la vida interdependiente que llevan los organismos en el arrecife. El peligro forma parte de la convivencia de estos organismos. La belleza es evidente en los colores de los peces y los corales, el ritmo de la actividad, la luz, etc.

17.

lo que las protege	lo que las amenaza
nadan rápidamente	el hombre
su caparazón	las águilas
el hombre	los lagartos
ponen sus huevos de noche	su lentitud al caminar en la arena

Composición
18. Un buena respuesta incluirá a varios miembros de la comunidad (por ejemplo, un maestro, el cartero, el papá) y las relaciones que se establecen entre ellos.

Respuestas a fondo
14. Aunque mucha gente quiera que cambie una situación, la mayoría de la gente no quiere arriesgarse a cambiarla.
15. Los cuentos ilustran una lección de manera concreta. Además no ofenden a nadie porque no hablan directamente de ellos. Patronio, por ejemplo, implica que son tontos los labradores pero no el conde.

Composición
16. Las respuestas pueden variar.

Hoja de respuestas
Los dos labradores, José María Osorio Rodríguez
Los ratones, Lope de Vega
Edición del estudiante (página 185)

Vocabulario
1. pollino
2. dictar
3. culto
4. encrespar
5. cascabel
6. desasosegado
7. ronzal
8. prudencia

Lectura a fondo
9. b
10. a
11. c
12. d
13. Y, encrespando el grueso lomo
    dijo al senado romano,
    después de hablar culto un <u>rato</u>:
    ¿quién de todos ha de s<u>er</u>
    el que se atreva a pon<u>er</u>
    ese cascabel al g<u>ato</u>?

Hoja de respuestas
La canción del árbol, Ana María Fagundo
El ruego del libro, Gabriela Mistral
Edición del estudiante (páginas 213 y 218)

Vocabulario
1. liviano
2. aliento
3. amapolas
4. marchitar
5. recobre

Lectura a fondo
6. a
7. b
8. b
9. c
10. d

Respuestas a fondo
11. El árbol se siente triste, solo, abandonado, viejo...como lo muestran las imágenes del poema.
12. historias infantiles; el sol; las flores; la patria; la religión; las hadas.

Composición
13. Las respuestas pueden variar.

**Hoja de respuestas
de *Yo sé por qué canta el pájaro enjaulado*
Maya Angelou
Edición del estudiante (página 224)**

Vocabulario
1. proponerse
2. alabar
3. vestigio
4. substraer
5. integridad
6. afable
7. facciones
8. afrentosa
9. infalible
10. maña

Lectura a fondo
11. c
12. c
13. d
14. c

Respuesta a fondo
15. El alumno indicará que Maya es tímida y que resiente que los adultos la critiquen por su falta de belleza.
16. Hermoso, simpático, travieso, cariñoso, juguetón, listo, etc.
17. La admiración que siente Maya hacia Bailey sugiere que ella es muy distinta de él. Sabemos que no es guapa y como resultado, es más tímida, más reservada. Parece más seria y formal. El alumno debe explicar por qué se identifica con ella o con Bailey.

**Hoja de respuestas
Los dos ruiseñores
José Martí
Edición del estudiante (página 241)**

Vocabulario
1. e
2. h
3. a
4. d
5. g
6. c
7. f
8. b

Lectura a fondo
9. c
10. a
11. c
12. d

Respuesta a fondo
13. ingenioso; comprensivo; dadivoso; humilde.

Composición
14. Las respuestas pueden variar. Una composición apropiada será aquella en la cual el estudiante utilice sus experiencias para explicar lo que se le pide.

**Hoja de respuestas
Los dos príncipes
José Martí
Los dos reyes y los dos laberintos
Jorge Luis Borges
Edición del estudiante (páginas 255 y 261)**

Vocabulario
1. congregar
2. álamo
3. vedado
4. estragado
5. proferir

Lectura a fondo
6. a
7. c
8. a
9. c
10. b

Respuesta a fondo
11. Las respuestas pueden variar. Un desierto aparenta ser lo opuesto a un laberinto porque no tiene paredes. Sin embargo, es muy difícil salir de los dos.

12.

entierro del hijo del rey	semejanzas	entierro del hijo del pastor
lujoso	sus animales sufren	humilde
coronas de laurel	los padres sufren	ponen una flor
todo el mundo fue al entierro		el pastor cava la fosa de su hijo

Composición
13. Las respuestas pueden variar. Una composición adecuada será aquella en la cual el estudiante utilice algún tema de las historias leídas y escriba una moraleja.

Hoja de respuestas
El árbol de oro
Ana María Matute
Edición del estudiante (página 275)

Vocabulario
1. codiciar
2. zozobra
3. hucha
4. embustero
5. desasosegar
6. estafado

Lectura a fondo
7. c
8. b
9. b
10. c
11. a

Respuesta a fondo
12. Para Ivo, el árbol de oro es la ilusión de su vida y la continuidad de ella en la muerte. El árbol representa el mundo de la imaginación, de la poesía, una visión mágica de la realidad. El idealismo es algo real.

13. El cariño de la maestra; los libros; los sueños de un niño; la amistad entre los niños.

Composición
14. Las respuestas pueden variar. El final distinto podrá expresar alegría, tristeza, decepción, asombro, etc.

Hoja de respuestas
La leyenda del maíz
Maricarmen Ohara
Edición del estudiante (página 283)

Vocabulario
1. belicoso
2. alternativa
3. oprimido
4. convocar
5. pasmado
6. sepultar

Lectura a fondo
7. a
8. b
9. b
10. a

Respuesta a fondo

11. La unión de los dos jóvenes prevalece con el nacimiento del maíz, alimento básico en varias culturas de América. El odio entre los dos pueblos no permite el amor entre los jóvenes; resulta en la guerra y la muerte. Maiza Chojclu muere y se convierte en maíz porque los dioses escuchan su petición.
12. Los dientes; el pelo rubio; la ropa; la flecha.
13. El alumno podrá optar por la muerte de Maiza Chojclu o presentar otra solución al conflicto.

Hoja de respuestas
Cuentos de junio
Susana Mendoza
Edición del estudiante (página 295)

Vocabulario
1. rocío
2. jadeante
3. hálito
4. poniente
5. husmear
6. impertinencia
7. colérico
8. destello
9. escollo
10. cañada

Lectura a fondo
11. c
12. c
13. b

Respuesta a fondo
14. El alumno podrá dar distintas respuestas, como por ejemplo, que el tigre es un dios bondadoso o el sol es fuente de vida.
15. Se abren las flores; los girasoles se mueven siguiéndolo; calienta las piedras; los gallos cantan.
16. El alumno podrá dar varias respuestas siempre y cuando las justifique.

Index of Authors and Titles

El adivinador de máscaras 20
Adivinanzas 26
Angelou, Maya 76
El árbol de oro 96

La bamba 33
Borges, Jorge Luis 90
Bradbury, Ray 48

La cabra Zlateh 12
La canción del árbol 72
Cardoso, Onelio Jorge 9
Una carta a Dios 17
La casa de las tres viudas, de *Memorias* 22
Castillo Guilbault, Rose Del 6
Chanclas 36
Cisneros, Sandra 36
Cuando era puertorriqueña 2
El cuendú 44
Cuentos de junio 102

Darío, Rubén 50
Los dos labradores 59
Los dos príncipes 88
Los dos reyes y los dos laberintos 90
Los dos ruiseñores 83

Fagundo, Ana María 72

Guilbault Del Castillo, Rose *ver* Castillo Guilbault, Rose Del
Guillén, Nicolás 26, 55

Huynh Quang Nhuong 38

La isla Sangalakki 52

Jiménez, Juan Ramón 105
Juan Manuel, Infante Don 59

Lacasa, Cristina 78
La leyenda del maíz 99
Lope de Vega *ver* Vega, Lope de
López y Fuentes, Gregorio 17

Las manos de la abuela 78
Manuel, Infante Don Juan *ver* Juan Manuel, Infante Don
Martí, José 83, 88
Matute, Ana María 96
Mendoza, Susana 102
Mistral, Gabriela 74

Negrita 9
Neiva, Santo 30
Neruda, Pablo 22

Ohara, Maricarmen 99

La Osa Mayor 55
Osorio Rodríguez, José María 59

El pájaro libre 105
Pérez, Emma 67
El pescador y la Madre del Agua 30

Quiroga, Horacio 44

Los ratones 64
Robles, Antonio 20
El ruego del libro 74

Santiago, Esmeralda 2
Se cayó la luna 67
Singer, Isaac Bashevis 12
Soto, Gary 33

La tierra que perdí 38
Todo el verano en un día 48
Trabajo de campo 6
El trópico 50

Vega, Lope de 64

Wu, Norbert 52

Yo sé por qué canta el pájaro enjaulado 76